SERMONS *for* LENT *and* EASTER

Including Ascension Day, Pentecost Sunday, and Trinity Sunday

SERMONS
for LENT
and EASTER

Including Ascension Day,
Pentecost Sunday, and
Trinity Sunday

MARTIN
LUTHER

HENDRICKSON
PUBLISHERS

Sermons for Lent and Easter: Including Ascension Day, Pentecost Sunday, and Trinity Sunday

© 2017 Hendrickson Publishers Marketing, LLC
P. O. Box 3473
Peabody, Massachusetts 01961-3473
www.hendrickson.com

ISBN 978-1-61970-889-1

Originally published by Hendrickson Publishers in *Through the Year with Martin Luther*.

Printed in the United States of America

First Printing — January 2017

Cover photo credit: © Exkalibur

Contents

Preface

Martin Luther, 1483–1546

A safe stronghold our God is still,
A trusty shield and weapon;
He'll help us clear from all the ill
That hath us now o'ertaken.
The ancient prince of hell
Hath risen with purpose fell;
Strong mail of craft and power
He weareth in this hour,
On earth is not his fellow.

❧

God's word, for all their craft and force,
One moment will not linger,
But spite of hell, shall have its course;
'Tis written by his finger.
And, though they take our life,
Goods, honour, children, wife,
Yet is their profit small;
These things shall vanish all:
The city of God remaineth.

— *"A Safe Stronghold"* by Martin Luther, translated
by Thomas Carlyle, 1795–1881

For the modern reader, the long version of Martin Luther's story relies on an unusual vocabulary. A bull? (An official, sealed document issued by the pope.) A diet? (An assembled court of law.) Worms? (A city in Germany.) The Diet of Worms? (Consider the possibilities.)

Martin Luther was born in eastern Germany in 1483. That's some forty years after the German Johann Gutenberg invented a printing press using movable metal type and nearly a decade before Columbus sailed the ocean blue. Having not inherited the family's farm, Luther's father turned to mining and founding metals. Being his father's hope for a son with a secure academic profession, Martin was educated in Latin and then attended the University of Erfurt, receiving a bachelor's and master's in law in 1505.

Martin was a particularly sensitive child, subject to mood swings—highs and lows. Influenced by his region's Germanic, peasantry brand of Christianity, he was haunted by fear—of demons and devils as well as of God the Judge, quick to condemn sinners to interminable punishment. Becoming a monk or priest was considered one sure way of gaining God's favor. For Martin, the decision to enter a monastery came in a July 1505 thunderstorm, when a bolt of lightning knocked him off his feet. On the brink of eternity, he cried out, imploring the aid of Saint Anne: "Help me," and promised, "I will become a monk."

Ordained in an Augustinian order in 1507, he continued educational pursuits, eventually being assigned to the University of Wittenberg to teach moral theology. Young Martin was not a happy man. How could he love God the Judge who was appeased at such a high price? He felt the burden of perfection, including stringent fasting and deprivations that he hoped would "compensate for his sins," to quote Roland Bainton in his acclaimed 1950 biography *Here I Stand*. There was the burden of confession, for scrupulous Martin several hours a day, wracking his brain to find offenses that would potentially separate him from God. There was the financial or physical cost of indulgences; papal bulls decreed that people could buy a proportioned amount of the righteousness of Jesus or a saint and thereby decrease a predeceased loved one's time in purgatory; some bulls went further, offering forgiveness of sin to a living person. Some indulgences were accessible only at churches or shrines containing relics, such as bones of saints. During a 1510 trip to Rome, Martin crawled up the purported (and displaced) steps of Pilate's palace, hopefully praying his grandfather out of purgatory.

After earning a theological doctorate, Martin taught biblical studies at Wittenberg, lecturing principally on the Psalms and then Romans and Galatians. In the writings of Paul, he rediscovered some classical theology of Augustine. Roland Bainton describes what Luther saw in Romans: "It is not that the Son by his sacrifice has placated the irate Father....It is that in some inexplicable way, in the utter desolation of the forsaken Christ, God was able to reconcile the world to himself."

Luther's long-time arguments with, even animosity toward, God withered. He later explained that he had previously taken the phrase "the righteousness of God" to mean "that righteousness whereby God is righteous and deals righteously in punishing the unrighteous." But after much grappling, "I grasped the truth that the righteousness of God is that righteousness whereby, through grace and sheer mercy, he justifies us by faith. Thereupon I felt myself to be reborn and to have gone through open doors into paradise. The whole of Scripture took on a new meaning, and whereas before 'the righteousness of God' had filled me with hate, now it became to me inexpressibly sweet in greater love."

At first Martin thought that his new insight would change the emphasis of his preaching and classroom teaching. But things got complicated. The small university town of Wittenberg was becoming a known center for acclaimed relics and the selling of indulgences. In surrounding areas, some Dominicans were selling even more indulgences, with geographical and cultural implications; German money was being whisked away to Rome to pay for the greatest reliquary of all: Saint Peter's Basilica. This political element helped to fuel the fire that resulted after Martin posted "Ninety-five Theses"—largely against the indulgences industry—in Latin on the door of the Castle Church in Wittenberg on October 31, 1517. If his intent was to engage academic debate, in actuality, he changed the course of the Western church and world.

Translated into German the document was reproduced by an enterprising printer and widely distributed, agitating local peasants. A copy went to Rome. Dominicans took sides against Augustinians. Luther dug in his heels, hitting at the authority of the pope by appealing to the higher authority of Scripture.

By the next summer, like the apostle Paul, Martin was subpoenaed, to appear in Rome, to answer charges of heresy and insubordination. But Luther's local political ruler, Frederick the Wise, had previously assured him that any trial would take place in Germany. A long, three-year tussle—including Luther's claim that the pope was the Antichrist and a papal bull decreeing Luther's excommunication in 1520—resulted in Luther's secular trial, at the Diet of Worms in early 1521.

The Holy Roman emperor himself, Charles V, presided over the trial. First-hand reports quote Martin as holding his ground, refusing to recant, saying, "Here I stand. I can do no other." Found guilty by a depleted number of jurors, Luther might well have been martyred, if not for one friend on the court, Saxony's elector, Frederick the Wise, who organized an abduction, in which Luther was spirited away to a fortress, Wartburg Castle. For about a year in hiding, Luther translated the New Testament from Greek into German, intent on getting the Scriptures into the hands of his people, even though his translation was outlawed by Charles V.

Martin Luther's message spoke freedom for and empowered German's "common man." His early writings (1520) include an *Appeal to the German*

Ruling Class, in which he rallied local rulers to reform the church and protect their people from its extortion and oppression. Here he laid out his understanding of the "priesthood of all believers," in contrast to the prevailing view of the clergy as a caste set apart with special access to God. Here he also proposed that priests be allowed to marry.

The title and contents of another document fueled unrest: *Babylonian Captivity of the Church* (1520) in which he discounted five of seven church sacraments, claiming that only two, Eucharist and Baptism, were biblically instituted. In terms of Eucharist, he insisted that "the cup" to be offered to all believers, not reserved for the clergy only, and he argued against the literalness of transubstantiation—that in the Mass the bread and wine in substance became flesh and blood.

In a third early document (1520), *The Freedom of a Christian,* he explained the tenet of justification by grace through faith alone, not as a result of good works, which were the fruit rather than a contributing source of salvation.

The Diet of Worms decreed that these publications be burned. Many bonfires blazed, but the public had been churned up, and other academics, clerics, and some public officials caught Luther's vision, which opened roads to political as well as spiritual freedom. Priests were marrying. Congregants were sipping Communion wine. The Mass was being said in German. Though it was not part of Martin's "agenda," pictures and statues of the saints were being desecrated. The Wittenberg community was ideologically split, to the point of violence, and in 1522 the city council boldly asked Martin to return to town, in Bainton's view, "probably...to exert a moderating influence" in the fray. Cautiously, courageously Martin returned to Wittenberg and indeed he preached "patience, charity, and consideration for the weak....No one can be intimidated into belief." Returning to Wittenberg, Luther was in effect its mayor and priest, leading the town to real reform. Another diet, at Nürnberg, in 1523 revisited charges made at Worms, but a juridical impasse allowed Luther to continue his work, writing, teaching, preaching, leading in circles beyond Wittenberg.

Politics and religion. It's hard for us to understand how intricately intertwined the two were in central Europe in Luther's day. Two publications later that year reflect the scope of Luther's influence. *On Civil Government* was followed by *On the Order of Worship,* an initial attempt at a revised Eucharistic liturgy in which he introduced the idea of congregational singing. In *Christian History* magazine Paul Grime notes, "Music in congregational worship remains one of Luther's most enduring legacies." To fill a gap he'd created, Martin accepted yet another task—that of writing hymns not in Latin but in

German. With ramifications he didn't even understand, Luther was empowering his people. His appeal to all believers to take their stand as equal before God, even to rally in song, contributed to such unrest that by 1525 he was surrounded by a populist uprising known as the Peasants' War. Again he tried to serve as a mediator, writing an *Admonition to Peace,* exhorting the rulers to be less severe and the populace to honor and obedience of secular authority. But when the rebellion didn't subside, Luther sided with the princes (*Against the Robbing and Murdering Horde of Peasants*), advocating a controversially harsh repression.

Into this whirlwind life, and despite some Pauline reservations ("my mind is averse to marriage because I daily expect the death decreed to the heretic"), he brought a bride. Katherina von Bora was a former nun fifteen years younger than himself. Though he married feeling some obligation to provide a home for her, she became a steadying, still point in his life, prompting him eventually to say, "I would not give my Katie for France and Venice together." In red-haired, feisty, Katie, Martin had met his match. While Martin was changing the landscape of Europe, Katie was reining him in at home; he was known to call her "my Lord Kate." She had her hands full, managing him, eventually their growing family (six children in all), and their large home (the very Augustinian monastery that Martin had lived in as a young man), which served in effect as a hotel for people passing through or a hostel for the needy and a hospital for the sick, especially in a 1527 plague epidemic that devastated Wittenberg. Some of Luther's best known writings are known as his *Table Talk,* more than 6,500 short discourses he gave to visitors, including disciples, around his dinner table.

One statement about his marriage sheds light back on Martin's public, spiritual persona. "In domestic affairs I defer to Katie. Otherwise, I am led by the Holy Ghost." Luther was sure he spoke for God, though often in exaggerated tones. As he aged his rancor and anger at his enemies is disturbing. He wrote, for instance, "I cannot deny that I am more vehement than I should be. …But they assail me and God's Word so atrociously and criminally that… these monsters are carrying me beyond the bounds of moderation." The word *Protestant* even then seemed an apt description. That word was first used at the 1529 Diet of Speyer, at which Emperor Charles V again attempted to enforce the Diet of Worms. *Protestant* stuck as a descriptor of the anti-Catholic group(s). Any number of theologians supported Luther in his stand against papal power and extrabiblical traditions and abuses. But as Rome itself headed toward a Counter-Reformation and lost some power in central Europe, Protestant reformers took issue with—even turned on—each other.

Points of doctrine and worship, such as the predestination versus free will, the baptism of infants, the role of music and art, the exact role and meaning of the Lord's Supper, caused rifts among groups of disciples, sometimes along regional lines, notably the Swiss and Dutch disagreeing with the Germans.

The most contentious issue became the "real presence" of Christ in the Eucharistic bread and wine. Though Luther disavowed the Catholic "hocus pocus" of the elements becoming flesh and blood, he appealed to Jesus' "This is my body...This is my blood" to counter Ulrich Zwingli's position that Christ's presence in the elements was not real but symbolic and dependent on the faith of the receiver. In 1529 a German prince, Philip of Hesse, persuaded Luther to meet with Ulrich Zwingli and others in Marburg to restore Protestant unity. But there was no compromise and to this day the Reformed and Lutheran traditions are set apart from each other.

Though Luther was making enemies of reformers, he still was in conflict with the Holy Roman Empire. Again under virtual house arrest at a castle fortress, he could not attend a 1530 Diet of Augsburg, at which the Lutheran apologetic, coauthored by Luther and his colleague Philipp Melanchthon, was presented. Professor Eugene Klug of Concordia Theological Seminary notes that for Lutherans, this *Augsburg Confession* became a "standard" for theology, "a document with the weight of a Declaration of Independence."

In midlife Luther was juggling not only matters of state, but also the education of the common man, writing a long and a short version of a *Catechism* that in question and answer format lay out the basics of the faith. The *Small Catechism*, which has been called "the gem of the Reformation," was taught in homes, generation after generation, instilling basic doctrines to the youngest children; it includes phrase-by-phrase explanations of the Ten Commandments, the Apostles' Creed, and the Lord's Prayer. In his spare time, he also continued translating the Old Testament from Hebrew, his complete German Bible being published in 1534.

And, lest we forget, Luther at heart was a teacher and preacher; he left a legacy of more than two thousand sermons, only a portion of those he delivered. The nineteen sermons selected for this volume reflect seasonal themes of the liturgical calendar, the very purpose for which they were written. In 1520, Luther's benefactor, Frederick the Wise, requested that Luther prepare a postil, or sermon, for every Sunday in the church year. His postils were expository studies of the lectionary readings assigned to the Sunday, and were intended to serve as expository guides for other priests, to help them prepare their own preaching. These writings were completed over a period of years and finally became known as the *Church Postils*.

As one would expect, Luther's sermons are grounded in a particular scriptural passage. But from that jumping off point, especially in his later years, Luther slipped in an agenda that not only supported his theological points, but also bitterly denounced groups that disagreed with him, particularly Catholics and also Jews. These tirades against Jews were theological, not racial. (Anthropological distinction between "Aryans" and "Semites" was a nineteenth-century categorization.) His complaint was not that the first-century Jews had killed Jesus, but rather that Jews subsequently did not accept and believe in him. Roland Bainton says, "The supreme sin for him was the persistent rejection of God's revelation of himself in Christ." Where Luther took that line of thought, and how, had drastic consequences in Europe for centuries.

Threads of his disrespect of his contrarians are evident in the sermons in this volume, which should be read for their positive and scriptural insights rather than for their accusative harangues. In his lifetime Luther wrote some 60,000 pages of prose. He welcomed listeners and readers, and yet his deeper desire was that "the Holy Scriptures alone be read." In a similar spirit, may these selected sermons prompt you to search the Scriptures themselves, looking for the basics of Luther's theology, which has been reduced to four points: *sola Scriptura* (Scripture alone being the authority, rather than extraneous tradition), *sola fide* (faith alone, not works, being the channel of our righteousness), *sola gratia* (grace alone—a gift of God—being the cause of our salvation)—all anchored in *solo Christo* (Christ alone). Dr. Timothy George notes that "each *sola* affirmed the centrality of Jesus Christ."

Martin Luther died in 1546, at age sixty-two, after years of continued productivity despite declining health. A year after his death, the emperor declared war on Protestants, set in motion at the Diet of Augsburg. The emperor initially defeated the Protestants, but the tide turned. The 1555 Peace of Augsburg allowed local princes to determine the religion of their districts. This legally recognized Protestantism, though Germany suffered sectarian violence, including the Thirty Years' War, for another century.

Historians feel that early-sixteenth-century Europe was ready for sweeping reform, seeded by John Wycliffe, John Huss, and Desiderius Erasmus, among others. If not Luther it would have been another cleric or academic bridging medieval and Renaissance culture. But it was Martin Luther, a powerful personality, a charismatic motivator, and systematic teacher who shook not just the church but the political world with a basic premise—that we cannot buy or work our way into the kingdom of God.

The First Sunday in Lent

The Fast and the Temptation of Christ

Then was Jesus led up of the Spirit into the wilderness to be tempted of the devil. And when he had fasted forty days and forty nights, he afterward hungered. And the tempter came and said unto him, "If thou art the Son of God, command that these stones become bread." But he answered and said, "It is written, Man shall not live by bread alone, but by every word that proceedeth out of the mouth of God." Then the devil taketh him into the holy city; and he set him on the pinnacle of the temple, and saith unto him, "If thou art the Son of God, cast thyself down: for it is written, 'He shall give his angels charge concerning thee: 'and,' On their hands they shall bear thee up, lest haply thou dash thy foot against a stone.'"

Jesus said unto him, Again it is written, Thou shalt not make trial of the Lord thy God. Again, the devil taketh him unto an exceeding high mountain, and showeth him all the kingdoms of the world, and the glory of them; and he said unto him, All these things will I give thee, if thou wilt fall down and worship me. Then saith Jesus unto him, Get thee hence, Satan: for it is written, Thou shalt worship the Lord thy God, and him only shalt thou serve. Then the devil leaveth him; and behold, angels came and ministered unto him. — MATTHEW 4:1–11

I. THE FASTING OF CHRIST

1. This Gospel is read today at the beginning of Lent in order to picture before Christians the example of Christ, that they may rightly observe Lent, which has become mere mockery: first, because no one can follow this example and fast forty days and nights as Christ did without eating any food. Christ rather followed the example of Moses, who fasted also forty days and nights, when he received the law of God on Mount Sinai. Thus Christ also wished to fast when he was about to bring to us, and give expression to, the new law. In the second place, Lent has become mere mockery because our

fasting is a perversion and an institution of man. For although Christ did fast forty days, yet there is no word of his that he requires us to do the same and fast as he did. Indeed, he did many other things, which he wishes us not to do; but whatever he calls us to do or leave undone, we should see to it that we have his Word to support our actions.

2. But the worst of all is that we have adopted and practiced fasting as a good work: not to bring our flesh into subjection, but, as a meritorious work before God, to atone for our sins and obtain grace. And it is this that has made our fasting a stench and so blasphemous and shameful, so that no drinking and eating, no gluttony and drunkenness, could have been as bad and foul. It would have been better had people been drunk day and night than to fast thus. Moreover, even if all had gone well and right, so that their fasting had been applied to the mortification of the flesh, but since it was not voluntary, and it was not left to each to do according to their own free will, but was compulsory by virtue of human commandment, and they did it unwillingly, it was all lost and to no purpose. I will not mention the many other evils as the consequences, as that pregnant mothers and their offspring, the sick and the weak, were thereby ruined, so that it might be called a fasting of Satan instead of a fasting unto holiness. Therefore, we will carefully consider how this Gospel teaches us by the example of Christ what true fasting is.

3. The Scriptures present to us two kinds of true fasting: one, by which we try to bring the flesh into subjection to the spirit, of which Saint Paul speaks in 2 Corinthians 6:5, "In labors, in watchings, in fastings." The other is that which we must bear patiently, and yet receive willingly, because of our need and poverty, of which Saint Paul speaks in 1 Corinthians 4:11, "Even unto this present hour we both hunger, and thirst," and Christ in Matthew 9:15, "When the bridegroom shall be taken away from them, then will they fast." This kind of fasting, Christ teaches us here while in the wilderness alone, without anything to eat, and while he suffers his penury without murmuring. The first kind of fasting, one can end whenever he wills, and can satisfy it by food; but the other kind, we must observe and bear until God himself changes it and satisfies us. Hence it is much more precious than the first, because it moves in greater faith.

4. This is also the reason that the evangelist with great care places it first: Then was Jesus led up of the Spirit into the wilderness, that he might there fast and be tempted, so that no one might imitate his example of their own choice and make of it a selfish, arbitrary, and pleasant fasting; but instead wait for the Spirit, who will send him enough fastings and temptations. For whoever, without being led by the Spirit, wantonly resorts to the danger of hunger or

to any temptation, when it is truly a blessing of God that he can eat and drink and have other comforts, tempts God. We should not seek want and temptation; they will surely come of themselves. We ought then do our best and act honestly. The text reads, Jesus was led up of the Spirit into the wilderness, and not, Jesus himself chose to go into the wilderness. "For as many as are led by the Spirit of God, these are sons of God," Romans 8:14. God gives his blessings for the purpose that we may use them with thanksgiving, and not that we may let them lie idle, and thus tempt him; for he wishes it, and forces us to fast by the Spirit or by a need which we cannot avoid.

5. This narrative, however, is written both for our instruction and admonition. First, for instruction, that we should know how Christ has served and helped us by his fasting, hunger, temptation, and victory; also, that whoever believes on Christ shall never suffer need, and that temptation shall never harm him; but we shall have enough in the midst of want and be safe in the midst of temptation; because his Lord and Head triumphed over these all in his behalf, and of this he is assured, as Christ says in John 16:33, "Be of good cheer; I have overcome the world." God, who was able to nourish Christ forty days without any food, can nourish also his Christians.

6. Secondly, this is written for our admonition, that we may in the light of this example also cheerfully suffer want and temptation for the service of God and the good of our neighbor, like Christ did for us, as often as necessity requires it, which is surely accomplished if we learn and confess God's Word. Therefore, this Gospel is sweet consolation and power against the unbelief and infamy of the stomach, to awaken and strengthen the conscience, that we may not be anxious about the nourishment of our bodies, but be assured that he can and will give us our daily bread.

II. THE TEMPTATION OF CHRIST

7. But as to how temptation takes place and how it is overcome, is all very beautifully pictured to us here in Christ. First, that he is led up into the wilderness, that is, he is left solitary and alone by God, angels, and men, by all creatures. What kind of a temptation would it be, if we were not forsaken and stood not alone? It is, however, painful when we do not feel anything that presents its back to us; as, for example, that I should support myself and have not a nickel, not a thread, not a twig, and I experience no help from others, and no advice is offered. That means to be led into the desert and to be left alone. There I am in the true school, and I learn what I am, how weak my faith is, how great and rare true faith is, and how deeply unbelief is entrenched in the hearts of all men. But whoever has his purse, cellar, and fields full, is not

yet led into the desert, neither is he left alone; therefore, he is not conscious of temptation.

8. Secondly, the tempter came forward and attacked Christ with these very same cares of food for the body and with the unbelief in the goodness of God, and said, "If thou art the Son of God, command that these stones become bread," as if he should say, Yes, trust thou in God and bake and cook nothing; only wait patiently until a roasted fowl flies into your mouth; do you now say that you have a God who cares for you; where is now your heavenly Father, who has charge of you? Yea, it seems to me he lets you in a fine condition; eat now and drink from your faith; let us see how you will satisfy your hunger; yea, when you have stones for bread. What a fine Son of God you are! How fatherly he is disposed toward you in that he fails to send you a slice of bread and permits you to be so poor and needy; do you now continue to believe that you are his son and he is your father? With like thoughts, he truly attacks all the children of God. And Christ surely felt this temptation, for he was no stock nor stone; although he was and remained pure and without sin, as we cannot do.

9. That Satan attacked Christ with the cares for daily food or with unbelief and avarice, Christ's answer proves, in that he says, "Man shall not live by bread alone"; that sounds as if he said, Thou wilt direct me to bread alone and dost treat me as though I thought of nothing but the sustenance of my body. This temptation is very common also among pious people, and they especially feel it keenly who have children and a family, and have nothing to eat. Therefore, Saint Paul says in 1 Timothy 6:10, that avarice is a root of all kind of evil; for it is a fruit of unbelief. Do you not think that unbelief, care, and avarice are the reasons people are afraid to enter married life? Why do people avoid it and live in unchastity, unless it be the fear that they must die of hunger and suffer want? But here we should consider Christ's work and example, who suffered want forty days and nights, and finally was not forsaken, but was ministered to even by angels.

10. Thirdly, behold how Christ resists this temptation of bread, and overcomes; he sees nothing but stones and what is uneatable, then he approaches and clings to the Word of God, strengthens himself by it, and strikes the devil to the ground with it. This saying all Christians should lay hold of when they see that there is lack and want and everything has become stones, so that courage trembles, and they should say, What were it if the whole world were full of bread, still man does not live by bread alone, but more belongs to life, namely, the Word of God. The words, however, are so beautiful and powerful that we must not pass over them lightly, but carefully explain them.

11. These words Christ quotes from Deuteronomy 8:3, where Moses says, "Thy God humbled thee, and suffered thee to hunger, and fed thee with manna, which thou knewest not, neither did thy fathers know; that he might make thee know that man doth not live by bread only, but by everything that proceedeth out of the mouth of Jehovah doth man live." That is as much as to say, Since God permits you to hunger and you still continue to live, you ought indeed to grasp the thought that God nourishes you without bread through his Word; for if you should live and sustain yourself by bread alone, then you must continually be full of bread. But the Word that nourishes us is, that he promises us, and causes it to be published, that he is our God and desires to be our God.

12. Thus now, the meaning of Moses and of Christ is, Whoever has here God's Word and believes, has both blessings: the first, where he is in want and has nothing, but must suffer hunger, that Word will sustain him, so that he will not die of hunger nor perish, just as well as if he had abundance to eat; for the Word he has in his heart nourishes and sustains him without eating and drinking. But has he little to eat, then a bite or slice of bread will feed and nourish him like a kingly meal; for not only bread but the Word of God also nourishes the body naturally, as it creates and upholds all things, in Hebrews 1:3. The other blessing he will also enjoy, namely, that finally bread will surely be at hand, come whence it will, and should it rain from heaven like manna where none grows and none can grow. In these two thoughts, every person can freely trust, namely, that he must in time of hunger receive bread or something to eat or, if not, then his hunger must become so moderate and bearable that it will nourish him even as well as bread does.

13. What has been said of eating and feeding the body should be understood also of drinking, clothing, house, and all our needs, namely, that although he still permits us to become naked and suffer want for clothing, house, etc., clothing must finally be at hand, and before it fails the leaves of the trees must become coats and mantles; or, if not, then the coats and garments that we wear must never grow old; just as happened to the children of Israel in the desert, in Deuteronomy 8:2–4, whose clothing and shoes never wore out. Likewise the wild wilderness must become their houses, and there must be a way where there is no way; and water, where there is no water; stones must become water. For here stands God's Word, which says, "He cares for you"; and Saint Paul in 1 Timothy 6:17, "God giveth us richly all things to enjoy"; and in Matthew 6:33–34, "But seek ye first the kingdom of God and his righteousness; and all these things shall be added unto you. Be not therefore anxious for the morrow." These and like words must continue true and stand forever firm.

14. All this one may indeed learn from his own daily experiences. For it is held, and I almost believe it, that there are not as many sheaves of wheat grown as there are people living on the earth; but God daily blesses and increases the wheat in the sack, the flour in the tray, the bread on the table and in the mouth, as Christ did, in John 6:12ff. It is also noticeable that as a rule poor people and their children are fatter and their food reaches farther and agrees with them better than is the case among the rich with all their provisions. However, that the godless at times suffer need, or in times of famine many die of hunger, is caused by a special plague as pestilence, war, etc. In other ways, we see that in all things it is not the food, but the Word of God that nourishes every human being.

15. Now that God sustains all mankind by bread, and not by the Word alone, without bread, is done to the end, that he conceals his work in the world in order to exercise believers; just as he commanded the children of Israel to arm themselves and to fight, and yet it was not his pleasure that victory should come through their own sword and deeds; but he himself was to slay their enemies and triumph with their swords and through their deeds. Here it might also be said, The warrior was not victorious through his sword alone, but by every Word that proceeded out of the mouth of God, as David sings, in Psalm 44:6, "For I will not trust in my bow, neither shall my sword save me." Also, in Psalm 147:10 and in Psalm 33:16–17, "He taketh no pleasure in the legs of a man. A mighty man is not delivered by great strength. A horse is a vain thing for safety." Yet he uses man and the horse, the sword and bow: but not because of the strength and power of man and of the horse, but under the veil and covering of man and the horse he fights and does all. This he proves in that he often did and daily does the same without man and the horse, where there is need and he is not tempted.

16. Thus he does also with the bread; since it is at hand, he nourishes us through it and by means of it, so that we do not see it and we think the bread does it; but where it is not at hand, there he nourishes us without the bread, only through the Word, as he does by means of the bread; so that thus bread is God's helper, as Paul says in 1 Corinthians 3:9, "We are God's fellow workers," that is, through and under our outward ministerial office, he gives inwardly his grace, which he also could give and does give indeed without our office; but since the office is at hand, one should not despise it nor tempt God. Thus God sustains us outwardly by bread; but only inwardly he gives that growth and permanency, which the bread cannot give. And the summary is, All creatures are God's larva and mummery, which he permits to work with him and to help to do everything that he can do and does do otherwise without their

cooperation, in order that we may cleave alone to his Word. Thus if bread is at hand, that we do not therefore trust the more; or if there is no bread present, that we do not therefore despair the more; but use it when it is at hand, and do without it, when there is none; being assured that we shall still live and be sustained at both times by God's Word, whether there be bread or no bread. With such faith, one overcomes avarice and temporal care for daily bread in the right way.

17. Christ's second temptation is opposed to the first and is repugnant to common sense. Its substance is that the devil teaches us to tempt God; as he here calls to Christ to cast himself down from the pinnacle of the temple, which was not at all necessary, since there were surely good steps upon which he could descend. And that this temptation was for the purpose of tempting or making trial of God, the answer of Christ also clearly proves, when he says, "Thou shalt not make trial of the Lord thy God." By this, he shows that the devil wished to lead him into temptation.

18. And this very appropriately follows the first temptation. For where the devil feels a heart trusts God in times of want and need, he soon ceases his temptation of bread and avarice and thinks, Wait, wilt thou be very spiritual and believing, I will assist you: He approaches and attacks on the other side, that we might believe where God has not commanded us to believe, nor wills that we should believe. For example, if God gave you bread in your homes, as he does yearly everywhere in the world, and you would not use it, but instead you would cause need and want yourselves, and say, Why, we are to believe God; I will not eat the bread, but will patiently wait until God sends me manna from heaven. See, that would be tempting God; for that is not believing where all is at hand that we need and should have. How can one believe that he will receive what he already has?

19. Thus you see here that Satan held before Christ want and need where there was neither want nor need, but where there was already good means by which to descend from the temple without such a newly devised and unnecessary way of descending. For this purpose, Satan led Christ to the top of the temple, in the holy city, says the evangelist, and placed him in a holy place. For he creates such precious thoughts in man that he thinks he is filled with faith and is on the true way of holiness; and yet he does not stand in the temple, but is only on the outside of the temple, that is, he is not in the true holy mind or life of faith; and yet he is in the holy city; that is, such persons are found only in Christendom and among true Christians, who hear a great deal of preaching about faith. To these persons, he applies the sayings of Scripture. For such persons learn Scripture also by daily hearing it; but not

farther than they can apply it to their erroneous opinions and their false faith. For Satan here quotes from the Psalter, in Psalm 91:11–12, that God commanded the angels that they should protect the children of God and carry them on their hands. But Satan, like a rogue and cheat, fails to quote what follows, namely, that the angels shall protect the children of God in all their ways. For the psalm reads thus, "For he will give his angels charge over thee to keep thee in all thy ways. They shall bear thee up in their hands, lest thou dash thy foot against a stone"; hence the protection of the angels does not reach farther, according to the command of God, than the ways in which God has commanded us to walk. When we walk in these ways of God, his angels take care of us. But the devil omits to quote "the ways of God" and interprets and applies the protection of the angels to all things, also to that which God has not commanded; then it fails and we tempt God.

20. Now, this temptation seldom takes place in outward material things as bread, clothing, house, etc. For we find many foolhardy people, who risk and endanger their body and life, their property and honor, without any need of doing so; as those do who willfully enter into battle or jump into the water, or gamble for money, or in other ways venture into danger, of whom the wise man says in Sirach 3:27, "Whoever takes pleasure in danger, will thereby be overcome"; for in the degree one struggles to get a thing, will he succeed in obtaining it; and good swimmers are likely to drown and good climbers likely to fall. Yet it is seldom that those of false faith in God abstain from bread, clothing, and other necessities of life, when they are at hand. As we read of two hermits who would not accept bread from the people, but thought God should send it to them directly from heaven: so the consequence was that one died and went to his father, the devil, who taught him such faith and left him fall from the pinnacle.

21. But in spiritual matters, this temptation is powerful when one has to do with the nourishment not of the body but of the soul. Here God has held before us the person and way by which the soul can be forever nourished in the richest manner possible without any want, namely, Christ, our Savior. But this way, this treasure, this provision, no one desires. Everybody seeks another way, other provisions, to help their souls. The real guilty ones are those who would be saved through their own work; these the devil sets conspicuously on the top of the temple. They follow him and go down where there is no stairway; they believe and trust in their own work where there is no faith nor trust, no way nor bridge, and break their necks. But Satan makes use of and persuades them through the Scriptures to believe that the angels will protect them, and that their way, works, and faith are pleasing to God, and who called

them through the Scriptures to do good works; but they do not care how falsely they explain the Scriptures.

22. Who these are, we have identified often enough and very fully, namely, work-righteous persons and unbelieving hypocrites under the name of being Christians and among the congregation of Christian people. For the temptation must take place in the holy city, and one temptation is seldom against another. In the first temptation, want and hunger are the reasons that we should not believe, and by which we become anxious to have a full sufficiency, so that there is no chance for us to believe. In the second temptation, however, the abundance and the full sufficiency are the reasons that we do not believe, by which we become tired of the common treasure, and everyone tries to do something through his own powers to provide for his soul. So we do; if we have nothing, then we doubt God and believe not; if we have abundance, then we become tired of it and wish to have something different and, again, we fail to believe. There we flee and turn against want and seek abundance: here we seek want and flee from the abundance we have. No, whatever God does for us, is never right. Such is the bottomless wickedness of our unbelief.

23. Christ's third temptation consists in temporal honor and power; as the words of the devil clearly teach, when Satan shows and offers Christ all the kingdoms of the world if he would worship him. To this class those belong who fall from their faith for the sake of honor and power, that they may enjoy good days, or not believe further than their honor and power extend. Such are also the heretics who start sects and factions in matters of faith among Christians, that they may make a great parade before the world and soar aloft in their own honor. Hence one may place this third temptation on the right, and the first on the left side. The first is the temptation of misfortune, by which man is stirred to anger, impatience, and unbelief; the third and last, the temptation of prosperity, by which man is enticed to lust, honor, joy, and whatever is high. The second or middle temptation is spiritual, and deals with the blind tricks and errors that mislead reason from faith.

24. For whom the devil cannot overcome with poverty, want, need, and misery, he attacks with riches, favor, honor, pleasure, power, and the like, and contends on both sides against us; yea, "he walketh about," says Saint Peter, in 1 Peter 5:8, so that if he cannot overthrow us either with suffering or love, that is, with the first temptation on the left or the third on the right, he retires to a higher and different method and attacks us with error, blindness, and a false understanding of the Scripture. If he wins there, we fare ill on all sides and in all things; and whether one suffers poverty or has abundance, whether he fights or surrenders, all is lost. For when one is in error, neither

patience in misfortune nor firmness in prosperity helps him; seeing that in both heretics are often powerful and the devil deliberately acts as if he were overcome in the first and last temptations, although he is not, if he has only won in the middle or second temptation. For he lets his own children suffer much and be patient, even at times to spurn the world, but never with a true and honest heart.

25. Now these three temptations taken together are heavy and hard; but the middle one is the greatest, for it attacks the doctrine of faith itself in the soul, and is spiritual and in spiritual matters. The other two attack faith in outward things, in fortune and misfortune, in pleasure and pain, etc., although both severely try us. For it is sad that one should lay hold of heaven and ever be in want and eat stones where there is no bread. Again, it is sad to despise favors, honor and possessions, friends and associates, and let go what one already has. But faith, rooted in God's Word, is able to do all things; is faith strong, then it is also easy for the believer to do this.

26. The order of these temptations, as they met Christ, one cannot absolutely determine; for the evangelists give them in different order. The temptation Matthew places as the middle one, Luke places last, in Luke 4:4ff.; and again, the temptation Luke places in the middle, Matthew places last, as if little depended on the order. But if one wished to preach or speak of them, the order of Luke would be the better. For it is a fine opportunity to repeat and relate that the devil began with want and misfortune; when that did not work, then he began with prosperity and honor; and last, when all fails, that he wantonly and wickedly springs forth and strikes people with terror, lies, and other spiritual tricks. And since they have no order in practice and experience, but as it happens that a Christian may be attacked at one time with the last, and another time with the first, etc., Matthew gave little attention to the order for a preacher to observe in speaking of this theme. And perhaps it was also the same with Christ through the forty days that the devil held to no order, but today attacked him with this and tomorrow with another temptation, and again in ten days with the first, and so on, just as occasion was given.

27. At last, angels approached and served him. This must have taken place in a literal sense, that they appeared in a bodily form and gave him to eat and drink, and just as at a table, they ministered to all his wants. For the service is offered outwardly to his body, just like, no doubt, the devil, his tempter, also appeared in a bodily form, perhaps like an angel. For, seeing that he places him on the pinnacle of the temple and shows him all the kingdoms of the world in a moment, he must have been a higher being than a man, since he represents himself as a higher being, in that he offers him all the kingdoms

of the world and permits himself to be worshiped. But he surely did not bear the form of the devil, for he desires to be beautiful when he lies and deceives, as Saint Paul says of him in 2 Corinthians 11:14, "For even Satan fashioneth himself into an angel of light."

28. This, however, is written for our comfort, that we may know that many angels minister also to us, where one devil attacks us; if we fight with a knightly spirit and firmly stand, God will not let us suffer want; the angels of heaven would sooner appear and be our bakers, waiters, and cooks, and minister to all our wants. This is not written for Christ's sake, for he does not need it. Did the angels serve him, then they may also serve us.

The Second Sunday in Lent

༺✻༻

The Faith of the Syrophenician Woman, and the Spiritual Interpretation of This Gospel

And Jesus went out thence, and withdrew into the parts of Tyre and Sidon. And behold, a Canaanitish woman came out from those borders and cried, saying, "Have mercy on me, O Lord, thou son of David; my daughter is grievously vexed with a demon." But he answered her not a word. And his disciples came and besought him, saying, "Send her away; for she crieth after us." But he answered and said, "I was not sent but unto the lost sheep of the house of Israel." But she came and worshiped him, saying, "Lord, help me." And he answered and said, "It is not meet to take the children's bread and cast it to the dogs." But she said, "Yea, Lord: for even the dogs eat of the crumbs which fall from their masters' table." Then Jesus answered and said unto her, "O woman, great is thy faith: be it done unto thee even as thou wilt." And her daughter was healed from that hour.

— Matthew 15:21–28

I. HER FAITH

1. This Gospel presents to us a true example of firm and perfect faith. For this woman endures and overcomes in three great and hard battles, and teaches us in a beautiful manner the true way and virtue of faith, namely, that it is a hearty trust in the grace and goodness of God as experienced and revealed through his Word. For Saint Mark says, she heard some news about Jesus, in Mark 7:25. What kind of news? Without doubt, good news, and the good report that Christ was a pious man and cheerfully helped everybody. Such news about God is a true Gospel and a word of grace, out of which sprang the faith of this woman; for had she not believed, she would not have thus run after Christ, etc. In like manner, we have often heard how Saint Paul,

in Romans 10:17, says that faith cometh by hearing, that the Word must go in advance and be the beginning of our salvation.

2. But how is it that many more have heard this good news concerning Christ, who have not followed him, and did not esteem it as good news? Answer: The physician is helpful and welcome to the sick; the healthy have no use for him. But this woman felt her need, hence she followed the sweet scent, as is written in the Song of Solomon 1:3. In like manner, Moses must precede and teach people to feel their sins in order that grace may be sweet and welcome to them. Therefore, all is in vain, however friendly and lovely Christ may be pictured, if man is not first humbled by a knowledge of himself and he possesses no longing for Christ, as Mary's song says, "The hungry he hath filled with good things; and the rich he hath sent empty away," in Luke 1:53. All this is spoken and written for the comfort of the distressed, the poor, the needy, the sinful, the despised, so that they may know in all times of need to whom to flee and where to seek comfort and help.

3. But see in this example how Christ like a hunter exercises and chases faith in his followers in order that it may become strong and firm. First when the woman follows him upon hearing of his fame and cries with assured confidence that he would according to his reputation deal mercifully with her, Christ certainly acts differently, as if to let her faith and good confidence be in vain and turn his good reputation into a lie, so that she could have thought, Is this the gracious, friendly man? or, Are these the good words, that I have heard spoken about him, upon which I have depended? It must not be true; he is my enemy and will not receive me; nevertheless he might speak a word and tell me that he will have nothing to do with me. Now he is as silent as a stone. Behold, this is a very hard rebuff, when God appears so earnest and angry and conceals his grace so high and deep; as those know so well, who feel and experience it in their hearts. Therefore, she imagines he will not fulfill what he has spoken, and will let his Word be false; as it happened to the children of Israel at the Red Sea and to many other saints.

4. Now, what does the poor woman do? She turns her eyes from all this unfriendly treatment of Christ; all this does not lead her astray, neither does she take it to heart, but she continues immediately and firmly to cling in her confidence to the good news she had heard and embraced concerning him, and never gives up. We must also do the same and learn firmly to cling to the Word, even though God with all his creatures appears different than his Word teaches. But, oh, how painful it is to nature and reason, that this woman should strip herself of self and forsake all that she experienced, and cling

alone to God's bare Word, until she experienced the contrary. May God help us in time of need and of death to possess like courage and faith!

5. Secondly, since her cry and faith avail nothing, the disciples approach with their faith, and pray for her, and imagine they will surely be heard. But while they thought he should be more tenderhearted, he became only the more indifferent, as we see and think. For now he is silent no more nor leaves them in doubt; he declines their prayer and says, "I was not sent but unto the lost sheep of the house of Israel." This rebuff is still harder since not only our own person is rejected, but the only comfort that remains to us, namely, the comfort and prayers of pious and holy persons, are rejected. For our last resort, when we feel that God is ungracious or we are in need, is that we go to pious, spiritual persons, and there seek counsel and help, and they are willing to help as love demands; and yet, that may amount to nothing, even they may not be heard and our condition becomes only worse.

6. Here one might upbraid Christ with all the words in which he promised to hear his saints as, in Matthew 18:19, "If two of you shall agree on earth as touching anything that they shall ask, it shall be done for them." Likewise, in Mark 11:24, "All things whatsoever ye pray and ask for, believe that ye receive them, and ye shall have them"; and many more like passages. What becomes of such promises in this woman's case? Christ, however, promptly answers, and says, Yes, it is true, I hear all prayers, but I gave these promises only to the house of Israel. What do you think? Is not that a thunderbolt that dashes both heart and faith into a thousand pieces, when one feels that God's Word, upon which one trusts, was not spoken for him, but applies only to others? Here all saints and prayers must be speechless, yea, here the heart must let go of the Word, to which it would gladly hold, if it would consult its own feelings.

7. But what does the poor woman do? She does not give up, she clings to the Word although it be torn out of her heart by force, is not turned away by this stern answer, still firmly believes his goodness is yet concealed in that answer, and still she will not pass judgment that Christ is or may be ungracious. That is persevering steadfastness.

8. Thirdly, she follows Christ into the house, as Mark 7:24–25 informs us, perseveres, falls down at his feet, and says, "Lord, help me!" There she received her last mortal blow, in that Christ said, in her face, as the words tell, that she was a dog, and not worthy to partake of the children's bread. What will she say to this! Here he presents her in a bad light, she is a condemned and an outcast person, who is not to be reckoned among God's chosen ones.

9. That is an eternally unanswerable reply, to which no one can give a satisfactory answer. Yet she does not despair, but agrees with his judgment

and concedes she is a dog, and desires also no more than a dog is entitled to, namely, that she may eat the crumbs that fall from the table of the Lord. Is not that a masterly stroke as a reply? She catches Christ with his own words. He compares her to a dog, she concedes it, and asks nothing more than that he let her be a dog, as he himself judged her to be. Where will Christ now take refuge? He is caught. Truly, people let the dog have the crumbs under the table; it is entitled to that. Therefore, Christ now completely opens his heart to her and yields to her will, so that she is now no dog, but even a child of Israel.

II. THE SPIRITUAL INTERPRETATION OF THIS GOSPEL

10. All this, however, is written for our comfort and instruction, that we may know how deeply God conceals his grace before our face, and that we may not estimate him according to our feelings and thinking, but strictly according to his Word. For here you see, though Christ appears to be even hard-hearted, yet he gives no final decision by saying "no." All his answers indeed sound like no, but they are not no, they remain undecided and pending. For he does not say, I will not hear thee; but is silent and passive, and says neither yes nor no. In like manner, he does not say she is not of the house of Israel; but he is sent only to the house of Israel; he leaves it undecided and pending between yes and no. So he does not say, Thou art a dog, one should not give thee of the children's bread; but it is not meet to take the children's bread and cast it to the dogs; leaving it undecided whether she is a dog or not. Yet all those trials of her faith sounded more like no than yes; but there was more yea in them than nay; aye, there is only yes in them, but it is very deep and very concealed, while there appears to be nothing but no.

11. By this is set forth the condition of our heart in times of temptation; Christ here represents how it feels. It thinks there is nothing but no and yet that is not true. Therefore, it must turn from this feeling and lay hold of and retain the deep spiritual yes under and above the no with a firm faith in God's Word, as this poor woman does, and say God is right in his judgment which he visits upon us; then we have triumphed and caught Christ in his own words. As, for example, when we feel in our conscience that God rebukes us as sinners and judges us unworthy of the kingdom of heaven, then we experience hell, and we think we are lost forever. Now, whoever understands here the actions of this poor woman and catches God in his own judgment, and says, Lord, it is true, I am a sinner and not worthy of thy grace; but still thou hast promised sinners forgiveness, and thou art come not to call the righteous, but, as Saint Paul says in 1 Timothy 1:15, "to save sinners." Behold, then must God according to his own judgment have mercy upon us.

12. King Manasseh did likewise in his penitence as his prayer proves; he conceded that God was right in his judgment and accused himself as a great sinner, and yet he laid hold of the promised forgiveness of sins. David also does likewise in Psalm 51:4, and says, "Against thee, thee only, have I sinned, and done that which is evil in thy sight; that thou mayest be justified when thou speakest, and be clear when thou judgest." For God's disfavor in every way visits us when we cannot agree with his judgment nor say yea and amen, when he considers and judges us to be sinners. If the condemned could do this, they would that very moment be saved. We say indeed with our mouth that we are sinners; but when God himself says it in our hearts, then we are not sinners, and eagerly wish to be considered pious and free from that judgment. But it must be so; if God is to be righteous in his words that teach you are a sinner, then you may claim the rights of all sinners that God has given them, namely, the forgiveness of sins. Then you eat not only the crumbs under the table as the little dogs do, but you are also a child and have God as your portion according to the pleasure of your will.

13. This is the spiritual meaning of our Gospel and the scriptural explanation of it. For what this poor woman experienced in the bodily affliction of her daughter, whom she miraculously caused to be restored to health again by her faith, that we also experience when we wish to be healed of our sins and of our spiritual diseases, which is truly a wicked devil possessing us; here she must become a dog and we become sinners and brands of hell, and then we have already recovered from our sickness and are saved.

14. Whatever more there is in this Gospel worthy of notice, as that one can obtain grace and help through the faith of another without his own personal faith, as took place here in the daughter of this poor woman, has been sufficiently treated elsewhere. Furthermore, that Christ and his disciples along with the woman in this Gospel exhibit to us an example of love, in that no one acts, prays, and cares for himself but each for others, is also clear enough and worthy of consideration.

The Third Sunday in Lent

❦

Christ's Defense Against Those Who Slandered Him

And he was casting out a demon that was dumb. And it came to pass, when the demon was gone out, the dumb man spake; and the multitudes marveled. But some of them said, By Beelzebub the prince of the demons casteth he out demons. And others trying him, sought of him a sign from heaven. But he, knowing their thoughts, said unto them, Every kingdom divided against itself is brought to desolation; and a house divided against a house falleth. And if Satan also is divided against himself, how shall his kingdom stand? because ye say that I cast out demons by Beelzebub. And if I by Beelzebub cast out demons, by whom do your sons cast them out? therefore shall they be your judges. But if I by the finger of God cast out demons, then is the kingdom of God come upon you. When the strong man fully armed guardeth his own court, his goods are in peace: but when a stronger than he shall come upon him, and overcome him, he taketh from him his whole armor wherein he trusted, and divideth his spoils.

— Luke 11:14–23

I. CHRIST'S DEFENSE AGAINST HIS SLANDERERS

1. This is a beautiful Gospel from which we learn many different things, and in which nearly everything is set forth as to what Christ, his kingdom, and his Gospel are: what they accomplish and how they fare in the world. In the first place, like all the Gospels, this one teaches us faith and love; for it presents Christ to us as a most loving Savior and helper in every need, and tells us that he who believes this is saved. For we see here that Christ had nothing to do with people who were healthy, but with a poor man who was greatly afflicted with many ills. He was blind, as Matthew says; also dumb and possessed with a demon, as Luke tells us here. Now, all mutes are also deaf, so that in the Greek language deaf and dumb are one word. By this act, Christ

draws us to himself, leads us to look to him for every blessing, and to go to him in every time of need. He does this that we also, according to the nature of love, should do unto others as he does unto us. This is the universal and the most precious doctrine of this Gospel and of all the Gospels throughout the church year. This poor man, however, did not come to Christ without the Word; for those who brought him to Christ must have heard his love preached and were moved thereby to trust in him. We learn, therefore, that faith comes through the Word; but more of this elsewhere.

2. Secondly, it is here demonstrated how Christ and his Gospel fare in the world, namely, that there are three kinds of hearers. Some marvel at him; these are pious and true Christians, who consider this deed so great that they are amazed at it. Some blaspheme the Gospel; these are the Pharisees and scribes, who were vexed because they could not do the like, and were worried lest the people should hold Christ in higher esteem than themselves. Some tempt him, like Herod desired a sign after his own heart, that they may make sport of it. But he answers both parties; at first, the blasphemers in this Gospel, and later on the tempters, saying that no sign shall be given this wicked generation except the sign of the prophet Jonah, of which we read in the verses following. He answers the blasphemers in a friendly way and argues five points with them.

3. In the first place, with honest and reasonable arguments, he concludes from two comparisons that one devil cannot cast out another; for if that were so, the devils would be divided among themselves and Satan's kingdom would indeed not stand. For nature teaches that if a kingdom is divided against itself and its citizens drive out each other, it is not necessary to go to war against it, for it will come to ruin soon enough of itself. Likewise, a house divided against itself needs no other destruction. Even the heathen author Sallust, teaching only from the light of nature and experience, says, "Great wealth passes away through discord, but through concord small means become large." If now the devils were divided among themselves to such a degree that one should drive out the other, Satan's dominion would be at an end, and we would have rest from his attacks.

4. What, then, were these blasphemers able to say to such clear arguments? They were put to silence, but their hearts were hardened, so that they did not heed his words. A hardened heart will not be instructed, no matter how plainly and clearly the truth is presented; but the faith of the righteous is strengthened when they see that the ground of their faith is right and good. And for the sake of such we must answer those whose hearts are hardened, and put them to silence. Even though they will not be converted nor keep

silence, still it serves to reveal their hardened hearts, for the longer they talk the more foolish they become, and they are caught in their folly, and their cause is robbed of the appearance of being right and good, as Solomon also says in Proverbs 26:5, "Answer a fool according to his folly, lest he be wise in his own conceit." That is, answer him according to his folly that his folly may be put to shame for the sake of others, that they may not follow him and be deceived, thinking that he is right. Otherwise, where no such condition exists, it is better to keep silent, as Solomon also says in the same chapter, verse 4, "Answer not a fool according to his folly, lest thou also be like unto him."

5. Nor could they say here that the devils only pretended to be divided among themselves and to yield to one another in order to deceive the people, for it is publicly seen how they resist and contend, cry and rave, tear and rage, when they see that Christ means to expel them. It is then clearly seen that they are opposed to Christ and his Spirit, and they are not united with him, to whom they must yield so unwillingly. Therefore, it is only a flagrant, blasphemous lie, in which they are caught and put to shame, by which they try in venomous hate to give the devil credit for a work of God. From this, we learn not to be surprised when our doctrine and life are blasphemed, and stubborn hearts will not be convinced nor converted, although they are overwhelmed, as it were, with tangible truth and completely put to silence. It is enough that through our arguments their obstinate folly is revealed, acknowledged, and made harmless to pious people, so that the latter may not be misled by its fine pretension. They may then go whither they will; they have condemned themselves, as Saint Paul says, in Titus 3:11.

6. In the second place, he replies with a public example and a similar work, when he says, "By whom do your sons cast them out?" As if he would say, "Is this not simple idiocy? Just what you praise in your sons, you condemn in me. Because your sons do it, it is of God; but because I do it, it must be of the devil." So it is in this world. What Christ does, is of the devil; if someone else did it, it would be all right. Thus the tyrants and enemies of the Gospel do now, when they condemn in us what they themselves do, confess, and teach; but they must proceed thus in order that their judgment may be publicly approved, when they are condemned by all justice. The sons, of whom Christ here says that they drive out devils, were, I think, certain exorcists among the people, for God, from the beginning, had given this people manifold spiritual gifts and he calls them their "sons," as though to say, I am the Son of God and must be called a child of the devil, while those who are your sons, begotten by you, do the same things and are not to be considered children of the devil.

7. "Therefore shall they be your judges," that is, I appeal to them. They will be forced to decide that you wrongfully blaspheme me, and thus condemn yourselves. For if one devil does not drive out another, then some other power must do it that is neither satanic nor human, but divine. Hence the words, "But if I by the finger of God cast out demons, then is the kingdom of God come upon you." This finger of God is called in Matthew 12:28, the Holy Ghost, for the words read thus, "But if I by the Spirit of God cast out demons," etc. In short, Christ means to say, If the kingdom of God is to come unto you, the devil must be driven out, for his kingdom is against God's kingdom, as you yourselves must confess. But demon is not driven out by demon, much less by men or the power of men, but alone by the Spirit and power of God.

8. From this follows that where the finger of God does not cast out the devil, there the devil's kingdom still exists; where Satan's kingdom still exists, there the kingdom of God cannot be. The unavoidable conclusion then is that, as long as the Holy Spirit does not enter our hearts, we are not only incapable of any good, but are of necessity in the kingdom of Satan. And if we are in his kingdom, then we can do nothing but that which pleases him, else it could not be called his kingdom. As Saint Paul says to Timothy, "The people are taken captive in the snares of the devil unto his will," in 2 Timothy 2:26. How could Satan suffer one of his people to take a notion to do something against, and not for, his kingdom? Oh, it is a striking, terrible, and powerful statement that Christ here admits such a dominion, which we cannot escape except by the power of God; and that the kingdom of God cannot come to us until that kingdom is driven out by divine, heavenly power.

9. This truth is proved in the case of this poor man, who was bodily possessed of the devil. Tell me, what could he and all mankind do to free him from the devil? Without a doubt, nothing. He had to do and suffer just as his master the devil willed, until Christ came, with the power of God. Now then, if he could not free himself from the devil as to his body, how could he, by his own power, deliver his soul from Satan's spiritual dominion? Especially is this the case since the soul, because possessed of sin, is the cause of all bodily possession as a punishment, and sins are more difficult to remove than the punishment of them, and the soul is always more firmly possessed than the body. This is proved by the fact that the devil permits the body to have its natural powers and functions; but he robs the soul of reason, judgment, sense, understanding, and all its powers, as you readily see in the case of this possessed man.

10. He answers them in the third place, by a comparison taken from life, namely, that of a strong man overcome by one stronger, and robbed of all his

armor and goods, etc. By this, he testifies also that no one but God can over-come the devil, so that again no man can boast of being able of himself to drive out either sin or the devil. Notice how he pictures the devil! He calls him a mighty giant who guards his court and home, that is, the devil not only pos-sesses the world as his own domain, but he has garrisoned and fortified it, so that no one can take it from him. He rules it also with undisputed sway, so that it does whatever he commands. Just as little as a house or court may withstand or contend against the tyrant who is its master, can man's free will and natural powers oppose sin and Satan, that is, not at all; but they are subject to them. And as that house must be conquered by a stronger man and thus wrested from the tyrant, so must man also be ransomed through Christ and wrested from Satan. We see again, therefore, that our works and righteousness contribute absolutely nothing toward our salvation; it is effected alone by the grace of God.

11. He answers them fourthly, with pointed proverbs and teachings, as, "He that is not with me is against me," and, "He that gathereth not with me, scattereth." "The devil is not with me for I drive him out, hence he must of necessity be against me." But this saying does not apply to the devil alone, but also to the blasphemers whom he here convicts and condemns, as being against him since they are not for him. "To be with Christ" is to have the same mind and purpose as Christ, that is, to believe in Christ that his works save us and not our own, for this is what Christ holds and teaches. But "to gather with Christ" is to do good out of love to him, and to become rich in good works. He that does not believe is, by his own free will, not with Christ but against him, because he depends upon his own works. Therefore, he that does not love, does not gather with Christ, but by fruitless works becomes only more sinful and drifts farther and farther from the faith.

12. In the fifth place, he answers with a threat, namely, that the last state always is worse than the first. Therefore, we should take heed that we not only refrain from blaspheming the Gospel and Christ, who does such great things for us and drives the devil out of us; but with zeal and fear hold fast to them, in order that we may not become possessed of seven worse devils whereas one possessed us before. For thus it was with the Jews, who had never been so wicked as while the Gospel was being preached to them. So also under the papacy, we have become seven times (that is, many times) worse heathen under the name of Christ than we ever had been before; as Saint Peter says, "The last state is become worse with them than the first," in 2 Peter 2:20. And if we neglect the great light which we now have, it will come to pass in our case also, that we shall become worse than we were before, for the devil does not slumber. This should be sufficient warning.

13. Finally, when the woman cries out to Christ and praises him, saying, "Blessed is the mother that bore such a son," etc., he opposes her carnal worship and takes occasion to teach all of us the substance of this Gospel, namely, that we should not go gaping after the works or merits of the saints but rather see to it that we hear and keep the Word of God. For it does not concern or profit us in the least to know how holy and honorable the mother of this child might be, nor how noble this Son of hers may be; but rather what this Son has done for us, namely, that, by grace, without any merit or worthiness on our part, he has redeemed us from the devil. This fact is proclaimed to us through the Word of God, and this we are to hear and hold in firm faith; then shall we, too, be blessed like this mother and her child.

Although such a Word and work will be blasphemed, we should suffer it and give an answer with meekness, as Saint Peter teaches, for the improvement of others.

II. THE SPIRITUAL MEANING OF THIS GOSPEL

14. This dumb, deaf, blind, and demon-possessed man represents all the children of Adam, who through the flesh are possessed of Satan in original sin, so that they must be his slaves and do according to his will. Hence they are also blind, that is, they do not see God. They are deaf, for they do not hear God's Word, and are not obedient or submissive to it. They are also dumb, for they do not give him one word of thanks or praise, nor do they preach and proclaim Christ and the grace of God. But they are all too talkative about the teachings of the devil and the opinions of men. In these things, they see only too well and are wiser than the children of light in their undertakings, opinions, and desires. In these things, they hear with both ears and readily adopt the suggestions of flesh and blood. So then, whatever we do, in word and deed, as to both body and soul, is of the devil, whether it be externally good or bad, and must be redeemed through the work of God. We are in his kingdom and, therefore, we acknowledge him, see, hear, and follow him, and praise and proclaim his name. All this takes place through the Spirit of God in his Word, which casts out the devil and his kingdom.

15. The Jews called the chief of the devils Beelzebub. The Hebrew word "zebub" means a fly; "baal" or "beel," a man or ruler, as a householder. When the two words form a combination, they mean an archfly or chief fly or, in plain German, "Fliegenkoenig oder grosse Hummel," that is, king fly or the great drone. They gave Satan this contemptuous epithet as though they were entirely free from him, secure against him, and lords over him. That is the way all conceited, corrupt hypocrites do; they imagine they are so pure and holy,

that the devil is a helpless, feeble fly compared with them, and that they do not need the grace of Christ nor the Word of God. Still, they think he is strong enough for others, yet, that whatever God-fearing people teach and do must be the devil's own work, and they consider it such a trifling thing as though it were a dead fly. The devil can well endure such contempt, for by it he is placed above the true God in their hearts.

16. The tyrant in the court or palace is the devil, as I said before. He is in peace, however, as long as God's Word and finger do not oppose him and, just like this deaf-mute, his people do whatever he wishes, for they know no better. His weapons and armor are the carnal conceit, doctrines, and traditions of men, by which he terrifies the conscience and protects himself.

17. But when the stronger man, the Gospel, comes, peace flees, and he rages like a madman, for he resents being condemned, unmasked, punished, and publicly branded. Then he gathers up his armor, the powerful, wise, rich, and holy people, and sets them all to attacking God's Word, as we see in the persecution of the teachers of the Gospel. Such rage and persecution signify that the devil retires very unwillingly and raves in his whole body; for as he acts in the body and its members when he must depart, so he also behaves in the whole world, resisting with all his power when he is to give place to the Gospel; but it is all in vain; he must be expelled.

18. For a stronger one, that is, Christ, comes and overpowers him, and takes away his whole armor, that is, he converts some of those same persecutors and, to that extent, makes him weaker and his own kingdom stronger. He divides the spoils, too, that is, those he converts he uses for various offices, graces, and works in Christendom, of which Paul writes, in Romans 12:6. He is also in the courtyard or anteroom of the palace, for the devil's kingdom consists in outward appearances and pretenses of wisdom, holiness, and strength; but when it is captured by the Gospel, it is found to consist of pure folly, sin, and weakness.

19. The text continues, "When the unclean spirit has gone out, he wanders through dry places, seeking rest," etc. This means as much as the saying, "The devil never takes a vacation" and "The devil never sleeps," for he is seeking how he may devour man. "Dry places" are not the hearts of the ungodly, for in such he rests and dwells like a mighty tyrant, as the Gospel here says; but there are dry and waste places here and there in the country where no people live, as forests and wildernesses. To these he flees in wicked rage because he is driven out. You will remember that the devil found Christ in the wilderness. Now, in Judea, there is not much water; hence we read that it contains many arid wastes. In other countries, however, as in our own, which are well

watered, the devils stay in rivers and lakes, and there they sometimes drown those who bathe or sail upon them. Furthermore, at some places, there are water spirits, who entice the children from the shores into the water and drown them. These are all devils.

20. That he comes again and finds the house swept and garnished (Matthew adds "empty"), signifies that the man is sanctified and adorned with beautiful spiritual gifts, and that the evil spirit clearly sees that he can do nothing there with his familiar tricks, for he is too well known. Thus when the worship of idols was driven from the heathen, he never attacked the world with that device again. But what did he do then? He tried something else, went out, took with him seven spirits, more evil than himself, and entered in with them and dwelt there, and the last state of that man was worse than the first. So he has dealt with us. When Christ had become known in the world and the devil's former kingdom with its idol worship had been destroyed, he adopted another plan and attacked us with heresy and introduced and established the papacy, in which Christ was entirely forgotten, and men became worse heathen under the name of Christ than before he was preached, as we can see now with our own eyes. Such also was the lot of the Jews after the destruction of Jerusalem, and of the Greeks under the Turks [Muslims]. And so all will fare, who at first hear the Word of God and afterward become secure and weary of it. Saint Matthew says, in Matthew 12:14, that Satan finds the house empty. And, in Matthew 13:25, he sowed tares among the wheat, by night, while men slept. Therefore, it is necessary for us to watch as the apostles always admonish us, especially Saint Peter, in 1 Peter 5:3, "Brethren, be sober, be watchful: your adversary the devil, as a roaring lion, walketh about, seeking whom he may devour"; for wherever he overthrows faith, he easily restores again all former vices.

The Fourth Sunday in Lent

❧❀❧

The Feeding of the Five Thousand

A fter these things Jesus went away to the other side of the sea of Galilee, which is the sea of Tiberias. And a great multitude followed him, because they beheld the signs which he did on them that were sick. And Jesus went up into the mountain, and there he sat with his disciples. Now the Passover, the feast of the Jews, was at hand. Jesus therefore lifting up his eyes, and seeing that a great multitude cometh unto him, saith unto Philip, "Whence are we to buy bread, that these may eat?" And this he said to prove him: for he himself knew what he would do. Philip answered him, "Two hundred shillings' worth of bread is not sufficient for them, that every one may take a little." One of his disciples, Andrew, Simon Peter's brother, saith unto him, "There is a lad here, who hath five barley loaves, and two fishes: but what are these among so many?" Jesus said, "Make the people sit down." Now there was much grass in the place. So the men sat down, in number about five thousand. Jesus therefore took the loaves; and having given thanks, he distributed to them that were set down; likewise also of the fishes as much as they would. And when they were filled, he saith unto his disciples, "Gather up the broken pieces which remain over, that nothing be lost." So they gathered them up, and filled twelve baskets with broken pieces from the five barley loaves, which remained over unto them that had eaten. When therefore the people saw the sign which he did, they said, This is of a truth the prophet that cometh into the world.

Jesus therefore perceiving that they were about to come and take him by force, to make him king, withdrew again into the mountain himself alone. — JOHN 6:1–15

I. THE FEEDING OF THE FIVE THOUSAND

1. In today's Gospel, Christ gives us another lesson in faith, that we should not be overanxious about our daily bread and our temporal existence, and

stirs us up by means of a miracle; as though to say by his act what he says by his words in Matthew 6:33, "Seek ye first the kingdom of God, and his righteousness, and all these things shall be added unto you." For here we see, since the people followed Christ for the sake of God's Word and the signs, and thus sought the kingdom of God, he did not forsake them but richly fed them. He hereby also shows that, rather than those who seek the kingdom of God should suffer need, the grass in the desert would become wheat, or a crumb of bread would be turned into a thousand loaves; or a morsel of bread would feed as many people and just as satisfactorily as a thousand loaves; in order that the words in Matthew 4:4 might stand firm, that "Man shall not live by bread alone, but by every word that proceedeth out of the mouth of God." And to confirm these words, Christ is the first to be concerned about the people, as to what they should eat, and asks Philip, before they complain or ask him; so that we may indeed let him care for us, remembering that he cares more and sooner for us than we do for ourselves.

2. Secondly, he gives an example of great love, and he does this in many ways. First, in that he lets not only the pious, who followed him because of the signs and the Word, enjoy the food; but also the slaves of appetite, who only eat and drink, and seek in him temporal honor; as follows later when they disputed with him at Capernaum about the food, and he said to them in John 6:26, "Ye seek me, not because ye saw signs, but because ye ate of the loaves," etc., and also because they desired to make him king; thus here also he lets his sun shine on the evil and the good, in Matthew 5:45. Secondly, in that he bears with the rudeness and weak faith of his disciples in such a friendly manner. For that he tests Philip, who thus comes with his reason, and Andrew speaks so childishly on the subject, all is done to bring to light the imperfections of the disciples, and on the contrary to set forth his love and dealings with them in a more beautiful and loving light, to encourage us to believe in him, and to give us an example to do likewise; as the members of our body and all God's creatures in their relation to one another teach us. For these are full of love, so that one bears with the other, helps, and preserves what God has created.

3. That he now takes the five loaves and gives thanks, etc., teaches that nothing is too small and insignificant for him to do for his followers, and he can indeed so bless their pittance that they have an abundance, whereas even the rich have not enough with all their riches; as Psalm 34:11 says, "They that seek Jehovah shall not want any good thing; but the rich must suffer hunger." And Mary, in her song of praise, says, "The hungry he hath filled with good things; and the rich he hath sent empty away," in Luke 1:53.

4. Again, that he tells them so faithfully to gather up the fragments, teaches us to be frugal and to preserve and use his gifts, in order that we may not tempt God. For just as it is God's will that we should believe when we have nothing and be assured that he will provide, so he does not desire to be tempted, nor to allow the blessings he has bestowed to be despised, or lie unused and spoil, while we expect other blessings from heaven by means of miracles. Whatever he gives, we should receive and use, and what he does not give, we should believe and expect he will bestow.

II. THE ALLEGORICAL INTERPRETATION

5. That Christ by the miraculous feeding of the five thousand has encouraged us to partake of a spiritual food, and taught that we should seek and expect from him nourishment for the soul, is clearly proved by the whole sixth chapter of John, in which he calls himself the bread from heaven and the true food, and says, "Verily, verily, I say unto you, ye seek me, not because ye saw signs, but because ye ate of the loaves, and were filled. Work not for the food which perisheth, but for the food which abideth unto eternal life, which the Son of man shall give unto you," in John 6:26–27. In harmony with these words, we will explain also this evangelical history in its spiritual meaning and significance.

6. First, there was much hay or grass in the place. The evangelist could not fail to mention that, although it appears to be unnecessary; however, it signifies the Jewish people, who flourished and blossomed like the grass through their outward holiness, wisdom, honor, riches, etc., as Isaiah 40:6–7 says, "All flesh is grass, and all the goodliness thereof is as the flower of the field. The grass withereth, the flower fadeth, because the breath of Jehovah bloweth upon it; surely the people is grass." From the Jewish people, the Word of God went forth and the true food was given to us; for salvation is of the Jews, in John 4:22. Now, as grass is not food for man, but for cattle, so is all the holiness of the outward Jewish righteousness nothing but food for animals, for fleshly hearts, who know and possess nothing of the Spirit.

7. The very same is taught by the people sitting on the grass; for the true saints despise outward holiness, as Paul does in Philippians 3:8, in that he counted his former righteousness to be filth and even a hindrance. Only common and hungry people receive the Word of God and are nourished by it. For here you see that neither Caiaphas nor Annas, neither the Pharisees nor the scribes, follow Christ and see Christ's signs, but they disregard them; they are grass and feed on grass. This miracle was also performed near the

festive time of the Jewish Passover; for the true Easter festival, when Christ should be offered as a sacrifice, was near, when he began to feed them with the Word of God.

8. The five loaves signify the outward, natural word formed by the voice and understood by man's senses; for the number five signifies outward things pertaining to the five senses of man by which he lives; as also the five and five virgins illustrate in Matthew 25:1. These loaves are in the basket, that is, locked up in the Scriptures. And a lad carries them, that means the servant class and the priesthood among the Jews, who possessed the sayings of God, which were placed in their charge and entrusted to them, in Romans 3:2, although they did not enjoy them. But that Christ took these into his own hands, and they were thereby blessed and increased, signifies that by Christ's works and deeds, and not by our deeds or reason, are the Scriptures explained, rightly understood, and preached. This he gives to his disciples, and the disciples to the people. For Christ takes the Word out of the Scriptures; so all teachers receive it from Christ and give it to the people, by which is confirmed what Matthew 23:10 says, "For one is your master, even the Christ," who sits in heaven, and he teaches all only through the mouth and the word of preachers by his Spirit, that is, against false teachers, who teach their own wisdom.

9. The two fishes are the example and witness of the patriarchs and prophets, who are also in the basket; for by them the apostles confirm and strengthen their doctrine, and the believers like Saint Paul does in Romans 4:2–6, where he cites Abraham and David, etc. But there are two, because the examples of the saints are full of love, which cannot be alone, as faith can, but must go out in exercise to its neighbor. Furthermore, the fishes were prepared and cooked; for such examples are indeed put to death by many sufferings and martyrdoms, so that we find nothing carnal in them, and they comfort none by a false faith in his own works, but always point to faith and put to death works and their assurance.

10. The twelve baskets of fragments are all the writings and books the apostles and evangelists bequeathed to us; therefore, they are twelve, like the apostles, and these books are nothing but that which remains from and has been developed out of the Old Testament. The fishes are also signified by the number five (Moses' books); as John 21:25 says, "Even the world itself would not contain the books that should be written" concerning Christ, all which nevertheless was written and proclaimed before in the Old Testament concerning Christ.

11. That Philip gives counsel as how to feed the people with his few shillings, and yet doubts, signifies human teachers, who would gladly aid the

soul with their teachings; but their conscience feels it helps nothing. For the discussion Christ here holds with his disciples takes place in order that we may see and understand that it is naturally impossible to feed so many people through our own counsel, and that this sign might be the more public. Thus he lets us also disgrace ourselves and labor with human doctrines, that we may see and understand how necessary and precious God's Word is and how doctrines do not help the least without God's Word.

12. That Andrew pointed out the lad and the loaves, and yet doubted still more than Philip, signifies the teachers who wish to make the people pious and to quiet them with God's laws; but their conscience has no satisfaction or peace in them, but only becomes continually worse, until Christ comes with his Word of grace. He is the one, and he alone, who makes satisfaction, delivers from sin and death, gives peace and fullness of joy, and does it all of his own free will, gratuitously, against and above all hope and presumption, that we may know that the Gospel is devised and bestowed, not through our own merit, but out of pure grace.

13. Finally, you see in this Gospel that Christ, though he held Gospel poverty in the highest esteem and was not anxious about the morrow, as he teaches in Matthew 6:34, had still some provisions, as the two hundred shillings, the five loaves, and the two fishes; in order that we may learn how such poverty and freedom from care consist not in having nothing at all, as the barefooted fanatics and monks profess, and yet they themselves do not hold to it; but it consists in a free heart and a poor spirit. For even Abraham and Isaac had great possessions, and yet they lived without worry and in poverty, like the best Christians do.

The Fifth Sunday in Lent

Christ's Defense Against His Enemies

"W hich of you convicteth me of sin? If I say truth, why do ye not believe me? He that is of God heareth the words of God: for this cause ye hear them not, because ye are not of God." The Jews answered and said unto him," Say we not well that thou art a Samaritan, and hast a demon? Jesus answered, "I have not a demon; but I honor my Father, and ye dishonor me. But I seek not mine own glory; there is one that seeketh and judgeth. Verily, verily, I say unto you, If a man keep my word, he shall never see death." The Jews said unto him. "Now we know that thou hast a demon. Abraham died, and the prophets; and thou sayest, 'If a man keep my Word, he shall never taste of death.' Art thou greater than our Father Abraham who died? and the prophets died: whom makest thou thyself?" Jesus answered, "If I glorify myself, my glory is nothing: it is my Father that glorifieth me; of whom ye say, that he is your God; and ye have not known him: but I know him; and if I should say, 'I know him not,' I shall be like unto you, a liar; but I know him and keep his Word. Your father Abraham rejoiced to see my day; and he saw it, and was glad." The Jews therefore said unto him, "Thou art not yet fifty years old, and thou hast seen Abraham?" Jesus said unto them, "Verily, verily, I say unto you, Before Abraham was born, I am." They took up stones therefore to cast at him: but Jesus hid himself, and went out of the temple.

— JOHN 8:46–59

I. HOW AND WHY CHRIST IN HIS DEFENSE DEMANDS A REASON WHY HIS ENEMIES DO NOT BELIEVE

1. This Gospel teaches how hardened persons become the more furious, the more one teaches them and lovingly stirs them to do their duty. For Christ asks them here in a very loving way for a reason why they still disbelieve, since

they can find fault neither with his life nor with his teaching. His life is blameless, for he defies them and says, "Which of you convicteth me of sin?" His teaching also is blameless, for he adds, "If I say truth, why do ye not believe me?" Thus Christ lives, as he teaches.

2. And every preacher should prove that he possesses both: first, a blameless life, by which he can defy his enemies and no one may have occasion to slander his teachings; secondly, that he possesses the pure doctrine, so that he may not mislead those who follow him. And thus he will be right and firm on both sides: with his good life against his enemies, who look much more at his life than at his doctrine, and despise the doctrine for the sake of the life; with his doctrine among his friends, who have much more respect for his doctrine than for the kind of life he leads, and will bear with his life for the sake of his teaching.

3. For it is indeed true that no one lives so perfect a life as to be without sin before God. Therefore, it is sufficient that he be blameless in the eyes of the people. But his doctrine must be so good and pure as to stand not only before man but also before God. Therefore, every pious pastor may well ask, Who among you can find fault with my life? Among you, I say, who are men; but before God I am a sinner. Thus Moses also boasts in Numbers 16:15, [sic] that he took nothing from the people and he did them no injustice. Samuel did likewise, in 1 Samuel 12:3; also Jeremiah and Hezekiah, who rightly boasted of their blameless life before the people, in order to stop the mouths of blasphemers. But Christ does not speak thus of his doctrine; he says not, "Who among you can find fault with my doctrine"; but, "If I tell you the truth." For one must be assured that his doctrine is right before God and that it is the truth and, accordingly, care not how it is judged by the people.

II. HOW AND WHY IN HIS DEFENSE HE PASSES SUCH A SEVERE JUDGMENT UPON HIS ENEMIES

4. Hence the Jews have no ground for their unbelief than that they are not the children of God; therefore, he passes judgment upon them, and says, "He that is of God heareth the words of God; for this cause ye hear them not, because ye are not of God," which cannot mean anything else than that you are of the devil.

5. The Jews could not stand this, for they wished to be God's children and people; therefore, they are now raging and slander both Christ's life and his doctrine; his doctrine, in that they say, "Thou hast a devil," that is, thou speakest moved by the devil and thy doctrine is his lie; and they slander his life, in that they say, "Thou art a Samaritan," which sounds among the Jews

worse than any other crime. In this way, Christ teaches us here the fate that awaits us Christians and his Word; both our life and our doctrine must be condemned and reviled, and that by the foremost, wisest, and greatest of earth. Thus one knows the corrupt tree by its fruits, as they, under the pretense of being good, are so bitter, angry, impatient, cruel, and mad as to condemn and pass sentence when one touches them at their tender spot and rejects their ideas and ways.

III. HOW AND WHY CHRIST IN HIS DEFENSE DID NOT ESTEEM HIS OWN LIFE, BUT POWERFULLY DEFENDED HIS TEACHINGS

6. What does Christ do here? His life he abandons to shame and dishonor, is silent and suffers them to call him a Samaritan while he takes pains to defend his doctrine. For the doctrine is not ours, but God's, and God dare not suffer in the least, here patience is at an end; but I should stake all that I have and suffer, all that they do, in order that the honor of God and of his Word may not be injured. For if I perish, no great harm is done; but if I let God's Word perish, and I remain silent, then I do harm to God and to the whole world. Although I cannot now close their mouth nor prevent their wickedness, I shall nevertheless not keep silent, nor act as if they are right, as I do about my good life, so that they retain their right. Although they do me injustice at the time, yet it remains right before God. Further, Christ excuses himself, and says, "I have not a demon," that is, my doctrine is not of the devil's lies; "but I honor my Father," that is, I preach in my doctrine the grace of God, through which he is to be praised, loved, and honored by believers. For the evangelical office of the ministry is nothing but glorifying God, in Psalm 19:2, "The heavens declare the glory of God," etc. "But you dishonor me," that is, you call me the devil's liar, who reviles and dishonors God.

7. Why does he not say, I honor my Father, and ye dishonor him, but says, "Ye dishonor me"? Impliedly, he proves by this, that the Father's and his honor are alike and the same, as he and the Father are one God; yet along with this, he also wishes to teach that if the office of the ministry, which God honors, is to be duly praised, then it must suffer disgrace. In like manner, we will also do to our princes and priests; when they attack our manner of life, we should suffer it and show love for hatred, good for evil; but when they attack our doctrine, God's honor is attacked. Then love and patience should cease, and we should not keep silent, but also say, I honor my Father, and you dishonor me; yet I do not inquire whether you dishonor me, for I do not seek my own honor. But, nevertheless, be on your guard; there is one

who seeks it and judges, that is, the Father will require it of you, and judge you, and never let you go unpunished. He seeks not only his honor, but also mine, because I seek his honor, as he says in 1 Samuel 2:30, "Them that honor me I will honor." And it is our consolation that we are happy; although the whole world reviles and dishonors us, we are assured that God will advance our honor and, therefore, will punish, judge, and revenge. If one could only believe it and persevere, he will surely come.

"Verily, verily, I say unto you, if a man keep my word, he shall never see death."

IV. HOW CHRIST IN HIS DEFENSE ASCRIBES A VERY POWERFUL EFFICACY TO HIS DOCTRINE

8. By these words, he spoils it entirely, in that he does not only defend his doctrine as right and good, which they attribute to the devil, but also ascribes such virtue to his teaching that it becomes a powerful emperor over Satan, death, and sin, to give and sustain eternal life. Behold here, how divine wisdom and human reason conflict with one another. How can a human being grasp the thought, that a corporeal, an oral word should redeem forever from death? But let blindness run its course; we shall consider this beautiful saying. Christ is speaking here not of the word of the law, but of the Gospel, which is a discourse about Christ, who died for our sins, etc. For God did not wish to impart Christ to the world in any other way; he had to embody him in the Word and thus distribute him, and present him to everybody; otherwise, Christ would have existed for himself alone and remained unknown to us; he would have thus died for himself. But since the Word places before us Christ, it thus places us before him who has triumphed over death, sin, and Satan. Therefore, he who grasps and retains Christ, has thus also eternal deliverance from death. Consequently, it is a Word of Life, and it is true, that whoever keeps the Word shall never see death.

9. And from this, we may well understand what Christ meant by the word "keep"; it does not refer to such keeping as one keeps the law by good works; for this word of Christ must be kept in the heart by faith and not with the fist or by good works, as the Jews in this case understand it. They fearfully rage against Christ, that Abraham and the prophets are dead; they know nothing of what it is "to keep," "to die," or "to live." And it is not called "to keep" in vain, for there is a conflict and battle when sin bites, death presses, and hell faces us; then we are to be in earnest in holding firmly to the Word and let nothing separate us from it. Thus see now how Christ answers the Jews and praises his own teachings. You say, my Word is of the devil and wish to sink it to the

bottom of perdition; on the contrary, I say to you that it has divine power in it, and I exalt it higher than the heaven of heavens, and above all creatures.

10. How does it then come to pass that man does not see nor taste death, and yet Abraham and all the prophets are dead, who notwithstanding had the Word of God as the Jews say? Here we must give attention to the words of Christ, who makes the distinction that death is a different thing than to see or taste death. We all must face death and die; but a Christian neither tastes nor sees it, that is, he does not feel it, he is not terrified before it, and he enters death calmly and quietly, as though falling asleep, and yet he does not die. But a godless person feels and experiences death, and is terrified before it forever. Thus to taste death may well be called the power and reign or the bitterness of death, yea, it is the eternal death and hell. The Word of God makes this difference. A Christian has that Word and clings firmly to it in death; therefore, he does not see death, but his eyes are filled with the life and the Christ in that Word; therefore, he never feels death. But the godless possess not that Word, therefore, they see no life, but only death; and they must also feel death; that is then the bitter and eternal death.

11. Now, Christ means here that whoever clings to his Word will in the midst of death neither feel nor see death, as he also says in John 11:25, "I am the resurrection, and the life: he that believeth in me though he die, yet shall he live," that is, he will not experience real death. Here we see now what a glorious estate it is to be a Christian, who is already released from death forever and can never die. For his death or dying seems outwardly indeed like the dying of the godless, but inwardly there is a difference as great as between heaven and earth. For the Christian sleeps in death and in that way enters into life, but the godless departs from life and experiences death forever; thus we may see how some tremble, doubt and despair, and become senseless and raging in the midst of the perils of death. Hence death is also called in the Scriptures a sleep. For just as he who falls asleep does not know how it happens, and he greets the morning when he awakes, so shall we suddenly arise on the last day, and never know how we entered and passed through death.

12. Let us take another example. When Israel marched out of Egypt and came to the Red Sea, they were free and experienced no death, but only life. However when King Pharaoh arrived behind them with all his forces, then they stood in the midst of death, then no life was in sight. For before them was the sea, through which they could not pass, behind them King Pharaoh, and on both sides of them high mountains; on all sides they were seized and enclosed by death, so that they said to Moses, "Because there were no graves in Egypt, hast thou taken us away to die in the wilderness?" in Exodus 14:11,

so completely and wholly did they despair of life. Just then, Moses came and brought them God's Word that comforted them in the midst of death and preserved them alive, when he said, in Exodus 14:13, "Fear not, stand still, and see the salvation of Jehovah, which he will work for you today: for the Egyptians whom ye have seen today, ye shall see them again no more for ever." They clung to this Word and held out until victory came; through it life appeared in the presence of death, because they believed the Word, that it would come to pass, and relying upon it they marched into the midst of the Red Sea, which stood on both sides of them like two walls. Then it came to pass that nothing but life and safety were in the sea, where before there were only death and danger. For they would have never become so bold as to go into the sea, had it divided a hundred times, if God's Word had not been present, which comforted them and promised life. Thus man triumphs over death through the Word of Life, if he cleaves to it and believes, and marches into death with it.

13. Likewise, Christ also says here in replying to the Jews, that Abraham and the prophets still live and they never died, but have life in the midst of death; they, however, only lie and sleep in death. For "Abraham," he says, "rejoiced to see my day; and he saw it, and was glad." Thus the prophets also saw it. Where and when did Abraham see it? Not with his bodily eyes, as the Jews interpret it, but with the sight of faith in the heart; that is, he recognized Christ when he was told in Genesis 22:18, "In thy seed shall all the nations of the earth be blessed." Then he saw and understood that Christ, born of his seed through a pure virgin, so as not to be cursed with Adam's children but to remain blessed, should suffer for the whole world, cause this to be preached, and thus overwhelm the whole world with blessing, etc. This is the day of Christ, the dispensation of the Gospel, that is, the light of this day, which radiates from Christ as from the sun of righteousness, and shines and enlightens the whole world. This is a spiritual day, yet it arose at the time Christ was on the earth in the flesh, a day like Abraham saw. But the Jews understood nothing about such a day because of their carnal minds, and hence they reviled Christ as a liar.

14. Therefore, Christ proceeds farther and gives the ground and reason why it is just his Word and not the word of anyone else, that gives life, and says it is because he was before Abraham or, in other words, because he was the one true God. For if the person who offered himself as a sacrifice for us were not God, it would not help or avail anything, even if he were born of the Virgin Mary and suffered a thousand deaths. But the fact that the Seed of Abraham, who gave himself for us, is also true God, secures blessing and

victory for all sinners. Therefore, Christ speaks not of his human nature that they saw and experienced, for they could easily see he was not yet fifty years of age, and did not live before Abraham, but with that nature by which he existed long before the time of Abraham, by which he existed also before all creatures and before the whole world. Just as he was man according to his spiritual nature before Abraham, that is, in his Word and in the knowledge of faith was he in the saints; for they all knew and believed that Christ, as God and man, should suffer for us, as is written, in Hebrews 13:8, "Jesus Christ is the same yesterday and today, yea and for ever"; and, in Revelation 13; 8, "The Lamb of God that hath been slain from the foundation of the world." Yet now he [John] is speaking here especially of his divine nature.

15. But here reason is terribly offended and becomes mad and furious because God should become man; this reason cannot harmonize and understand. And this is the article of faith to which the Jews still in our day cannot reconcile themselves; hence they cannot cease their throwing stones and their blasphemy. But Christ also continues on the other hand to hide himself from them and to go out of their temple so that they cannot see nor find him in the Scriptures, in which they search daily. Again, this narrative is not a little terror to all who are so foolhardy about the Scriptures and never approach them with a humble spirit. For even in our day it happens, that many read and study in the Scriptures and yet they cannot find Christ; he is hid and has gone out of the temple. And how many there are who say with their mouth that God is become man, and yet they are without the spirit in their hearts; who, whenever tested, prove that they were never in real earnest. This is sufficient on this subject.

Palm Sunday

꽃

Christic: An Example of Love

Have this mind in you, which was also in Christ Jesus: who, existing in the form of God, counted not the being on an equality
with God a thing to be grasped, but emptied himself, taking the form of
a servant, being made in the likeness of men; and being found in fashion as a man, he humbled himself, becoming obedient even unto death,
yea, the death of the cross. Wherefore also God highly exalted him,
and gave unto him the name which is above every name; that in the
name of Jesus every knee should bow, of things in heaven and things
on earth and things under the earth, and that every tongue should
confess that Jesus Christ is Lord, to the glory of God the Father.
— PHILIPPIANS 2:5–11

1. Here Paul again presents to us as a powerful example of the celestial
and eternal fire, the love of Christ, for the purpose of persuading us to exercise a loving concern for one another. The apostle employs fine words and precious admonitions, having perceived the indolence and negligence displayed
by Christians in this matter of loving. For this, the flesh is responsible. The
flesh continually resists the willing spirit, seeking its own interest and causing sects and factions. Although a sermon on this same text went forth in my
name a few years ago, entitled "The Twofold Righteousness," the text was
not exhausted; therefore, we will now examine it word by word.

Have this mind in you, which was also in Christ Jesus.

2. You are Christians; you have Christ, and in him and through him all
fullness of comfort for time and eternity: therefore, nothing should appeal
to your thought, your judgment, your pleasure, but that which was in the
mind of Christ concerning you as the source of your welfare. For his motive
throughout was not his own advantage; everything he did was done for your

sake and in your interest. Let men, therefore, in accord with his example, work every good thing for one another's benefit.

> *Who, existing in the form of God, counted not the being on an equality with God a thing to be grasped, but emptied himself, taking the form of a servant.*

> [*Who, being in the form of God, thought it not robbery to be equal with God; but made himself of no reputation, and took upon him the form of a servant.*]

3. If Christ, who was true God by nature, has humbled himself to become servant of all, how much more should such action befit us who are of no worth, and are by nature children of sin, death, and the devil! Were we similarly to humble ourselves, and even to go beyond Christ in humility—a thing, however, impossible—we should do nothing extraordinary. Our humility would still reek of sin in comparison with his. Suppose Christ to humble himself in the least degree—but a hair's breadth, so to speak—below the most exalted angels; and suppose we were to humble ourselves to a position a thousand times more abased than that of the devils in hell; yet our humility would not compare in the least with that of Christ. For he is an infinite blessing—God himself—and we are but miserable creatures whose existence and life are not for one moment secure.

4. What terrible judgment must come upon those who fail to imitate the ineffable example of Christ; who do not humble themselves below their neighbors and serve them, but rather exalt themselves above them! Indeed, the example of Christ may well terrify the exalted, and those high in authority; and still more the self-exalted. Who would not shrink from occupying the uppermost seat and from lording it over others when he sees the Son of God humble and eliminate himself?

5. The phrase "form of God" does not receive the same interpretation from all. Some understand Paul to refer to the divine essence and nature in Christ; meaning that Christ, though true God, humbled himself. While Christ is indeed true God, Paul is not speaking here of his divine essence, which is concealed. The word he uses, *"morphe,"* or *"forma,"* he employs again where he tells of Christ taking upon himself the form of a servant. "Form of a servant" certainly cannot signify "essence of a real servant"—possessing by nature the qualities of a servant. For Christ is not our servant by nature; he has become our servant from good will and favor toward us. For the same reason, "divine form" cannot properly mean "divine essence"; for divine essence is not visible, while the divine form was truly seen. Very well; then let us use the vernacular, and thus make the apostle's meaning clear.

6. "Form of God," then, means the assumption of a divine attitude and bearing, or the manifestation of divinity in port and presence; and this not privately, but before others, who witness such form and bearing. To speak in the clearest possible manner: Divine bearing and attitude are in evidence when one manifests in word and deed that which pertains peculiarly to God and suggests divinity. Accordingly, "the form of a servant" implies the assumption of the attitude and bearing of a servant in relation to others. It might be better to render "*Morphe tu dulu,*" by "the bearing of a servant," that means, manners of such character that whoever sees the person must take him for a servant. This should make it clear that the passage in question does not refer to the manifestation of divinity or servility as such, but to the characteristics and the expression of the same. For, as previously stated, the essence is concealed, but its manifestation is public. The essence implies a condition, while its expression implies action.

7. As regards these forms, or manifestations, a threefold aspect is suggested by the words of Paul. The essence may exist without the manifestation; there may be a manifestation without the corresponding essence; and finally, we may find the essence together with its proper manifestation. For instance, when God conceals himself and gives no indication of his presence, there is divinity, albeit not manifest. This is the case when he is grieved and withdraws his grace. On the other hand, when he discloses his grace, there is both the essence and its manifestation. But the third aspect is inconceivable for God, namely, a manifestation of divinity without the essence. This is rather a trick of the devil and his servants, who usurp the place of God and act as God, though they are anything but divine. An illustration of this we find in Ezekiel 28:2, where the king of Tyre is recorded as representing his heart, which was certainly decidedly human, as that of a god.

8. Similarly, the form, or bearing, of a servant may be considered from a threefold aspect. One may be a servant and not deport himself as such, but as a lord, or as God; as in the instance just mentioned. Of such a one Solomon speaks, in Proverbs 29:21, saying, "He that delicately bringeth up his servant from a child shall have him become a son at the last." Such are all the children of Adam. We who are rightly God's servants would be God himself. This is what the devil taught Eve when he said, "Ye shall be as God," in Genesis 3:5. Again, one may be a servant and conduct himself as one, as all just and faithful servants behave before the world; and as all true Christians conduct themselves in God's sight, being subject to him and serving all men. Thirdly, one may be not a servant and yet behave as one. For instance, a king might minister to his servants before the world. Before God, however, all men being

servants, this situation is impossible with men; no one has so done but Christ. He says at the Supper, in John 13:13–14, "Ye call me, Teacher, and, Lord: and ye say well; for so I am," and yet I am among you as a servant. And in another place, Matthew 20:28, "The Son of man came not to be ministered unto, but to minister."

9. From these explanations, Paul's meaning must have become clear. His thought is, Christ was in the form of God; that is, both the essence and the bearing of deity were his. He did not assume the divine form as he did that of a servant. He was, I repeat it; he was in the form of God. The little word "was" expresses that divinity was his both in essence and form. The meaning is, Many assume and display an appearance of divinity, but are not themselves actually divine; the devil, for instance, and Antichrist and Adam's children. This is sacrilege—the assumption of divinity by an act of robbery. See Romans 2:22. Though the offender does not look upon such conduct as robbery, it is none the less robbing divine honor, and is so regarded by God and angels and saints, and even by his own conscience. But Christ, who had not come by divinity through arrogating it to himself, but was divine by nature according to his very essence, did not deem his divinity a thing he had grasped, nor could he, knowing divinity to be his very birthright, and holding it as his own natural possession from eternity.

10. So Paul's words commend Christ's essential divinity and his love toward us and, at the same time, correct all who falsely assume a divine form. Such are we all so long as we are the devil's members. The thought is, The devil's members all would be God, would rob the divinity they do not possess; and they must admit their action to be robbery, for conscience testifies, indeed must testify, that they are not God. Though they may despise the testimony of conscience and fail to heed it, yet the testimony stands, steadfastly maintaining the act as not right—as a malicious robbery.

But the one man, Christ, who did not assume the divine form but was in it by right and had a claim upon it from eternity, who did not and could not hold it robbery to be equal with God, this man humbled himself, taking upon him the form of a servant—not his rightful form—that he by the power of his winning example, might induce them to assume the bearing of servants who possessed the form and character of servants, but who, refusing to own them, appropriated the appearance of divinity upon which they had no claim, since the essence of divinity was forever beyond them.

11. That some fail to understand readily this great text, is due to the fact that they do not accept Paul's words as spoken, but substitute their own ideas of what he should have said, namely, Christ was born true God and

did not rob divinity, etc. The expression "who, existing in the form of God" sounds, in the Greek and Latin, almost as if Christ had merely borne himself as God, unless particular regard be given to the words "existing in," which Paul contrasts with the phrase "took upon him." Christ took upon himself the form of a servant, it is true, but in that form was no real servant. Just so, while dispensing with a divine appearance, behind the appearance chosen was God. And we, likewise, take upon ourselves the divine form, but in the form we are not divine; and we spurn the form of servants, though that is what we are, irrespective of appearance. Christ disrobes himself of the divine form wherein he existed, to assume that of a servant, which did not express his essential character; but we lay aside the servant form of our real being and take upon ourselves, or arrogate to ourselves, the form of God to which we are not fitted by what we are in reality.

12. They are startled by this expression also, "Christ thought it not robbery to be equal with God." Now, at first sight, these words do not seem to refer solely to Christ, since even the devil and his own, who continually aspire to equality with God, do not think their action robbery in spite of the testimony of their conscience to the contrary. But with Paul, the little word "think," or "regard," possesses a powerful significance, having the force of "perfect assurance." Similarly, he says, in Romans 3:28, "We reckon therefore that a man is justified by faith apart from the works of the law"; and, in 1 Corinthians 7:40, "I think [deem] that I also have the spirit of God." But the wicked cannot boast it no robbery when they dare take upon themselves the form of God; for they know, they are satisfied in themselves, that they are not God. Christ, however, did not, nor could he, think himself not equal to God; in other words, he was confident of his equality with God, and knew he had not stolen the honor.

Paul's words are chosen, not as an apology for Christ, but as a severe rebuke for those who arrogate to themselves the form of God against the protest of conscience that it is not their own but stolen. The apostle would show how infinitely Christ differs from them, and that the divine form they would take by theft is Christ's by right.

13. Paul does not use this expression, however, when he refers to Christ's assumption of the servant form which is his, not by nature, but by assumption. The words produce the impression that Christ took by force something not his own. Paul should be expected to say, "He held it not robbery to assume the form of a servant." Why should he rather have chosen that form of expression in the first instance, since Christ did not assume the divine form, but possessed it as his very own—yes, laid it aside and assumed a form foreign

to his nature? The substance of the matter is that he who becomes a servant does not and cannot assume anything, but only gives, giving even himself. Hence there is no warrant here to speak of robbery or of a disposition to look upon the matter in this light.

On the other hand, assumption of the divine form necessarily involves taking, and altogether precludes giving. Hence there is warrant to speak of robbery in this connection, and of men who so view it. But this charge cannot be brought against Christ. He does not render himself guilty of robbery, nor does he so view his relation, as all others must do. Divinity is his by right, and so is its appropriate form a birthright.

14. Thus it seems to me, this text very clearly teaches that to have divine form is simply to assume in regard to others, in word and deed, the bearing of God and Lord; and that Christ meets this test in the miraculous signs and life-giving words, as the Gospels contend. He does not rank with the saints who lack the divine essence; he has, in addition to divine form, the divine essence and nature. On the other hand, the servant, or servile, form implies acting toward others, in word and deed, like a servant. Thus Christ did when he served the disciples and gave himself for us. But he served not as the saints, who are servants by nature. Service was, with him, something assumed for our benefit and as an example for us to follow, teaching us to act in like manner toward others, to disrobe ourselves of the appearance of divinity as he did, as we shall see.

15. Unquestionably, then, Paul proclaims Christ true God. Had he been mere man, what would have been the occasion for saying that he became like a man and was found in the fashion of other men? and that he assumed the form of a servant though he was in form divine? Where would be the sense in my saying to you, "You are like a man, are made in the fashion of a man, and take upon yourself the form of a servant"? You would think I was mocking you, and might appropriately reply, "I am glad you regard me as a man; I was wondering if I were an ox or a wolf. Are you mad or foolish?" Would not that be the natural rejoinder to such a foolish statement? Now, Paul not being foolish, nor being guilty of foolish speech, there truly must have been something exalted and divine about Christ. For when the apostle declares that he was made like unto other men, though the fact of his being human is undisputed, he simply means that the man Christ was God, and could, even in his humanity, have borne himself as divine. But this is precisely what he did not do; he refrained: he disrobed himself of his divinity and bore himself as a mere man like others.

16. What follows concerning Christ, now that we understand the meaning of "form of God" and "form of a servant," is surely plain. In fact, Paul

himself tells us what he means by "form of a servant." First: He makes the explanation that Christ disrobed, or divested himself; that is, appeared to lay aside his divinity in that he divested himself of its benefit and glory. Not that he did, or could, divest himself of his divine nature; but that he laid aside the form of divine Majesty—did not act as the God he truly was. Nor did he divest himself of the divine form to the extent of making it unfelt and invisible; in that case, there would have been no divine form left. He simply did not affect a divine appearance and dazzle us by its splendor; rather he served us with that divinity. He performed miracles. And during his suffering on the cross he, with divine power, gave to the murderer the promise of paradise, in Luke 23:43. And in the garden, similarly, he repelled the multitude by a word, in John 18:6.

Hence Paul does not say that Christ was divested by some outside power; he says Christ "made himself" of no repute. Just so the wise man does not in a literal way lay aside wisdom and the appearance of wisdom, but discards them for the purpose of serving the simple-minded who might fittingly serve him. Such man makes himself of no reputation when he divests himself of his wisdom and the appearance of wisdom.

17. Secondly: Christ assumed the form of a servant, even while remaining God and having the form of God; he was God, and his divine words and works were spoken and wrought for our benefit. As a servant, he served us with these. He did not require us to serve him in compensation for them, as in the capacity of a Lord he had a just right to do. He sought not honor or profit thereby, but our benefit and salvation. It was a willing service and gratuitously performed, for the good of men. It was a service unspeakably great, because of the ineffable greatness of the minister and servant—God eternal, whom all angels and creatures serve. He who is not by this example heartily constrained to serve his fellows, is justly condemned. He is harder than stone, darker than hell, and utterly without excuse.

18. Thirdly: "Being made in the likeness of men." Born of Mary, Christ's nature became human. But even in that humanity he might have exalted himself above all men and served none. But he forbore and became as other men. And by "likeness of men," we must understand just ordinary humanity without special privilege whatever. Now, without special privilege, there is no disparity among men. Understand, then, Paul says, in effect, Christ was made as any other man who has neither riches, honor, power, nor advantage above his fellows; for many inherit power, honor, and property by birth. So lowly did Christ become, and with such humility did he conduct himself, that no mortal is too lowly to be his equal, even servants and the poor. At the

same time, Christ was sound, without bodily infirmities, as man in his natural condition might be expected to be.

19. Fourthly: "And being found in fashion as a man." That is, he followed the customs and habits of men, eating and drinking, sleeping and waking, walking and standing, hungering and thirsting, enduring cold and heat, knowing labor and weariness, needing clothing and shelter, feeling the necessity of prayer, and having the same experience as any other man in his relation to God and the world. He had power to avoid these conditions; as God, he might have demeaned and borne himself quite differently. But in becoming man, as above stated, he fared as a human being, and he accepted the necessities of ordinary mortals while all the time he manifested the divine form which expressed his true self.

20. Fifthly: "He humbled himself," or debased himself. In addition to manifesting his servant form in becoming man and faring as an ordinary human being, he went farther and made himself lower than any man. He abased himself to serve all men with the supreme service—the gift of his life in our behalf.

21. Sixthly: He not only made himself subject to men, but also to sin, death, and the devil, and bore it all for us. He accepted the most ignominious death, the death on the cross, dying not as a man but as a worm, in Psalm 22:6; yes, as an archknave, a knave above all knaves, in that he lost even what favor, recognition, and honor were due to the assumed servant form in which he had revealed himself, and perished altogether.

22. Seventhly: All this Christ surely did not do because we were worthy of it. Who could be worthy of such service from such a one? Obedience to the Father moved him. Here Paul with one word unlocks heaven and permits us to look into the unfathomable abyss of divine Majesty and to behold the ineffable love of the fatherly heart toward us—his gracious will for us. He shows us how from eternity it has been God's pleasure that Christ, the glorious one who has wrought all this, should do it for us. What human heart would not melt at the joy-inspiring thought? Who would not love, praise, and thank God and, in return for his goodness, not only be ready to serve the world, but gladly to embrace the extremity of humility? Who would not so do when he is aware that God himself has such precious regard for him, and points to the obedience of his Son as the pouring out and evidence of his fatherly will? Oh, the significance of the words Paul here uses! such words as he uses in no other place! He must certainly have burned with joy and cheer. To gain such a glimpse of God—surely this must be coming to the Father through Christ. Here is truly illustrated the truth that no one comes to Christ except the

Father draw him; and with what power, what delicious sweetness, the Father allures! How many are the preachers of the faith who imagine they know it all, when they have received not even an odor or taste of these things! How soon are they become masters who have never been disciples! Not having tasted God's love, they cannot impart it; hence they remain unprofitable babblers.

Wherefore also God highly exalted him.

23. As Christ was cast to the lowest depths and subjected to all devils, in obeying God and serving us, so has God exalted him Lord over all angels and creatures, and over death and hell. Christ now has completely divested himself of the servant form—laid it aside. Henceforth, he exists in the divine form, glorified, proclaimed, confessed, honored, and recognized as God.

While it is not wholly apparent to us that "all things are put in subjection" to Christ, as Paul says, in 1 Corinthians 15:27, the trouble is merely with our perception of the fact. It is true that Christ is thus exalted in person and seated on high in the fullness of power and might, executing everywhere his will; though few believe the order of events is for the sake of Christ. Freely the events order themselves, and the Lord sits enthroned free from all restrictions. But our eyes are as yet blinded. We do not perceive him there nor recognize that all things obey his will. The last day, however, will reveal it. Then we shall comprehend present mysteries; how Christ laid aside his divine form, was made man, and so on; how he also laid aside the form of a servant and resumed the divine likeness; how as God he appeared in glory; and how he is now Lord of life and death, and the King of Glory.

This must suffice on the text. For how we, too, should come down from our eminence and serve others has been sufficiently treated of in other postils. Remember, God desires us to serve one another with body, property, honor, spirit, and soul, even as his Son served us.

Maundy Thursday

❧ ❀ ❧

Of Confession and the Lord's Supper

I. OF CONFESSION AND THE LORD'S SUPPER IN GENERAL

1. Although I have often preached and written on the Lord's Supper and Confession, yet annually the time appointed for the consideration of these subjects, for the sake of those who desire to commune, returns, and so we must review them in a summary and speak of them once more.

2. In the first place, I have often enough said that Christians are not obliged to commune on this particular festive day, but that they have the right and authority to come whenever they desire; for God established the office of the ministers for the purpose that they might at all times serve the people and provide them with God's Word and the sacraments. It is, therefore, unchristian to force people under pain of committing mortal sin to commune just at this time, as has been done heretofore, and is still done in many places. For it is not and cannot be in keeping with the Lord's Supper to force or compel anyone to partake of it; on the contrary, it is intended only for a hungry soul that compels itself and rejoices in being permitted to come; those who must be driven are not desired.

3. Therefore, until the present the devil has ruled with unrestrained power and authority through the pope, compelling him to drive and force the whole world to commune; and in fact, everybody did come running, like swine, because of the pope's command. In this way, so much dishonor and shame have been brought upon the Lord's Supper, and the world has been so filled with sin that one is moved with compassion to think of it. But since we know these things, we ought to let no command bind us, but to hold fast the liberty wherewith Christ has made us free. I say this for the sake of those who will not commune except at this time of the year, and who come only because of the custom and the common practice. There is, to be sure, no harm in coming at this Easter festival, if only the conscience be free and not bound to the time, and is properly prepared to receive the Lord's Supper.

II. OF CONFESSION

4. In the second place, we must say the same thing concerning Confession. First of all, we know that the Scriptures speak of three kinds of confession. The first is that which is made to God, of which the prophet David speaks in Psalm 32:5, "I acknowledged my sin unto thee, and my iniquity did I not hide: I said, I will confess my transgressions unto Jehovah; and thou forgavest the iniquity of my sin." Likewise, in the preceding third verse, David says, "When I kept silence, my bones wasted away as with the drought of summer"; that is, before God no one is able to stand unless he come with this confession, as Psalm 130:4 declares, "But there is forgiveness with thee, that thou mayest be feared"; that is, whoever would deal with thee must deal so that this confession proceeds from his heart, which says, Lord, if thou be not merciful, all is lost, no matter how pious I may be. Every saint must make this confession, as again we read, in the Psalm mentioned, verse 6, "For this let everyone that is godly pray unto thee."

This kind of confession, therefore, teaches us that we are all alike, wicked and sinners, as the saying is, If one of us is good, all of us are good. If anyone have special grace, let him thank God and refrain from boasting. Has anyone fallen into sin, it is because of his flesh and blood; nor has any fallen so low but that another who now stands may fall even lower. Therefore, as far as we are concerned, there is no difference among us, the grace of God alone is dividing us.

5. This kind of confession is so highly necessary that it dare not cease for a moment, but must constitute the entire life of a Christian, so that without ceasing he praise the grace of God and reproach his own life in the eyes of God. Otherwise, if he dare to plead some good work or a good life before God, his judgment, which can tolerate nothing of the kind, would follow; and no one is able to stand before it. Therefore, this kind of confession must be made, that you may condemn yourself as worthy of death and the fire of hell; thus you will anticipate God so that he will not be able to judge and condemn you, but must show you mercy. Concerning this kind of confession, however, we will not speak at this time.

6. The second kind of confession is that made to our neighbor, and is called the confession springing from love, as the other is called the confession springing from faith. Concerning this kind of confession we read in James 5:16, "Confess therefore your sins one to another." In this confession, whenever we have wronged our neighbor, we are to acknowledge our fault to him, as Christ declares in Matthew 5:23–25, "If therefore thou art offering

thy gift at the altar, and there rememberest that thy brother hath aught against thee, leave there thy gift before the altar, and go thy way, first be reconciled to thy brother, and then come and offer thy gift. Agree with thine adversary quickly, while thou art with him in the way, etc." God here requires of both parties that he who hath offended the other ask forgiveness, and that he who is asked, grant it. This kind of confession, like the former, is necessary and commanded; for God will be merciful to no one, nor forgive his sins, unless he also forgive his neighbor. In like manner, faith cannot be true unless it produce this fruit, that you forgive your neighbor, and that you ask for forgiveness; otherwise, a man dare not appear before God. If this fruit is absent, faith and the first kind of confession are not honest.

7. The third kind of confession is that ordered by the pope, which is privately spoken into the ears of the priest when sins are enumerated. This confession is not commanded by God; the pope, however, has forced the people to it and, in addition, has invented so many kinds and varieties of sin that no one is able to keep them in mind; thus consciences have been troubled and tortured in a manner that is pitiful and distressing. Concerning this, however, we will say that God does not force you to confess by faith to him, or by love to your neighbor, when you have no desire to be saved and to receive his grace. Neither does he want you to make confession against your will and desire; on the contrary, he wants you to confess of your own accord, heartily, with love and pleasure. In like manner, he does not compel you to make a private confession to the priest when you have no desire of your own to do so, and do not long for absolution.

This the pope disregarded, and proceeded as though it were a part of the civil government requiring that force be employed; he did not inquire whether a person felt willing or not, but he simply issued the order, that whosoever does not confess at this time shall not have burial in the cemetery. But God cares not whether a thing is done or not, as long as it is not done with pleasure. It is better, therefore, to postpone a duty than to perform it unwillingly. For no one can come to God unless he come gladly and of his own free will; hence no one can compel you to come. If you come because of the command and in order to show obedience to the pope, you do wrong. Yet it is the custom in the whole world that everybody runs to the Lord's Supper solely because it is commanded; hence this is very properly called the week of torture, since in it the consciences of the people are tortured and tormented so that they are really to be pitied, besides the injury and destruction of souls. Moreover, Christ himself is also tortured far more shamefully than when he hung upon the cross. Therefore, we may well lift up our hands and thank God for giving us such light. For although we do not bear much fruit and amend, still we have the right knowledge. Hence it is much better to stay away from confession and communion than to go unwillingly; then at least our consciences remain untortured.

8. Hence we say of private confession, that no one is compelled to observe it. Still it is for this reason a commendable and good thing. Wherever and whenever you are able to hear God's Word, you ought not to despise it, but receive it with heartfelt desire. Now, God has caused his Word to go forth through all the world, so that it fills every nook and corner, and wherever you go you find God's Word. If I preach the forgiveness of sins, I preach the true Gospel. For the sum of the Gospel is, Whosoever believeth in Christ shall receive the forgiveness of his sins. Thus a Christian preacher cannot open his mouth unless he pronounces an absolution. Christ also does the same in the Gospel lesson when he says, *"Pax vobiscum,"* Peace be unto you. That is, I proclaim unto you, as of God, that you have peace and forgiveness of sins; this is even the Gospel itself, and absolution. So also the words of the Lord's Supper, "This is my body which is given for you; this is my blood which is shed for you for the remission of sins, etc." If I were to say, I will not go to confession because I have the Word in the Lord's Supper, I will be like him who declares, Neither am I going to hear the preaching. The Gospel must ring and echo without ceasing in every Christian's mouth. We are, therefore, to accept it with joy wherever and whenever we can hear it, lift up our hands, and thank God that we can hear it everywhere.

9. Therefore, when you go to private confession, give more heed to the priest's word than to your own confessing; and make this distinction, What you say is one thing, and what he says who hears you is another. Do not place much value on what you do, but give heed to what he says, to wit, that in God's stead he proclaims to you the forgiveness of sins. It makes no difference whatever whether he be a priest, called to preach, or merely a Christian. The word which he speaks is not his, but God's Word; and God will keep it as surely as if he had spoken it. This is the way he has placed his holy Word into every corner of the world. Since, therefore, we find it everywhere, we ought to receive it with great thankfulness, and not cast it to the winds.

10. For in Confession as in the Lord's Supper, you have the additional advantage, that the Word is applied to your person alone. For in preaching it flies out into the whole congregation, and although it strikes you also, yet you are not so sure of it; but here it does not apply to anyone except to you. Ought it not to fill your heart with joy to know a place where God is ready to speak to you personally? Yea, if we had a chance to hear an angel speak we would

surely run to the ends of the earth. Are we not then foolish, wretched, and ungrateful people not to listen to what is told us? Here the Scriptures stand, and testify that God speaks through us, and that this is as valid as though he were to speak it with his own mouth; even as Christ declares in Matthew 18:20, "Where two or three are gathered together in my name, there am I in the midst of them"; again in John 20:23, "Whose soever sins ye forgive, they are forgiven unto them; whose soever sins ye retain, they are retained." Here God himself pronounces the absolution, just as he himself baptizes the child; and do you say we don't need Confession? For although you hear the same thing in the Lord's Supper, you ought not on that account to reject it, especially since it applies to you, as already stated, personally.

11. Besides this, you have another advantage: in Confession, you are enabled to disclose all your failings and to obtain counsel regarding them. And if there were no other reason, and God did not himself speak in Confession, I would not willingly give it up for this one reason, that here I am permitted to open my heart to my brother and tell him what troubles me. For it is a deplorable thing to have the conscience burdened and prostrate with fear, and to know neither counsel nor consolation.

This is why it is such an excellent and comforting thing for two to come together, and the one to offer advice, help, and consolation to the other, proceeding in a fine brotherly and affectionate manner. The one reveals his ailment, whereupon the other heals his wounds. I would, therefore, not give Confession up for all the treasure of the world. Still it dare not be made a command, lest it be turned into a matter of conscience, as though a person would not dare to commune without first making confession; nevertheless, we ought never to despise Confession; you cannot hear God's Word too frequently, nor impress it so deeply upon your heart that it could not be done still better.

12. Therefore, I said that confession and absolution must be carefully distinguished from each other, that you give attention chiefly to the absolution, and that you attend Confession not because of the command, or in order to do a good work by your confessing, thinking that because of this good work your sins are forgiven; on the contrary, we are to go only because we there hear God's Word and by it receive consolation. To this incline your ears, and be persuaded that God speaks through men and forgives you your sins; this, of course, requires faith.

Hitherto, the manner of our Confession was as follows: when people were absolved, so many works were required of them as to render satisfaction for their sins. This was called absolving, whereas in truth it meant binding worse than ever. Sins ought to be completely removed by the absolution; but they first imposed the task of rendering satisfaction for them, and thus force people away from faith and absolution, and induce them to rely upon their own works.

They should be taught thus, Behold, this word which I speak to you in God's stead you must embrace in true faith. If you have not this faith, postpone your confession; yet this does not mean that when your faith is too weak you are not to come and demand consolation and strength. If you cannot believe, tell the brother to whom you would confess of it, and say to him, I do indeed feel that I have need of confession and absolution, but I find I am too cold and too weak in faith. For to whom are you going to confide your weakness if not to God? And where can you find him except in your brother? He can strengthen and help you by his words. This is confessing in the right way; and would to God the whole world were brought far enough at least for everyone to confess that he cannot believe.

13. Let it be said now concerning Confession that everything ought to be free, so that each person attends without constraint, of his own accord. But what ought one to confess? Here is where our preachers in the past have pounded a great deal into us by means of the five senses, the seven deadly sins, the Ten Commandments, etc., thereby perplexing our consciences. But it should be, that you first of all feel that which weighs you down, and the sins that pain you most and burden your conscience you ought to declare and confess to your brother. Then you need not search long nor seek all kinds of sins; just take the ones that come to your mind, and say, This is how frail I am and how I have fallen; this is where I crave consolation and counsel. For confession ought to be brief. If you recall something that you have forgotten, it is not to trouble you; for you confessed not in order to do a good work, or because you were compelled, but in order to be comforted by the word of absolution. Moreover, you can easily confess to God in secret what was forgotten, or you can hear the absolution for it during the communion service.

We are, therefore, not to worry even if sins have been forgotten; though forgotten they are still forgiven; for God looks not to the excellence or completeness of your confession, but to his Word and how you believe it. So also the absolution does not state that some sins are forgiven and others not; on the contrary, it is a free proclamation declaring that God is merciful to you. But if God is merciful to you, all your sins must be blotted out. Hold fast, therefore, to the absolution alone and not to your confession; whether you have forgotten anything makes no difference; as much as you believe, so much are you forgiven. This is the way we must ever trust in God's Word in spite of sin and an evil conscience.

III. OF THE LORD'S SUPPER

14. In the third place, we must speak of the Lord's Supper. We said above that no one should be compelled to commune at any special time, but that this should be left free. It remains for us to speak of the two elements in the Lord's Supper. I have already said that among us one element alone is not to be offered to the communicant; he who wants the Lord's Supper should receive the whole of it. For we have preached and practiced this long enough and cannot assume that there should be anyone unable to understand it; yet if there be one so dense, or claiming to be so weak that he cannot grasp the true meaning of it, we will excuse him; it is just as well that he remains away. For anyone to hear God's Word so long, to have himself coddled like a child, and after all to continue saying, I do not understand, is no good sign. For it is impossible for you to hear so long and still be unenlightened; since then you remain blind, it is better for you not to receive the Lord's Supper. If you cannot grasp the Word that is bright, clear, and certain, you need not grasp the sacrament; for the sacrament would be nothing if there were no Word.

Moreover, this Word has now resounded again and again throughout the whole world, so that even they who oppose it, know it. These, however, are not weak but obdurate and hardened; they set their heads against the doctrine they hear us prove from the Scriptures with such clearness that they are unable to reply or establish the contrary; yet they simply remain in the Romish Church and try to force us to follow them. It is, therefore, out of the question for us any longer to yield or to endure them, since they defy us and maintain as their right what they teach and practice. Hence we wish to receive both elements in the Lord's Supper, just because they wish to prevent us from having them. The thought of causing offense no longer applies to those people.

But if there were a locality where the Gospel had not been heard, it would be proper and Christian to adapt one's self for a time to those who are weak, as also we did in the beginning when our cause was entirely new. Now, however, since so much opposition is offered, and so many efforts at violent suppression are made, forbearance is out of the question.

15. It is, moreover, a fine example of God's providential ruling and guidance that the Lord's Supper is not devoid of persecution, for in instituting it he intended it to be a token and mark whereby we might be identified as Christians. For if we were without it, it would be impossible to tell where to find Christians, and who are Christians, and where the Gospel has borne fruit. But when we go to the Lord's Supper, people can see who they are that have heard the Gospel; moreover, they can observe whether we lead Christian

lives. So this is a distinctive mark whereby we are recognized, whereby we also confess the name of God and show that we are not ashamed of his Word.

When now the pope sees me going to the Lord's Supper and receiving both elements, the bread and the wine, according to the Gospel, it is a testimony that I am determined to cling to the Gospel. If then he grows angry and endeavors to slay me, it is just as it was in the early days of Christianity when the Christians confessed God in the same way by this token of the Lord's Supper. Our bishops have forbidden both elements as contrary to God's ordinance and command. If now we mean to confess Christ, we must receive both elements, so that people may know that we are Christians and abide by the Word of God. If for this cause they slay us, we ought to bear it, knowing that God will abundantly restore life to us again. Hence it is proper for us to suffer persecution on this account; otherwise, if everything were to go smoothly, there would be no real confession. In this way, we remain in the right state, always expecting shame and disgrace, yea, even death, for the Lord's sake, as it was in the ancient church.

16. Furthermore, I said it is not enough to go to the Lord's Supper, unless you are assured and know a defense to which you can refer as the foundation and reason that you do right in going; in order that you may be armed when attacked, and able to defend yourself with the Word of God against the devil and the world. On this account, you dare not commune on the strength of another's faith; for you must believe for yourself, even as I must, just as you must defend yourself, as well as I must defend myself. Therefore, above all, you must know the words Christ used in instituting the Lord's Supper. They are these:

Our Lord Jesus Christ, the same night in which he was betrayed, took bread; and when he had given thanks, he broke it and gave it to his disciples and said, "Take, eat; this is my body which is given for you: this do in remembrance of me."

After the same manner also he took the cup, when he had supped, gave thanks and gave it to them, saying, "Take, drink ye all of it; this cup is the New Testament in my blood, which is shed for you for the remission of sins: this do ye, as oft as ye drink it, in remembrance of me."

17. These are the words which neither our opponents nor Satan are able to deny; on them we must stand. Let them make whatever comments they please; we have the clear Word of God, saying the bread is Christ's body given for us; and the cup, his blood shed for us. This he bids us do in remembrance of him; but the pope commands that it be not done.

Well, they say, we are only erring laymen, we do not understand, nor are we able to explain the words. But we reply, It is for us to explain just as much as it is for them; for we are commanded to believe in Christ, to confess our faith, and to keep all the commandments of God, just as well as they are. For we have the same God they claim to have. How, then, are we to believe without knowing and understanding his Word? Since I am commanded to believe, I must know the words I am to believe; for how can I believe without the words? Moreover, it is my duty to stand firm, and I must know how to defend myself and how to refute the arguments to the contrary. This is how you can stop their mouths and bring them to silence. My faith must be as good as yours; therefore, I must have and must know the Word as well as you. For example, the evangelist here says Jesus took the cup and gave it to his disciples, saying, "Take, drink ye all of it; this cup is the New Testament in my blood, which is shed for you," etc. These words are certainly clear enough; and there is no one so stupid that he cannot understand what is meant by, "Take, drink ye all of it; this cup is the New Testament in my blood," etc. Therefore we reply, Unless they prove to us that drinking here signifies something different from what all the world understands by the term, we shall stick to the interpretation, that we are all to drink of the cup. Let them bring forward what they please, custom or councils, we reply, God is older and greater than all things.

18. Likewise, the words are clear, "This do in remembrance of me." Tell me, who is to remember the Lord? Is this said to the priests alone, and not to all Christians? And to remember the Lord, what is that but to preach him and to confess him? Now if we are all to remember the Lord in his Supper, we must certainly be permitted to receive both elements, to eat the bread and to drink the cup; this surely no one can deny. There is, therefore, no use for you to cover up these words and tell us that we are not to know them. If we are not to know them, what are you here for? You claim to be a shepherd and, therefore, you ought to be here to teach these words and preach them to me and now, by your own rotten defense, you are forced to confess your own shame and bite your own tongue, having so shamefully spoken in contradiction of the truth.

19. Thus you see how we are to understand the words of the institution of the Lord's Supper and firmly hold to them, for in them all the virtue is centered; we all must know them, understand them, and cling to them in faith, so as to be able to defend ourselves and to repulse the foe. When you wish to go to the Lord's Supper, listen to the words spoken, and be assured that they contain the whole treasure on which you are to stand and rely, for they are really spoken to you. My body is given, my blood is shed, Christ

declares. Why? Just for you to eat and drink? No; but for the remission of sins. This is what strikes you; and everything else that is done and said has no other purpose than that your sins may be forgiven. But if it is to serve for the forgiveness of sins, it must be able also to overcome death. For where sin is gone, there death is gone, and hell besides; where these are gone, all sorrow is gone and all blessedness has come.

20. Here, here the great treasure lies; on this keep your eyes and dismiss the follies which occupy and trouble the great schools when they inquire how the body of Christ can be present and concealed in so small a space. Be not puzzled about the marvel, but cleave to the Word, and endeavor to obtain the benefit and fruit of the Lord's Supper, namely, that your sins be forgiven.

You must, therefore, act so that the words mean you. This will be when you feel the sting and terror of your sin, the assault of the flesh, the world, and the devil. At one time you are angry and impatient; at another you are assailed by the love of money and the cares of life, etc.; so that you are constantly attacked, and at times even gross sins arise, and you fall and injure your soul. Thus you are a poor and wretched creature, afraid of death, despondent, and unable to be happy. Then it is time, and you have reason enough to go, make confession, and confide your distress to God, saying, Lord, thou hast instituted and left us the sacrament of thy body and blood that in it we may find the forgiveness of sin. I now feel that I need it. I have fallen into sin. I am full of fear and despair. I am not bold to confess thy Word. I have all these failings, and these. Therefore, I come now that thou mayest heal, comfort, and strengthen me, etc.

21. For this reason, I made the statement that the Lord's Supper is to be given only to him who is able to say that this is his condition; that is, he must state what troubles him, and must long to obtain strength and consolation by means of the Word and the symbol. Let him who is unable to use the Lord's Supper in this way remain away, nor let him do like those who wretchedly torture themselves at this time, when they come to the sacrament, and have no idea what they are doing.

Now, when you have received the Lord's Supper, go forth and exercise your faith. The sacrament serves to the end that you may be able to say, I have the public declaration that my sins are forgiven; besides, my mouth has received the public symbol, this I can testify, as also I have testified before the devil and all the world. When death now and an evil conscience assail you, you can rely on this and defy the devil and sin, and thus strengthen your faith and gladden your conscience toward God, and amend your life day by day, where otherwise you would be slothful and cold, and the longer you

remained away the more unfit you would be. But if you feel that you are
unfit, weak, and lacking in faith, where will you obtain strength but here?
Do you mean to wait until you have grown pure and strong, then indeed
you will never come and you will never obtain any benefit from the Holy
Communion.

22. This is the right use of the Lord's Supper, serving not to torture, but
to comfort and gladden the conscience. For by instituting it for us, God did
not intend it to be poison and torture to frighten us; this is what we made
of it by our false doctrine, when we imagined we were to bring the offering
of our piety to God, and hid the words that were to give comfort and salvation, strengthen our consciences, refresh, gladden, and free them from every
distress. This is the meaning of the Lord's Supper, and we are to look upon
it only as containing sweet grace, consolation, and life. It is poison and death
to those who approach it with insolence, who feel no weakness, frailty, or
distress to impel them, who act as if they were pure and pious from the start.
The Lord's Supper welcomes those who perceive their frailties and feel that
they are not pious, yet would like to be. Thus it all depends on this feeling,
for we are all frail and sinful, only we do not all confess it.

23. Let this suffice on how we ought to prepare ourselves to receive the
communion and conduct ourselves toward it, namely, that we are to exercise
and strengthen our faith by the words of the institution of the Supper which
say that Christ's body and blood are given and shed for the remission of sins.
These words sufficiently show the benefit, fruit, and use of the Lord's Supper
as far as partaking of it for ourselves is concerned.

But the second thought springing from the first is Christian love, and this
also deserves attention. It is our duty to let the benefit and fruit of the Lord's
Supper become manifest, and we ought to show that we have received it with
profit. We at present see it received throughout all the world in so many cel-
ebrations of the Mass, but where do you see the least fruit following from it?

24. Now, this is the fruit, that even as we have eaten and drunk the body
and blood of Christ the Lord, we in turn permit ourselves to be eaten and
drunk, and say the same words to our neighbor, Take, eat and drink; and this
by no means in jest, but in all seriousness, meaning to offer yourself with all
your life, even as Christ did with all that he had, in the sacramental words. As
if to say, Here am I myself, given for you, and this treasure do I give to you;
what I have you shall have; when you are in want, then will I also be in want;
here, take my righteousness, life, and salvation, that neither sin, nor death,
nor hell, nor any sorrow may overcome you; as long as I am righteous and
alive, so long shall you also be righteous and alive.

These are the words he speaks to us; these we must take, and repeat them to our neighbor, not by the mouth alone, but by our actions, saying, Behold, my dear brother, I have received my Lord; he is mine, and I have more than enough and great abundance. Now you take what I have, it shall be yours, and I place it at your disposal. Is it necessary for me to die for you, I will even do that. The goal placed before us in the Lord's Supper is that the attainment of such conduct toward our neighbor may appear in us.

25. Of course, it is true, we will not become so perfect that one places his soul and body, goods, and honor at the disposal of the other. We still live in the flesh, and this is so deeply rooted in us that we are unable to furnish this symbol and evidence as perfectly as we should. On account of these our shortcomings, Christ has instituted the Lord's Supper for our training, that here we may obtain what we lack. For what will you do when you miss in yourself what we have described? You must even come and tell him, Behold, this is what I need. Thou dost give thyself to me so richly and abundantly, but I am unable to do likewise toward my neighbor; this I lament before thee, and I pray thee, let me grow rich and strong enough to accomplish it. Though it is impossible for us to reach such perfection, we are nevertheless to sigh for it, and not to despair when we fall short, only so the desire to obtain it continue in our hearts.

26. Yet the least part of love and devotion is not the sacrifice of my pride. I can indeed give my neighbor temporal goods and bodily service by my efforts and labor; I can also render him service by offering instruction and intercession; likewise, I can visit and comfort him when he is sick and in sorrow, feed him when hungry, loose him when bound, etc. But to bear my neighbor's weakness is far greater than all these. Yet with us the trouble will always be that we will not be able to do it as perfectly as Christ did. He is the bright, radiant sun without a single shadow, whereas our light, compared with this sun, is only a gleaming bit of lighted straw. Yonder a glowing oven full of fire and perfect love; and he is satisfied if we light only a little taper and endeavor somewhat to let love shine forth and burn.

This is the shortcoming we all see and feel in each other. But never let anyone conclude and say, This is not Christ. On the contrary, see what he did in the Gospel story when so often he suffered his disciples to stray and stumble, making his wisdom yield and serve their folly. He condemns them not, but endures their weakness, and tells them in John 13:7–33, "Whither I go, ye cannot come." Likewise, to Peter, "What I do, thou knowest not now." By such love, he abandons his righteousness, judgment, power, vengeance, and punishment, and his authority over us and our sins. He could indeed condemn us for our folly, but all he does is to say, You do wrong, you do not know; yet casts us not away, but comforts us. Therefore I said, it is no small evidence of love to be able to bear with one's neighbor when he is weak in faith or in love.

27. On the other hand, Christ's dealing so kindly with his disciples is no permission for us to approve of human weaknesses or of sin. For later he tells Peter, "What I do thou shalt understand hereafter." Here he merely gives his weakness time and bears with it. It is as though he said, I will bear with your ignorance and weak faith for your sake and will spare you as long as you understand that you must do better, and intend to later on; not that you may grow idle and secure.

28. Therefore, when we have received the Lord's Supper, we must not allow ourselves to become indolent, but must be diligent and attentive to increase in love, aid our neighbor in distress, and lend him a helping hand when he suffers affliction and requires assistance. When you fail to do this, you are not a Christian, or only a weak Christian, though you boast of having received the Lord and all that he is, in the Lord's Supper.

29. If, however, you would be sure of partaking profitably of the Lord's Supper, there is no better way than to observe your conduct toward your neighbor. You need not reflect on the great devoutness you experienced, or on the sweetness of the words in your heart. These indeed are good thoughts, but they will not give you assurance; they may deceive you. However, you will be sure as to whether the sacrament is efficacious in your heart if you watch your conduct toward your neighbor. If you discover that the words and the symbol soften and move you to be friendly to your enemy, to take an interest in your neighbor's welfare, and to help him bear his suffering and affliction, then it is well.

On the other hand, if you do not find it so, you continue uncertain even if you were to commune a hundred times a day with devotions so great as to move you to tears for very joy; for wonderful devotions like this, very sweet to experience, yet as dangerous as sweet, amount to nothing before God. Therefore, we must above all be certain for ourselves, as Peter writes in 2 Peter 1:10, "Give the more diligence to make your calling and election sure." The Word and the sacrament are indeed certain in themselves; for God himself, together with all the angels and saints, testify to this; the question is in regard to yourself, whether you furnish the same testimony. Therefore, even if all the angels and the whole world were to testify that you had received the Lord's Supper profitably, it would be weaker testimony than that furnished by yourself. This you cannot reach unless you consider your conduct, whether it shines forth, works in you, and bears fruit.

30. Now, when fruit fails to appear, when you feel that constantly you remain just as you were, and when you care nothing for your neighbor, then you have reason to take a different attitude in these things; for this is no good sign. Even Peter had to hear the same who was godly and ready to die and to do wonderful deeds for Christ. What then will you do? If you still experience evil desires, anger, impatience, etc., you are again in trouble, and that should urge and impel you to go to Christ and lay it before him, saying, I partake of the Lord's Supper, still I remain as I was, without fruit. I have received the great treasure, yet it remains inactive and dormant within me: This I lament before thee. As thou hast bestowed this treasure upon me, grant now that it may also produce fruit and a new life within me, manifesting themselves toward my neighbor. Now when you begin a little to prove this, you will continually grow stronger and break forth in good deeds to your neighbor more from day to day.

31. For this life is nothing more than a life of faith, of love, and of sanctified affliction. But these three will never be perfect in us while we live here on earth, and no one possesses them in perfection except Christ. He is the sun and is set for our example, which we must imitate. For this reason, there will always be found among us some that are weak, others that are strong, and again some that are stronger; these are able to suffer less, those more; and so they must all continue in the imitation of Christ. For this life is a constant progress from faith to faith, from love to love, from patience to patience, and from affliction to affliction. It is not righteousness, but justification; not purity, but purification; we have not yet arrived at our destination, but we are all on the road, and some are farther advanced than others. God is satisfied to find us busy at work and full of determination. When he is ready he will come quickly, strengthen faith and love, and in an instant take us from this life to heaven. But while we live on earth we must bear with one another, as Christ also bore with us, seeing that none of us is perfect.

32. Christ has shown this to us not only by his own example and by his Word, but he has also pictured it to us in the form of the Sacrament of the Altar, namely, by means of the bread and the wine. We believe that the true body and blood of Christ is under the bread and wine, even as it is. Here we see one thing and believe another, which describes faith. For when we hear the Word and receive the Lord's Supper, we have merely a word and an act, yet by it we embrace life and every treasure, even God himself. Likewise, love is pictured in these signs and elements—first of all, in the bread. For as long as the grains of wheat are in a pile before they are ground, each is a body separate for itself, and is not mingled with the others; but when they are ground,

they all become one body. The same thing takes place with the wine. As long as the berries are not crushed, each retains its own form; but when they are crushed, they all flow together and become one drink. You cannot say, this is the flour from this grain, or this is a drop from that berry; for each has entered the form of the other, and thus was formed one bread and one drink.

This is the interpretation of Saint Paul in 1 Corinthians 10:17, "Seeing that we, who are many, are one bread, one body: for we all partake of the one bread." We eat the Lord by the faith of the Word which the soul consumes and enjoys. In this way, my neighbor also eats me: I give him my goods, body, and life and all that I have, and let him consume and use it in his want. Likewise, I also need my neighbor; I, too, am poor and afflicted, and suffer him to help and serve me in turn. Thus we are woven one into the other, helping one another even as Christ helped us. This is what it means spiritually to eat and drink one another.

33. Let me say now in conclusion in regard to the Lord's Supper that when we have received it, we ought to give heed to love and, in this way, assure ourselves that we have received the sacrament profitably and, at the same time, furnish evidence to others; so that we may not always come and still continue unchanged. Therefore, as I said, we must turn from our devotions and thoughts to our conduct toward our neighbor, and examine ourselves in this mirror with all seriousness. The sacrament is to act upon us so that we may be transformed and become different people. For God's Word and work do not intend to be idle, but are bound to produce great things, to wit, set us free from sin, death, and the devil, and every kind of fear, and make us servants even of the least among men on earth, and this without the slightest complaint on our part, rejoicing rather to find someone in need of our help, and fearing only lest after receiving so much we may not apply it all.

34. Whenever the Lord's Supper fails to produce this result, there is reason to fear it has wrought injury. Nevertheless, even if the result is not great, we are not to reject those that are imperfect and weak, but those that are indolent and insolent, who imagine they have done enough when they have partaken of the sacrament. A change must take place in you, and there must be evidence of it, then you will be able to perceive through the symbol that God is with you, and your faith will grow sure and strong. For you can easily feel whether you have grown more joyous and bold than you were before. Formerly, the world seemed too narrow for us when we heard of death and thought of sin. If now we feel different, it is not because of our own strength, for in the past we could not get so far, although we put forth greater exertions and endeavored to help ourselves by means of works. Likewise, you can feel

whether you are kind to him who injured you, and whether you are merciful to him who is sick. Thus you can discover, whether the Lord's Supper is producing any fruit through your own life. If you experience nothing, go to God and tell him of your shortcomings and troubles; we all must do the same thing as long as we live, for, as we have said, not one of us is perfect. For the present, let this suffice on this subject.

Good Friday

How to Contemplate Christ's Holy Sufferings

THE TRUE AND THE FALSE VIEWS OF CHRIST'S SUFFERINGS

I. THE FALSE VIEWS OF CHRIST'S SUFFERINGS

1. In the first place, some reflect upon the sufferings of Christ in a way that they become angry at the Jews, sing and lament about poor Judas, and are then satisfied; just like by habit they complain of other persons, and condemn and spend their time with their enemies. Such an exercise may truly be called a meditation not on the sufferings of Christ but on the wickedness of Judas and the Jews.

2. In the second place, others have pointed out the different benefits and fruits springing from a consideration of Christ's Passion. Here the saying ascribed to Albertus is misleading, that to think once superficially on the sufferings of Christ is better than to fast a whole year or to pray the Psalter every day, etc. The people thus blindly follow him and act contrary to the true fruits of Christ's Passion; for they seek therein their own selfish interests. Therefore, they decorate themselves with pictures and booklets, with letters and crucifixes, and some go so far as to imagine that they thus protect themselves against the perils of water, of fire, and of the sword, and all other dangers. In this way, the suffering of Christ is to work in them an absence of suffering, which is contrary to its nature and character.

3. A third class so sympathize with Christ as to weep and lament for him because he was so innocent, like the women who followed Christ from Jerusalem, whom he rebuked, in that they should better weep for themselves and for their children. Such are they who run far away in the midst of the Passion season, and are greatly benefited by the departure of Christ from Bethany and by the pains and sorrows of the Virgin Mary, but they never get further. Hence they postpone the Passion many hours, and God only knows whether it is devised more for sleeping than for watching. And among these fanatics

are those who taught what great blessings come from the holy Mass and, in their simple way, they think it is enough if they attend Mass. To this we are led through the sayings of certain teachers, that the Mass *opere operati, non opere operantis*, is acceptable of itself, even without our merit and worthiness, just as if that were enough. Nevertheless, the Mass was not instituted for the sake of its own worthiness, but to prove us, especially for the purpose of meditating upon the sufferings of Christ. For where this is not done, we make a temporal, unfruitful work out of the Mass, however good it may be in itself. For what help is it to you, that God is God, if he is not God to you? What benefit is it that eating and drinking are in themselves healthful and good, if they are not healthful for you, and there is fear that we never grow better by reason of our many masses, if we fail to seek the true fruit in them?

II. THE TRUE VIEWS OF CHRIST'S SUFFERINGS

4. Fourthly, they meditate on the Passion of Christ aright, who so view Christ that they become terror-stricken in heart at the sight, and their conscience at once sinks in despair. This terror-stricken feeling should spring forth, so that you see the severe wrath and the unchangeable earnestness of God in regard to sin and sinners, in that he was unwilling that his only and dearly beloved Son should set sinners free unless he paid the costly ransom for them as is mentioned in Isaiah 53:8 "For the transgression of my people was he stricken." What happens to the sinner, when the dear child is thus stricken? An earnestness must be present that is inexpressible and unbearable, which a person so immeasurably great goes to meet, and suffers and dies for it; and if you reflect upon it really deeply, that God's Son, the eternal wisdom of the Father, himself suffers, you will indeed be terror-stricken; and the more you reflect, the deeper will be the impression.

5. Fifthly, that you deeply believe and never doubt the least, that you are the one who thus martyred Christ. For your sins most surely did it. Thus Saint Peter struck and terrified the Jews as with a thunderbolt in Acts 2:36–37, when he spoke to them all in common, "Him have ye crucified," so that three thousand were terror-stricken the same day and tremblingly cried to the apostles, "O beloved brethren what shall we do?" Therefore, when you view the nails piercing through his hands, firmly believe it is your work. Do you behold his crown of thorns, believe the thorns are your wicked thoughts, etc.

6. Sixthly, now see, where one thorn pierces Christ, there more than a thousand thorns should pierce thee, yea, eternally should they thus and even more painfully pierce thee. Where one nail is driven through his hands and feet, thou shouldest eternally suffer such and even more painful nails; as will

be also visited upon those who let Christ's sufferings be lost and fruitless as far as they are concerned. For this earnest mirror, Christ, will neither lie nor mock; whatever he says must be fully realized.

7. Seventhly, Saint Bernard was so terror-stricken by Christ's sufferings that he said, I imagined I was secure and I knew nothing of the eternal judgment passed upon me in heaven, until I saw the eternal Son of God took mercy upon me, stepped forward, and offered himself on my behalf in the same judgment. Ah, it does not become me still to play and remain secure when such earnestness is behind those sufferings. Hence he commanded the women, "Weep not for me, but weep for yourselves, and for your children," in Luke 23:28; and gives, in verse 31, the reason, "For if they do these things in the green tree, what shall be done in the dry?", as if to say, Learn from my martyrdom what you have merited and how you should be rewarded. For here it is true that a little dog was slain in order to terrorize a big one. Likewise, the prophet also said, "All generations shall lament and bewail themselves more than him"; it is not said they shall lament him, but themselves rather than him. Likewise, were also the apostles terror-stricken in Acts 2:27, as mentioned before, so that they said to the apostles, "O, brethren, what shall we do?" So the church also sings, I will diligently meditate thereon, and thus my soul in me will exhaust itself.

8. Eighthly, one must skilfully exercise himself in this point, for the benefit of Christ's sufferings depends almost entirely upon man's coming to a true knowledge of himself, and becoming terror-stricken and slain before himself. And where man does not come to this point, the sufferings of Christ have become of no true benefit to him. For the characteristic, natural work of Christ's sufferings is that they make all men equal and alike, so that as Christ was horribly martyred as to body and soul in our sins, we must also like him be martyred in our consciences by our sins. This does not take place by means of many words, but by means of deep thoughts and a profound realization of our sins. Take an illustration: If an evildoer were judged because he had slain the child of a prince or king, and you were in safety, and sang and played as if you were entirely innocent until one seized you in a horrible manner and convinced you that you had enabled the wicked person to do the act behold, then, you would be in the greatest straits, especially if your conscience also revolted against you. Thus much more anxious you should be, when you consider Christ's sufferings. For the evildoers, the Jews, although they have now judged and banished God, they have still been the servants of your sins, and you are truly the one who strangled and crucified the Son of God through your sins, as has been said.

9. Ninthly, whoever perceives himself to be so hard and sterile that he is not terror-stricken by Christ's sufferings and led to a knowledge of him, he should fear and tremble. For it cannot be otherwise; you must become like the picture and sufferings of Christ, be it realized in life or in hell; you must at the time of death, if not sooner, fall into terror, tremble, quake, and experience all Christ suffered on the cross. It is truly terrible to attend to this on your deathbed; therefore, you should pray God to soften your heart and permit you fruitfully to meditate upon Christ's Passion. For it is impossible for us profoundly to meditate upon the sufferings of Christ of ourselves, unless God sink them into our hearts. Further, neither this meditation nor any other doctrine is given to you to the end that you should fall fresh upon it of yourself, to accomplish the same; but you are first to seek and long for the grace of God, that you may accomplish it through God's grace and not through your own power. For in this way it happens, that those referred to above never treat the sufferings of Christ aright; for they never call upon God to that end, but devise out of their own ability their own way, and treat those sufferings entirely in a human and an unfruitful manner.

10. Tenthly, whoever meditates thus upon God's sufferings for a day, an hour, yea, for a quarter of an hour, we wish to say freely and publicly, that it is better than if he fasts a whole year, prays the Psalter every day, yea, than if he hears a hundred masses. For such a meditation changes a man's character and, almost as in baptism, he is born again, anew. Then Christ's suffering accomplishes its true, natural, and noble work; it slays the old Adam, banishes all lust, pleasure, and security that one may obtain from God's creatures, just like Christ was forsaken by all, even by God.

11. Eleventhly, since, then, such a work is not in our hands, it happens that sometimes we pray and do not receive it at the time; in spite of this, one should not despair nor cease to pray. At times it comes when we are not praying for it, as God knows and wills; for it will be free and unbound: then man is distressed in conscience and is wickedly displeased with his own life, and it may easily happen that he does not know that Christ's Passion is working this very thing in him, of which perhaps he was not aware, just like the others so exclusively meditated on Christ's Passion that in their knowledge of self they could not extricate themselves out of that state of meditation. Among the first, the sufferings of Christ are quite and true; among the others, a show and false, and according to its nature God often turns the leaf, so that those who do not meditate on the Passion, really do meditate on it; and those who hear the Mass, do not hear it; and those who hear it not, do hear it.

III. THE COMFORT OF CHRIST'S SUFFERINGS

12. Twelfthly, until the present we have been in the Passion week and have celebrated Good Friday in the right way: now we come to Easter and Christ's resurrection. When man perceives his sins in this light and is completely terror-stricken in his conscience, he must be on his guard that his sins do not thus remain in his conscience, and nothing but pure doubt certainly come out of it; but just as the sins flowed out of Christ and we became conscious of them, so should we pour them again upon him and set our conscience free. Therefore, see well to it that you act not like perverted people, who bite and devour themselves with their sins in their heart, and run here and there with their good works or their own satisfaction, or even work themselves out of this condition by means of indulgences and become rid of their sins; which is impossible, and, alas, such a false refuge of satisfaction and pilgrimages has spread far and wide.

13. Thirteenthly, then, cast your sins from yourself upon Christ, believe with a festive spirit that your sins are his wounds and sufferings, that he carries them and makes satisfaction for them, as Isaiah 53:6 says, "Jehovah hath laid on him the iniquity of us all"; and Saint Peter, in his 1 Peter 2:24, says, "Who his own self bare our sins in his body upon the tree" of the cross; and Saint Paul in 2 Corinthians 5:21, "Him who knew no sin was made to be sin on our behalf; that we might become the righteousness of God in him." Upon these and like passages you must rely with all your weight, and so much the more the harder your conscience martyrs you. For if you do not take this course, but miss the opportunity of stilling your heart, then you will never secure peace, and must yet finally despair in doubt. For if we deal with our sins in our conscience and let them continue within us and be cherished in our hearts, they become much too strong for us to manage, and they will live forever. But when we see that they are laid on Christ and he has triumphed over them by his resurrection and we fearlessly believe it, then they are dead and have become as nothing. For upon Christ they cannot rest; there they are swallowed up by his resurrection, and you see now no wound, no pain in him, that is, no sign of sin. Thus Saint Paul speaks in Romans 4:25, that he was delivered up for our trespasses and was raised for our justification; that is, in his sufferings he made known our sins and also crucified them; but by his resurrection, he makes us righteous and free from all sin, even if we believe the same differently.

14. Fourteenthly, now, if you are not able to believe, then, as I said before, you should pray to God for faith. For this is a matter in the hands of God that is entirely free, and is also bestowed alike at times knowingly, at times secretly, as was just said on the subject of suffering.

15. Fifteenthly, but now bestir yourself to the end: first, not to behold Christ's sufferings any longer; for they have already done their work and terrified you; but press through all difficulties and behold his friendly heart, how full of love it is toward you, which love constrained him to bear the heavy load of your conscience and your sin. Thus will your heart be loving and sweet toward him, and the assurance of your faith be strengthened. Then ascend higher through the heart of Christ to the heart of God, and see that Christ would not have been able to love you if God had not willed it in eternal love, to which Christ is obedient in his love toward you; there you will find the divine, good Father heart and, as Christ says, be thus drawn to the Father through Christ. Then will you understand the saying of Christ in John 3:16, "God so loved the world that he gave his only begotten Son," etc. That means to know God aright, if we apprehend him not by his power and wisdom, which terrify us, but by his goodness and love; there our faith and confidence can then stand unmovable and man is truly thus born anew in God.

16. Sixteenthly, when your heart is thus established in Christ, and you are an enemy of sin, out of love and not out of fear of punishment, Christ's sufferings should also be an example for your whole life, and you should meditate on the same in a different way. For hitherto we have considered Christ's Passion as a sacrament that works in us and we suffer; now we consider it, that we also work, namely, thus: if a day of sorrow or sickness weighs you down, think how trifling that is compared with the thorns and nails of Christ. If you must do or leave undone what is distasteful to you, think how Christ was led hither and thither, bound and a captive. Does pride attack you, behold, how your Lord was mocked and disgraced with murderers. Do unchastity and lust thrust themselves against you, think how bitter it was for Christ to have his tender flesh torn, pierced, and beaten again and again. Do hatred and envy war against you, or do you seek vengeance, remember how Christ with many tears and cries prayed for you and all his enemies, who indeed had more reason to seek revenge. If trouble or whatever adversity of body or soul afflict you, strengthen your heart, and say, Ah, why then should I not also suffer a little since my Lord sweat blood in the garden because of anxiety and grief? That would be a lazy, disgraceful servant who would wish to lie in his bed while his lord was compelled to battle with the pangs of death.

17. Behold, one can thus find in Christ strength and comfort against all vice and bad habits. That is the right observance of Christ's Passion, and that is the fruit of his suffering, and he who exercises himself thus in the same does better than by hearing the whole Passion or reading all masses. And they are called true Christians who incorporate the life and name of Christ into their

own life, as Saint Paul says in Galatians 5:24, "And they that are of Christ Jesus have crucified the flesh with the passions and the lusts thereof." For Christ's Passion must be dealt with not in words and a show, but in our lives and in truth. Thus Saint Paul admonishes us in Hebrews 12:3, "For consider him that hath endured such gainsaying of sinners against himself, that ye wax not weary, fainting in your souls"; and Saint Peter, in 1 Peter 4:1, "As Christ suffered in the flesh, arm ye yourselves also with the same mind." But this kind of meditation is now out of use and very rare, although the Epistles of Saint Paul and Saint Peter are full of it. We have changed the essence into a mere show, and painted the meditation of Christ's sufferings only in letters and on walls.

Easter Sunday

❧❧❧

Of Christ's Resurrection

A nd when the Sabbath was past, Mary Magdalene, and Mary the mother of James, and Salome, bought spices, that they might come and anoint him. And very early on the first day of the week, they came to the tomb when the sun was risen. And they were saying among themselves, "Who shall roll us away the stone from the door of the tomb?" and looking up, they saw that the stone is rolled back: for it was exceeding great. And entering into the tomb, they saw a young man sitting on the right side, arrayed in a white robe; and they were amazed. And he saith unto them, "Be not amazed: ye seek Jesus, the Nazarene, who hath been crucified: he is risen: he is not here: behold, the place where they laid him! But go tell his disciples and Peter, 'He goeth before you into Galilee: there shall ye see him, as he said unto you.'" And they went out, and fled from the tomb; for trembling and astonishment had come upon them: and they said nothing to any one; for they were afraid. —Mark 16:1–8

I. THE STORY OF CHRIST'S RESURRECTION

1. In the first place, we shall briefly examine the text of this narrative, and afterward speak of the benefits of the resurrection of Christ, and how we should build upon it. The text reads, "And when the Sabbath was past." Here we must remember Mark writes of the Sabbath according to the custom of the Hebrews, for according to the Jewish reckoning, the day began in the evening and lasted until the evening of the next day, as the first chapter of Genesis says, "And there was evening and there was morning, one day," "a second day," "a third day," and so forth. Thus the first and greatest Sabbath began on the evening of the day when Christ was crucified, that is to say, at the time of sunset on the evening of Friday. Our reckoning conveys the wrong sense. Yesterday was the great Sabbath, when Christ lay in the grave;

in addition to this, the Jews had seven full days which they celebrated, and all of which they called Sabbaths, counting them from the first holiday after the great Sabbath and calling it prima *sabbathorum* (first of the Sabbaths), and the third holiday *secundam sabbathorum* (second of the Sabbaths), and so forth. On these days, they ate only wafers and unleavened bread, for which reason they are also called by the evangelist the days of unleavened bread. From this, we must conclude that Christ rose before sunrise and before the angel descended in the earthquake. Afterward, the angel only came to open the empty grave, etc., as has been clearly described by the evangelists.

2. The question now arises, How can we say that he rose on the third day, since he lay in the grave only one day and two nights? According to the Jewish calculation, it was only a day and a half; how shall we then persist in believing there were three days? To this we reply that he was in the state of death for at least a part of all three days. For he died at about two o'clock on Friday and, consequently, was dead for about two hours on the first day. After that night, he lay in the grave all day, which is the true Sabbath. On the third day, which we commemorate now, he rose from the dead and so remained in the state of death a part of this day, just as if we say that something occurred on Easter Day, although it happens in the evening, only a portion of the day. In this sense, Paul and the evangelists say that he rose on the third day.

3. For this period and no longer, Christ was to lie in the grave, so that we might suppose that his body remained naturally uncorrupted and that decomposition had not yet set in. He came forth from the grave so soon that we might presume that corruption had not yet taken place according to the course of nature; for a corpse can lie no longer than three days before it begins to decompose. Therefore, Christ was to rise on the third day, before he saw corruption.

4. The great longing and love of the women for the Lord must also be particularly noted here, so that unadvised and alone they go early to the grave, not thinking of the great stone which was rolled before the tomb. They might have thought of this and taken a man with them. But they act like timid and sorrowing persons and, therefore, they go on their way without even thinking of the most necessary things. They do not even think of the watchers who were clad in armor, nor of the wrath of Pilate and the Jews, but boldly they freely risk it and alone they venture on their way. What urged these good women to hazard life and body? It was nothing but the great love they bore to the Lord, which had sunk so deeply into their hearts that for his sake they would have risked a thousand lives. Such courage they had not of themselves, but here the power of the resurrection of Christ was revealed, whose Spirit

makes these women, who by nature are timid, so bold and courageous that they venture to do things which might have daunted a man.

5. These women also show us a beautiful example of a spiritual heart that undertakes an impossible task, of which the whole world would despair. Yet a heart like this stands firm and accomplishes it, not thinking the task impossible. So much we say for the present on this narrative, and now let us see what are the fruits and benefits of the resurrection of Christ.

II. THE FRUITS AND BENEFITS OF THE RESURRECTION OF CHRIST

6. Saint Paul writes in Romans 4:25, as follows, "Christ was delivered up for our trespasses, and was raised for our justification." Paul is indeed the man who extols Christ in a masterly manner, telling us exactly why and for what purpose he suffered and how we should conform ourselves to his sufferings, namely, that he died for our sins. This is a correct interpretation of the sufferings of Christ, by which we may profit. And as it is not sufficient to know and believe that Christ has died, so it will not suffice to know and believe that he rose with a transfigured body and is now in a state of joy and blessedness, no longer subject to mortality, for all this would profit me nothing or very little. But when I come to understand the fact that all the works God does in Christ are done for me, nay, they are bestowed upon and given to me, the effect of his resurrection being that I also will arise and live with him, that will cause me to rejoice. This must be brought home to our hearts, and we must not merely hear it with the ears of our body nor merely confess it with our mouth.

7. You have heard in the story of the Passion how Christ is portrayed as our exemplar and helper, and that he who follows him and clings to him receives the Spirit, who will enable him also to suffer. But the words of Paul are more Christian and should come closer home to our hearts and comfort us more, when he says: "Christ was raised for our justification." Here the Lamb is truly revealed, of whom John the Baptist testifies, when he says in John 1:29, "Behold, the Lamb of God, that taketh away the sin of the world." Here is fulfilled that which was spoken to the serpent, "I will put enmity between thee and the woman, and between thy seed and her seed: he shall bruise thy head," which means that for all those who believe in him, hell, death, and the devil and sin have been destroyed. In the same manner, the promise is fulfilled today which God gave to Abraham, when he said in Genesis 22:18, "In thy seed shall all the nations of the earth be blessed." Here Christ is meant, who takes away our curse and the power of sin, death, and the devil.

8. All this is done, I say, by faith. For if you believe that by this seed the serpent has been slain, then it is slain for you; and if you believe that in this seed all nations are to be blessed, then you are also blessed. For each one individually should have crushed the serpent under foot and redeemed himself from the curse, which would have been too difficult, nay, impossible for us. But now it has been done easily, namely, by Christ, who has crushed the serpent once, who alone is given as a blessing and benediction, and who has caused this Gospel to be published throughout the world, so that he who believes, accepts it, and clings to it, is also in possession of it, and is assured that it is as he believes. For in the heart of such a man, the Word becomes so powerful that he will conquer death, the devil, sin, and all adversity, like Christ himself did. So mighty is the Word that God himself would sooner be vanquished than that his Word should be conquered.

9. This is the meaning of the words by Saint Paul, "Christ was raised for our justification." Here Paul turns my eyes away from my sins and directs them to Christ, for if I look at my sins, they will destroy me. I must, therefore, look unto Christ, who has taken my sins upon himself, crushed the head of the serpent, and become the blessing. Now, they no longer burden my conscience, but rest upon Christ, whom they desire to destroy. Let us see how they treat him. They hurl him to the ground and kill him. O God; where is now my Christ and my Savior? But then God appears, delivers Christ, and makes him alive; and not only does he make him alive, but he translates him into heaven and lets him rule over all. What has now become of sin? There it lies under his feet. If I then cling to this, I have a cheerful conscience like Christ, because I am without sin. Now I can defy death, the devil, sin, and hell to do me any harm. As I am a child of Adam, they can indeed accomplish it that I must die. But since Christ has taken my sins upon himself, has died for them, has suffered himself to be slain on account of my sins, they can no longer harm me, for Christ is too strong for them; they cannot keep him; he breaks forth and overpowers them, ascends into heaven (takes sin and sorrow captive, Ed. 1531), and rules there over all throughout eternity. Now I have a clear conscience, am joyful and happy, and am no longer afraid of this tyrant, for Christ has taken my sins away from me and made them his own. But they cannot remain upon him; what then becomes of them? They must disappear and be destroyed. This then is the effect of faith. He who believes that Christ has taken away our sin, is without sin, like Christ himself, and death, the devil, and hell are vanquished as far as he is concerned, and they can no longer harm him.

10. Here we also refer to the passage in Hosea 13:14, which Paul quotes in reference to the victory that Christ has won by his resurrection, and by

which he has conquered sin, death, hell, and all our enemies. Paul says that death is swallowed up in this victory, and he defies death with these words, "O death, where is thy victory? O death, where is thy sting?" Just as if Paul would say, O death, where are thy teeth? Come, bite off one of my fingers. Thou formerly hadst a spear, what has become of it now? Christ has taken it from thee. Death, where is now thy spear, etc.? Sin, where is now the edge of thy sword and thy power? Paul says that the power of sin is the law. The more clearly we understand the law, the more sin oppresses and stings us. For this reason, Paul says that Christ has completely destroyed and annihilated the spear and whetstone of death. Now, this Gospel he has not taken with him into heaven, but he caused it to be preached throughout the world, so that for him who believes in Christ, spear and whetstone, nay, sin and death, should be destroyed. This is the true Gospel, which bestows life, strength, power, and marrow, and of which all the passages of Scripture speak.

11. Therefore, seek and learn to know Christ aright, for the whole Scriptures confer upon us the righteousness of the true knowledge of Christ. But this must be brought about by the Holy Spirit. Let us, therefore, pray God that his Gospel may prosper, that we all may truly learn to know Christ and thus rise with him and be honored by God as he was honored.

12. The question now arises, If Christ has taken away death and our sins by his resurrection and has justified us, why do we then still feel death and sin within us? For our sins torment us still, we are stung by our conscience, and this evil conscience creates the fear of hell.

13. To this I reply, I have often said before that feeling and faith are two different things. It is the nature of faith not to feel, to lay aside reason and close the eyes, to submit absolutely to the Word, and follow it in life and death. Feeling, however, does not extend beyond that which may be apprehended by reason and the senses, which may be heard, seen, felt, and known by the outward senses. For this cause, feeling is opposed to faith, and faith is opposed to feeling. Therefore, the author of the Epistle to the Hebrews writes of faith, "Now faith is assurance of things hoped for, a conviction of things not seen." For if we would see Christ visibly in heaven, like the visible sun, we would not need to believe it. But since Christ died for our sins and was raised for our justification, we cannot see it nor feel it, neither can we comprehend it with our reason. Therefore, we must disregard our feeling and accept only the Word, write it into our heart, and cling to it, even though it seems as if my sins were not taken from me, and even though I still feel them within me. Our feelings must not be considered, but we must constantly insist that death, sin, and hell have been conquered, although I feel that I am still under

the power of death, sin, and hell. For although we feel that sin is still in us, it is only permitted that our faith may be developed and strengthened, that in spite of all our feelings, we accept the Word, and that we unite our hearts and consciences more and more to Christ. Thus faith leads us quietly, contrary to all feeling and comprehension of reason, through sin, through death, and through hell. Then we shall see salvation before our eyes, and then we shall know perfectly what we have believed, namely, that death and all sorrow have been conquered.

14. Take as an illustration the fish in the water. When they are caught in the net, you lead it quietly along, so that they imagine they are still in the water; but when you draw them to the shore, they are exposed and begin to struggle, and then they first feel they are caught. Thus it also happens with souls that are caught with the Gospel, which Christ compares with a net, in Matthew 13:47. When the heart has been conquered, the Word unites this poor heart to Christ and leads it gently and quietly from hell and from sin, although the soul still feels sin and imagines to be still under its power. Then a conflict begins, the feelings struggling against the Spirit and faith, and the Spirit and faith against our feelings; and the more faith increases, the more our feelings diminish, and vice versa. We have still sins within us, as for instance pride, avarice, anger, and so forth, but only in order to lead us to faith, so that faith may increase from day to day, and the man become finally a thorough Christian and keep the true Sabbath, consecrating himself to Christ entirely. Then the conscience must become calm and satisfied, and all the surging waves of sin subside. For as upon the sea one billow follows and buffets the other, as though they would destroy the shore, yet they must disappear and destroy themselves, so also our sins strive against us and would fain bring us to despair, but finally they must desist, grow weary, and disappear.

15. In the second place, death is still at our elbow. It also is to exercise the faith of him who believes that death has been killed and all his power taken away. Now, reason feels that death is still at our elbow and is continually troubling us. He who follows his feelings will perish, but he who clings to the Word with his heart will be delivered. Now, if the heart clings to the Word, reason will also follow; but if reason follows, everything will follow, desire and love and all that is in man. Yea, we desire that all may come to the point when they may consider death to be dead and powerless. But this cannot come to pass until the old man, that is, the old Adam, be entirely destroyed and, meanwhile, that process has been going on of which Christ speaks in Matthew 13:33, where he compares the kingdom of God to leaven, which a woman took and hid in three measures of meal. For even if the kneading

has begun, the meal is not yet thoroughly leavened. So it is here. Although the heart clings to the belief that death and hell are destroyed, yet the leaven has not yet worked through it entirely. For it must penetrate and impregnate all the members of the body, until everything becomes leavened and pure, and there remains nothing but a pure faith. This will not be brought about before the old man is entirely destroyed; then all that is in man is Christlike from center to circumference.

16. These two things, sin and death, therefore, remain with us to the end, that we might cultivate and exercise our faith, in order that it may become more perfect in our heart from day to day and finally break forth, and all that we are, body and soul, become more Christlike. For when the heart clings to the Word, feelings and reasoning must fail. Then in the course of time, the will also clings to the Word, and with the will everything else, our desire and love, until we surrender ourselves entirely to the Gospel, are renewed, and leave the old sin behind. Then there comes a different light, different feelings, different seeing, different hearing, acting, and speaking, and also a different outflow of good works. Now, our Scholastics and papists have taught an external piety; they would command the eyes not to see, and the ears not to hear, and would put piety into our hearts from the outside. Ah, how far this is from the truth! But it comes in this way: When the heart and conscience cling to the Word in faith, they overflow in works, so that, when the heart is holy, all the members become holy, and good works follow naturally.

17. This is signified by the Sabbath that was to be hallowed, and on which the Lord lay quietly in the grave. It signifies that we should rest from all our works, should not stir, nay, should not allow any sin to stir within us, but we should firmly believe that death, hell, sin, and the devil are destroyed by the death of Christ, and we are righteous, pious, holy, and, therefore, contented, experiencing no longer any sin. Then all the members are calm and quiet, being convinced that sin and death are vanquished and prostrated. But this cannot be brought about, as I have said, until this impotent, wretched body and the old Adam are destroyed. Therefore, it is indeed necessary that we are required to keep this Sabbath. For as Christ lies in the grave on the Sabbath, never feels nor moves, so it must be with us, as we have heard: Our feelings and actions must cease. And I say again that this cannot be accomplished before the old Adam is annihilated. Nevertheless, we still experience sin and death within us, wrestle with them and fight against them. You may tie a hog ever so well, but you cannot prevent it from grunting (until it is strangled and killed, Ed. 1531). Thus it is with the sins in our flesh. As they are not yet entirely conquered and killed, they are still active, but when death comes, they

must also die, and then we are perfect Christians and pure, but not before. This is the reason why we must die, namely, that we may be entirely freed from sin and death. These words on the fruits of the resurrection of Christ may suffice for the present, and with them we will close. Let us pray God for grace that we may understand them and learn to know Christ aright.

Easter Sunday

❧❀❧

The Manifestation of Christ After His Resurrection, and the Sermon He Preached to His Disciples

*A*nd as they spake these things, he himself stood in the midst of *them, and saith unto them, "Peace be unto you." But they were terrified and affrighted, and supposed that they beheld a spirit. And he said unto them, "Why are ye troubled? and wherefore do questionings arise in your heart? See my hands and my feet, that it is I myself: handle me, and see, for a spirit hath not flesh and bones, as ye behold me having". And when he had said this, he showed them his hands and his feet. And while they still disbelieved for joy, and wondered, he said unto them, "Have ye here anything to eat?" And they gave him a piece of a broiled fish. And he took it, and ate before them.*

And he said unto them, "These are my words which I spake unto you, while I was yet with you, that all things must needs be fulfilled, which are written in the law of Moses, and the prophets, and the psalms, concerning me." Then opened he their mind, that they might understand the Scriptures; and he said unto them, "Thus it is written, that the Christ should suffer, and rise again from the dead the third day; and that repentance and remission of sins should be preached in his name unto all the nations, beginning from Jerusalem." — LUKE 24:36–47

I. CHRIST'S MANIFESTATION AFTER HIS RESURRECTION

1. I think, beloved, you have heard enough in these days on the resurrection of Christ, what it works, why it came to pass, and what fruit it bears. But since the Lord has commanded those who preach the Gospel to be steadfast and diligent in this proclamation, we must dwell upon it ever more and more. Our Gospel shows, first, who hear of the Lord's resurrection profitably and fruitfully, namely, they that are here assembled in fear and dread behind closed doors. To them it ought also to be preached most of all, although it must be preached to all nations, as the Lord says at the end of the Gospel of

Matthew. Therefore, let us learn first of all what kind of persons hear the Gospel aright.

2. The disciples are gathered there together in seclusion. They are afraid of the Jews and are, indeed, in danger of their lives; they are fearful and fainthearted, and afraid of sin and death. Had they been strong and courageous, they would not thus have crept into a corner; even as afterward they were made so courageous, when the Holy Spirit came and strengthened and comforted them, that they stepped forth and preached publicly without fear. This is written for us, that we might learn that the Gospel of Christ's resurrection comforts only the fainthearted. And who are these? They are the poor, conscience-stricken ones, whose sins lie heavily upon them, who feel their faint heart, are loath to die, and are well-nigh startled by the sound of a rustling leaf. To these contrite, poor, and needy souls, the Gospel offers comfort; to them it is a sweet savor.

3. This is also learned from the nature of the Gospel, for the Gospel is a message and a testimony, which declares how the Lord Jesus Christ rose from the dead, that he might remove sin, death, and all evil from all who believe on him. If I recognize him as such a Savior, I have heard the Gospel aright, and he has in truth revealed himself to me. If now the Gospel teaches naught but that Christ has overcome sin and death by his resurrection, then we must indeed confess that it can be of service to none save those who feel sin and death. For they who do not feel their sin, and are not dismayed, nor see their infirmities, profit not a whit by it, nor do they delight in it. And though they hear the Gospel, it has no effect upon them, except that they learn the words, and speak of what they heard. They do not treasure them in their hearts, and receive neither comfort nor joy from them.

4. Hence it were well, if the Gospel could be preached only where such fainthearted and conscience-stricken ones are found. But this cannot be and, for this reason, it bears so little fruit. For this they reproach us, and say that we wish to preach many new things, and yet no one is better because of our doctrine. The fault is not in the Gospel, but in the hearers. They hear it, indeed, but they do not feel their own affliction and misery, nor have they ever tried to feel it; they simply go on, secure and reprobate, like dumb brutes. Hence none need marvel if the Gospel does not everywhere bring forth fruit. For besides the good hearers, of whom we have spoken, there are many others that have no regard for it at all, have neither a conscience nor a heart for it, and think neither of death nor of the salvation of souls. These must be driven by force, like asses and dumb brutes and, for this purpose, the civil sword is established. Again, there are some who do not despise the Gospel, but fully

understand it, yet do not amend their lives, nor strive to walk in it. They carry away only the words and prate much about them, but neither deeds nor fruit follow. The third class, however, are they that taste it and use it aright, so that it bears fruit in them.

5. This is then the conclusion of the matter: the Gospel is a testimony of the resurrection of Christ, which serves to comfort and refresh the poor, sorrowing, and terrified consciences. There is need that we have clearly apprehended this truth when we come to die, and also that we may provide for it in every other need. If you think, Behold, now death is approaching and staring me in the face; would that I had someone to comfort me that I might not despair; then know that for this purpose the Gospel is good; here it belongs, here its use is blessed and salutary. As soon as a man knows and understands this, and believes the Gospel, his heart finds peace, and says, If Christ, my Lord, has overcome my sin, and trodden it under foot by his resurrection, wherefore should I fear, and of what should I be afraid? Why should not my heart rejoice and be of good cheer? But such comfort, peace, and joy of heart are felt by none save by the small company which was before greatly dismayed and full of sorrow, and felt its infirmities. Hence also the rude and impenitent understand neither this nor any other Gospel, for he that has not tasted the bitter cannot relish the sweet, and he that has not seen adversity does not understand happiness. For as in the world, that man who neither cares nor attempts to do anything and endures naught, is good for nothing, so, in a more eminent degree in spiritual things, it is not possible that anyone should understand the Gospel except he who has such a dismayed and terrified heart.

6. From this, you should learn that it is no marvel, that many who hear the Gospel do not receive it nor live according to it. Everywhere there are many who reject and persecute it, but we must let them go and grow accustomed to their work. Where the Gospel is preached, such people will surely be found and, if it were otherwise, it would not be right, for there must be many kinds of hearers. Again, many will be found who do not persecute it and yet do not receive it, for they bear no fruit and continue to live as before. Be not worried because of this! for even though a man preach and continue in the Gospel for many years, he must still lament, and say, Aye, no one will come, and all continue in their former state. Therefore, you must not let that grieve nor terrify you.

7. For note what took place at Jerusalem, where the Gospel was first heard, and where there were so many people that it is said, there were in the city at the feast of the Passover eleven hundred thousand men. How many of

these were converted? When Saint Peter stood up and preached, they made
a mockery of it and considered the apostles drunken fools. When they had
urged the Gospel a long time, they gathered together three thousand men and
women. But what were they among so many? Yea, no one could discern that
the Gospel had accomplished anything, for all things continued in the same
state as before. No change was seen, and scarcely anyone knew that there
were Christians there. And so it will be at all times.

8. Hence the Gospel must not be measured by the multitude that hear,
but by the small company that receive it. They, indeed, appear as nothing; they
are despised and persecuted, and yet God secretly works in them.

9. Besides this, there is another thing that hinders the free movement
of the Gospel, namely, the infirmities of the believers. This we see in many
examples. Thus although Peter was filled with faith and the Holy Spirit, yet
he fell and stumbled, he and all that were with him, when he walked not
according to the Gospel nor according as he had taught, so that Paul had to
reprove him openly, in Galatians 2:14. There clung to him many great and
holy men, and all stumbled with him. Again, we read that Mark journeyed
with Paul, but afterward fell away and withdrew from him; and in Acts 15:37,
we read again that Paul and Barnabas strove together, and there arose a sharp
contention between them. And, before this, we read in the Gospels how often
the apostles erred in weighty matters, though they were the best of Christians.

10. These infirmities of Christians and believers darken the Gospel most
of all, so that men who deem themselves wise and learned stumble and are
offended in them. Few there are who can well reconcile these things so as
to take no offense and hence say, Yes, these desire to be good Christians, and
are still so wayward, envious, filled with hate and wrath, that one thinks the
Gospel has been preached in vain. This really signifies to be offended in the
weak and sick Christ.

11. It was also thus with the disciples. At first, when Christ wrought great
and excellent works, and gained great honors, and began the work only to
fulfill it, they remained steadfast, though many great and noble saints and
learned men were offended, because he would not join them. The common
man on the contrary was instructed, and the people clung to him, because
they saw that with great power he wrought such excellent works; and also
walked so that none could reproach him, but all must needs say, Truly this is
a great and holy prophet! But when his suffering began, they all turned back
and forsook him, and not one of his disciples continued with him. Why was
this? Because they considered him not the strong, but the weak Christ. He
now was in the hands of the Jews, did no more works and miracles just as if

he had lost all his power and was forsaken of God. Then perished completely his power and his great name. Before, they counted him a prophet, the like of whom had never appeared; now, he is rated as a murderer and a condemned man. Who could now see that this was Christ, the Son of God? Here all reason must fall, yea, all the great and holy saints; for they thought, If he were the Christ, there would needs appear the fruits whereby we might know that it is he, but now we see in him only weakness and sin and death.

12. Therefore, it is the highest wisdom on earth, though it is known by very few men, how to bear with the weak Christ. For if I see a pious, holy man leading a beautiful godly life, who will thank me for praising him, and saying, There is Christ, and there is righteousness? For although bishops and great dunces be offended in such a one, the common people will be instructed. But if he be feeble and falter, straightway everyone will be offended and say, Alas! I had imagined him to be a good Christian, but I see that he falls short of it. However, if they look about them, they will find none without like infirmities, yea, they will perceive it in themselves. Still they think that the Gospel has come to naught. Thus might they think, if God were not able, in his wisdom, to hide it, even as he put a covering over Christ when he drew over him death and weakness, and Christ was under it, though no man could see it. Hence he told his disciples in advance, in Matthew 26:31, "All, all ye, shall be offended in me, and shall no more think nor believe that I am the Christ." Hence if we judge the Gospel, as I have said, according to the infirmity and weakness of Christians, as they stumble at times, a very great obstacle is presented at which offense is taken, and the Gospel is thought to be without power.

13. Therefore, he that would know Christ aright must not give heed to the covering. And though you see another stumble, do not despair, nor think all hope is lost; but rather think, God, perchance, will have this one bear the weak Christ, even as another bears the strong; for both must be and abide on earth, though the greater part appear weak and are such especially in our day. But if you pierce through such weakness, you will find that Christ lies hidden in that weak person; he will come forth and show himself.

14. That is what Paul means when he says to the Corinthians, in 1 Corinthians 2:2, "I determined not to know anything among you, save Jesus Christ, and him crucified." What kind of glory is this that impels him to write that he knows nothing, save Christ crucified? It is a thing that neither reason nor human wisdom can understand, nor yet they who have studied and learned the Gospel; for this wisdom is mighty, hidden, and mysterious, and seems of no value, because he was crucified and emptied himself of all power and divine strength, and hung upon the cross like a wretched, forsaken man, and it

seemed as if God would not help him. Of him alone I speak and preach, says Saint Paul. For the Christ, that sits on high, does wonders, comes and breaks through with power, that all may see who he is, and may quickly come to know him. But to know the weak Christ, that is hanging upon the cross and lying in death, one needs great wisdom; for they who know him not, must needs stumble and be offended.

15. Yea, some are also found who really know the Gospel, but are offended at their own manner of life. They have a desire to walk in godliness, but they feel they make no progress. They begin to despair and think that with them all is lost because they do not feel the strength which they ought to have, also earnestly desire Christ to become strong in them and manifest himself in mighty deeds. But Jehovah, our God, hereby designs to humble us, that we may see what feeble creatures we are, what wretched, lost, and condemned men, if Christ had not come and helped us. Behold, that is the great wisdom we have, and at which all the world is offended.

16. But thereby we have no furlough, to continue for all time in weakness, for we do not preach that any should be weak, but that we should know the weakness of Christians and bear with it. Christ did not hang upon the cross, that he might appear as a murderer and evildoer, but that we might learn thereby how deeply strength lies hidden under weakness, and might learn to know God's strength in weakness. Thus our weakness is not to be praised, as though we should abide in it, but rather must we learn not to think that those who are weak are not Christians, nor yet to despair when we feel our own weakness. Therefore, it behooves us to know our own weaknesses and ever to seek to wax stronger, for Christ must not suffer always, nor remain in the grave, but must come forth again and live.

17. Hence let none say that this is the true course and condition. It is only a beginning, in which we must grow day by day, giving heed only that we turn not away and despair when we are so weak, as though all were lost. Rather must we continue to exercise ourselves until we wax stronger and stronger, and endure and bear the weakness, until God helps and takes it away. Hence even though you see your neighbor so weak that he stumbles, think not that he is beyond hope. God will not have one judge another and be pleased with himself, inasmuch as we are all sinners, but that one bear the infirmity of the other, Romans 14 and Galatians 5. And if you will not do that, he will let you fall and cast you down, and raise the other up. He desires to have us help one another and bear each other's weaknesses.

18. I have thus spoken of our infirmity in order that you may have a good understanding of it, for such knowledge is very necessary, especially at this

time. Oh, if our bishops, pastors, and prelates had had this wisdom, for they needed it the most, how much better would conditions be in Christendom! They would then be able to bear with the weak consciences, and would know how to minister to them. But now it has come to this, that they look only to the strong Christians, and can never bear with the weak; but deal only harshly with them and proceed with force. In times past, when conditions were yet good, the bishops were sorely wanting in this, for, though they were great and holy men, they yet constrained and oppressed the consciences too much. Such things do not take place among Christians, for it is Christ's will to be weak and sickly yet a while, and to have both flesh and bones together, as he says here in the Gospel, "Handle me and see, for a spirit hath not flesh and bones, as ye behold me having." He would have both, not bones only, nor flesh only. Thus we read, in Genesis 2:23, that when God created Eve, Adam said, "This is now bone of my bones, and flesh of my flesh." He says not flesh only nor bones only; he speaks of having both himself, for he, too, must needs have both. So it is also with Christ and with us, and hence he says here, I have both flesh and bones; you will find in me not only bones, nor yet only flesh; you will find that I am both strong and sick.

19. Thus also my Christians must be so mingled together, that some are strong and some weak. They that are strong walk uprightly, are hale and hearty, and must bear the others; they are the bones. The others are the weak that cleave unto the strong. They are also the greater number, as in a body there will always be found more flesh than bones. Hence Jesus was crucified and died, and likewise was quickened again and glorified, that he might not be a spirit, as the disciples here deem him to be and were filled with fear of him, thinking that because he is not only bone and the strong Christ, it is not he, but a ghost.

20. This wisdom was diligently urged by the apostles and by Christ himself and, besides this, I know of no book in which it is urged. It is, indeed, sometimes touched upon, but nowhere urged. Only this one book, the New Testament, urges it constantly, and everywhere strives to set before the people the weak and strong Christ. Thus says Saint Paul, in Romans 15:1–3, "Now we that are strong ought to bear the infirmities of the weak and not to please ourselves. Let each one of us please his neighbor for that which is good, unto edifying. For Christ also pleased not himself." Hence we must do the same, and this is the wisdom we are to learn here.

21. To this school belong all that are pictured here in this Gospel, whom Christ finds terrified and affrighted. The others, who do not belong here, are easily identified, for they reject and despise the Gospel. In like manner, everyone can know himself, whether he truly takes pleasure in the Gospel. And if

you see in another's behavior evidence of an earnest desire to be made holy, you should not despise him.

22. This Gospel, therefore, shows the following: first, that the Lord stands among the disciples and is now strong, having overcome sin, death, and the devil; but they do not stand as yet, but sit there, and he comes and stands in the midst of them. Where does he stand at the present time? In the midst of the weak and fainthearted company, that sit in fear and weakness, while he is strong and mighty, though it is not yet apparent to the world. But even though the world does not see it, God sees it. Secondly, he shows them his hands and his feet, and comforts them, saying, "Why are ye troubled? and wherefore do questionings arise in your hearts? See my hands and my feet, that it is I myself: handle me and see; for a spirit has not flesh and bones," etc.

23. This is nothing but a sermon that teaches us not to be offended in the weak Christ. He does not rebuke the disciples harshly, does not say, Away with you; I do not want you. You should be strong and courageous, but here you sit and are dismayed and terrified! He does not do these things, but lovingly comforts them, that he might make them strong and fearless. Hence they were also made strong and fearless, and not only this, but also cheerful and of good courage. Therefore, we ought not to cast away the weak, but so deal with them that, from day to day, we may bring them to a condition that they may become strong and of good cheer. This does not signify that it is well, if they are weak, and that they should continue weak; for Christ does not stand among them for that purpose, but that they might grow in faith and be made fearless.

24. Here we may also speak, as the text gives occasion, of ghosts or walking spirits, for we see here that the Jews and the apostles themselves held that spirits roam about and are seen by night and at other times. Thus, in Matthew 14:25ff., when the disciples sailed in a ship by night and saw Jesus walking on the sea, they were affrighted, as before a ghost, and cried out in fear. And here we learn that Jesus does not deny it but confirms it by his answer that spirits do appear, for he says, "A spirit has not flesh and bones," etc.

25. But the Scriptures do not say, nor give any example, that such are the souls of dead persons walking among the people and seeking help, as we, in our blindness and deluded by the devil, have heretofore believed. Hence the pope has, also, invented purgatory and established his shameful annual market of masses. We may well see in this false doctrine and abomination as a fruit, that the foundation on which it is built, namely, the doctrine of the migration of souls, comes from the father of lies, the devil, who has deluded the people in the name of the dead.

26. We have good reason not to believe such apparitions of roaming erring spirits that profess to be souls. First, because the Scriptures nowhere say that the souls of the deceased, that have not yet risen, should wander about among the people; whereas everything else we need to know, is clearly revealed in the Scriptures. Not one word concerning this is given for our instruction, nor is it possible that we should grasp and understand the state of the spirits that have departed from the body, before the resurrection and the day of judgment; for they are sundered and separated altogether from the world and from this generation. Moreover, it is clearly forbidden in the Scriptures to consult the dead or to believe them who do, in Deuteronomy 18:11 and in Isaiah 28:19. And, Luke 16:31 proves that God will neither let one rise from the dead nor preach, because we have Moses and the Scriptures.

27. Know, therefore, that all ghosts and visions, which cause themselves to be seen and heard, especially with din and noise, are not men's souls, but evidently devils that amuse themselves thus either to deceive the people with false claims and lies, or unnecessarily frighten and trouble them. Hence with a specter that makes a pretense in the name of a soul, a Christian should not deal otherwise than as with the very devil himself. He should be well girded with God's Word and faith, that he may not be deceived nor affrighted, but abide in the doctrine that he has learned and confessed from the Gospel of Christ, and cheerfully despise the devil with his noise. Nor does he tarry long where he feels a soul trusts in Christ and despise him. This I say that we may be wise and not suffer ourselves to be misled by such deception and lies, as in the past he deceived and mocked even excellent men, like Saint Gregory, under the name of being a soul.

28. Now what does it signify that he shows the disciples his hands and his feet? He would thereby say, Come, and learn to know me. Now I am strong, but you are weak, as I also was. Therefore, see to it now that you become strong also.

II. THE SERMON CHRIST PREACHED TO HIS DISCIPLES

29. The above is one chief part of this Gospel; the other follows at the end of the Gospel, where the Lord concludes by saying,

> *"Thus it is written, that the Christ should suffer, and rise again*
> *from the dead the third day; and that repentance and remission*
> *of sins should be preached in his name unto all the nations."*

30. Here you see that the Gospel is the preaching of repentance and remission of sins. And it should not be preached in a corner, but before all men,

whether it be received or not, for it is to spread even farther that it may be heard and bear fruit. Hence we are not to be offended though but few receive it, nor say it has been given in vain. We should, rather, be content with it, that Christ has given command to preach it in all the world, that he who will may receive it. But we must note here in particular, that he says,

31. First, let us consider two thoughts. By repentance he means a change for the better; not as we have called it repentance, when one scourges and castigates himself and does penance to atone for his sin, or when the priest imposes this or that upon anyone for penance. Scripture does not speak of it in this sense. Repentance rather signifies here a change and reformation of the whole life; so that when one knows that he is a sinner, and feels the iniquity of his life, he desists from it and enters upon a better course of life, in word and deed, and that he does it from his heart.

32. What then is repentance in his name? Hereby he singles out the repentance that is not made in his name, and hence the text compels us to consider two kinds of repentance. First, a repentance not in his name is, when I come with my own works and undertake to blot out sin with them, as we all have hitherto been taught and have tried to do. This is not repentance in God's name, but in the devil's name. For this is striving to propitiate God by our own works and by our own strength, a thing God cannot allow.

33. But on the other hand, to repent in his name is done thus: in those who believe in Christ, God, through the same faith, works a change for the better, not for a moment, nor for an hour, but for their whole life. For a Christian is not instantaneously or suddenly cleansed perfectly, but the reformation and change continue as long as he lives. Though we use the utmost diligence, we will always find something to sweep or clean. For even though all wickedness be overcome, we have not yet overcome the fear of death, for few have come so far as to desire death with a spirit of rejoicing; hence we must grow better day by day. This is what Paul means when he says in 2 Corinthians 4:16, "Though our outward man is decaying, yet our inward man is renewed day by day." For we hear the Gospel every day, and Christ shows us his hands and his feet every day that our minds may be still more enlightened, and we be made more and more godly.

34. For this reason, Christ would say, let no one strive to amend his life by his own works and in his own name; for of themselves no one is an enemy of sin, no one will come to repentance and think of amending his life. Nothing will be accomplished except in my name. That name alone has power to do it, and brings with it willingness and desire to be changed. But if the works and doctrines of men be taught, I will go and say to myself, O, that I might

not need to pray, nor make confession, nor go to the Lord's Supper! What will your repentance profit you, if you fail to do it gladly or willingly, but are constrained by the commandment or by fear of shame, otherwise you would rather not do it? But what is the reason? Because it is a repentance in the devil's name, in your own name, or in the pope's name. Hence you go on and do worse things, and wish there were no confession and sacrament, so that you might not be constrained to attend them. This is repentance in our own name, and proceeds from our own strength.

35. But when I begin to believe in Christ, lay hold of the Gospel, and doubt not that he has taken away my sin and blotted it out, and comforts me with his resurrection, my heart is filled with such gladness that I myself take hold willingly, not through persuasion, nor of necessity; I gladly do what I ought, and say, Because my Lord has done this for me, I will also do his will in this, that I may amend my ways and repent out of love to him and to his glory. In this way, a true reformation begins that proceeds from the innermost heart, and that is brought forth by the joy that flows from faith, when I apprehend the greatness of the love Christ has bestowed upon me.

36. Secondly, we should preach also forgiveness of sins in his name. This signifies nothing else than that the Gospel should be preached, which declares unto all the world that in Christ the sins of all the world are swallowed up, and that he suffered death to put away sin from us, and arose to devour it and blot it out. All did he do, that whoever believes, should have the comfort and assurance, that it is reckoned unto him even as if he himself had done it; that his work is mine and thine and all men's; yea, that he gives himself to us with all his gifts to be our own personal property. Hence as he is without sin and never dies by virtue of his resurrection, even so I also am, if I believe in him; and I will, therefore, strive to become more and more godly, until there be no more sin in me. This continues as long as we live, until the day of judgment. As he is without sin, he sets before us an example, that we might be fashioned like unto him, though while we live here, we shall be fully like the image.

37. Saint Paul speaks of this in writing to the Corinthians, "We all, with unveiled face beholding as in a mirror the glory of the Lord, are transformed into the same image from glory to glory," in 2 Corinthians 3:18. Christ, even as he is risen, is the image, and is set before us that we might know that he rose from the dead to overcome our sin. This image stands before us and is set before our eyes by the Gospel, and is so mirrored in our hearts that we may grasp it by faith, if we hold it to be true and daily exercise ourselves in it. Thus the glory is imparted by him to us, and it comes to pass that we become ever more glorious, and grow into the same image that he is. Hence

he also says that we are not at once made perfect and strong, but must grow from day to day until we become like him. Many similar passages are here and there in the Scriptures.

38. This then is preaching the forgiveness of sins in his name, that we do not point only to confession, or to a certain hour; for we must act in view of the fact that it deals not with our works but with the whole person. Even when we begin to believe, our sin and infirmity are always present so that there is nothing pure in us, and we are indeed worthy of condemnation. But now forgiveness is so great and powerful, that God not only forgives the former sins you have committed but looks through his fingers and forgives the sins you will yet commit. He will not condemn us for our daily infirmities, but forgives all, in view of our faith in him, if we only strive to press onward and get rid of sin.

39. Here you may see what a difference there is between this and that which has heretofore been preached, of buying letters of indulgence, and of confessions, by which it was thought sin could be blotted out. So far as this pressed and such confidence was there put in it, that men were persuaded if anyone should die upon it, he would straightway mount to heaven. They did not know that we have still more sin and will not be rid of it, as long as we live. They supposed that all is well if only we have been to confession. Hence this is a forgiveness in the name of the devil. But see that you understand it correctly: By absolution you are absolved and declared free from sin, that is, you are put into that state, where there is forgiveness of sin that never ends. And not only is there forgiveness of past sins, but of those also you now have, if you believe that God overlooks and forgives your sins; and although you stumble still, yet he will neither reject nor condemn you, if you continue in faith. This teaching is heard indeed in all the world, but few there be that understand it.

40. Thus you have heard what the Gospel is, and what repentance and forgiveness of sins are, whereby we enter into another, a new state, out of the old. But take heed, lest you trust in this and become sluggish, thinking that when you sin there is no danger, and thus boldly persist in sin. This would be sinning in spite of God's mercy and would tempt God. But if you desire to be delivered from sin, it is well with you, and all is forgiven. So much then on the second part of this Gospel, and with it we shall, for the present, content ourselves.

The Sunday After Easter

Of True Piety, the Law and Faith, and of Love to Our Neighbor

W hen therefore it was evening, on that day, the first day of the week, and when the doors were shut where the disciples were, for fear of the Jews, Jesus came and stood in the midst, and saith unto them, "Peace be unto you." And when he had said this, he showed unto them his hands and his side. The disciples therefore were glad, when they saw the Lord. Jesus therefore said to them again, "Peace be unto you: as the Father hath sent me, even so send I you." And when he had said this, he breathed on them, and saith unto them, "Receive ye the Holy Spirit: whose soever sins ye forgive, they are forgiven unto them; whose soever sins ye retain, they are retained."

But Thomas, one of the twelve, called Didymus, was not with them when Jesus came. The other disciples therefore said unto him, "We have seen the Lord." But he said unto them, "Except I shall see in his hands the print of the nails, and put my finger into the print of the nails, and put my hand into his side, I will not believe."

And after eight days again his disciples were within, and Thomas with them. Jesus cometh, the doors being shut, and stood in the midst, and said, "Peace be unto you." Then said he to Thomas, "Reach hither thy finger, and see my hands; and reach hither thy hand, and put it into my side: and be not faithless, but believing". Thomas answered and said unto him, "My Lord and my God." Jesus saith unto him, "Because thou hast seen me, thou hast believed: blessed are they that have not seen, and yet have believed."

Many other signs therefore did Jesus in the presence of the disciples, which are not written in this book: but these are written, that ye may believe that Jesus is the Christ, the Son of God; and that believing ye may have life in his name. — JOHN 20:19–31

I. OF TRUE GODLINESS; OF THE LAW AND FAITH

1. In today's Gospel is presented to us, what the life of a Christian is to be and that it consists of two parts: first, that the Lord shows Thomas his hands and feet; secondly, that he is sent as Christ is sent. This is nothing else than faith and love, the two thoughts that are preached to us in all the Gospel texts.

2. Formerly you heard, and alas! it is preached in all the world, that if anyone desires to become righteous, he must begin with human laws. This was done under the reign of the pope, and nearly all the very best preachers preached nothing else than how one is to be outwardly pious, and about good works which glitter before the world. But this is still far from the true righ-teousness that avails before God.

3. There is another way to begin to become righteous, which commences by teaching us the laws of God, from which we learn to know ourselves, what we are, and how impossible it is for us to fulfill the divine commandments. The law speaks thus, Thou shalt have one God, worship him alone, trust in him alone, seek help and comfort from him alone, in Exodus 20. The heart hears this and yet it cannot do it. Why then does the law command such an impossible thing? In order, as I have said, to show us our inability, and that we may learn to know ourselves and to see ourselves as we are, even as one sees himself in a mirror. When now the conscience, thus smitten by God's law, begins to quake and finds that it does not keep God's commandment, then the law does its proper work; for the true mission of the law is only to terrify the conscience.

4. But there are two classes of men who fulfill the law, or who imagine they fulfill it. The first are those who, when they have heard it, begin with outward works; they desire to perform and fulfill it by works. How do they proceed? They say, God has commanded thou shalt have one God; I surely will worship no other God; I will serve him and no idol, and will have no heathen idolatrous image in my house or in my church; why should I do this? Such persons make a show with their glittering, fabricated service of God, like the clergy in our day, and they think they keep this law, when they bend their knees and are able to sing and prate much about God. By this show, the poor laity also are deceived; they follow after and also desire to obey the law by their works. But the blind guides the blind and both fall into a pit, in Luke 6:39. This is the first class, who take hold and imagine they will keep the law, and yet they do not.

5. The other class are those who know themselves by the law and study what it seeks and requires. For instance, when the law speaks, "Thou shalt have one God, and worship and honor him alone," this same heart meditates,

What does this mean? Shalt thou bend the knees? Or what is it to have one God? It surely is something else than a bodily, outward reverence; and finally it perceives that is a very different thing than is generally supposed; that it is nothing but having trust and hope in God, that he will help and assist in all anxiety and distress, in every temptation and adversity, that he will save him from sin, from death, from hell, and from the devil, without whose help and salvation he alone can do nothing. And this is the meaning of having one God. A heart, so thoroughly humble, desires to have God, namely, a heart that has become quite terrified and shaken by this commandment, and in its anxiety and trouble flees to God alone.

6. This now the hypocrites and work saints, who lead a fine life before the world, are not able to do; for their confidence is based alone upon their own righteousness and outward piety. Therefore, when God attacks them with the law and causes the poor people to see that they have not kept the law, aye, not the least of it, and when overwhelmed by anxiety and distress, and an evil conscience, and they perceive that external works will not suffice and that keeping the commandments of God is a very different thing from what they thought, then they rush ahead and seek ever more and more, and other and still other works, and fancy that they will thereby quiet their conscience, but they greatly miss the right way. Hence it comes to pass that one wishes to do it by rosaries, another by fasting; this one by prayer and that one by torturing his body; one runs to Saint James, another to Rome, this man to Jerusalem, that to Aix; here one becomes a monk, another a nun, and they seek their end in so many ways that they can scarcely be enumerated.

7. Why do they do all this? Because they wish to save themselves, to rescue and help themselves. The consequence of this is great blasphemy of God, for they also boast mightily of these works, and vaunt, and say, I have been in an order so long, I have prayed so many rosaries, have fasted so much, have done this and that; God will give me heaven as a reward. This then means to have an idol. This also is the meaning of Isaiah, when he says, "They worship the work of their own hands," in Isaiah 2:8. He is not speaking of stone and wood, but of the external works, which have a show of goodness and beauty before men. These hypocrites are ingenious enough to give the chaff to God and to keep the wheat for themselves. This then is true idolatry, as Saint Paul writes to the Romans, "Thou that abhorrest idols, dost thou rob temples?" in Romans 2:22. This is spiritual robbery.

8. Therefore, you will find that there is nothing good in any man of himself. But you have this distinction, that the upright, in whom the law has exercised its work, when they feel their sickness and weakness, say, God will

help me; I trust in him; I build upon him; he is my rock and hope. But the others, as hypocrites and work saints, when trial, distress, and anxiety are at hand, lament, and say, Oh, whither shall I go? They must at last despair of God, of themselves, and of their works, even if they have ever so many of them.

9. Such in the first place are these false and unrighteous pupils of the law, who presume to fulfill it by their works. For they have an appearance and glitter outwardly, but in their hearts they have nothing but filth and uncleanness. Therefore, they also merit nothing before God, who regards not external works that are done without any heart in them.

10. In the second place, they are the true and real pupils, who keep the law, who know and are conscious that they do evil, and make naught of themselves, surrender themselves, count all their works unclean in the eyes of God, and despair of themselves and all their own works. They who do this, shall have no trouble, except that they must not deceive themselves with vain fruitless thoughts and defer this matter until death; for if anyone persistently postpones this until death, he will have a sad future.

11. But we must give heed that we do not despair, even if we still feel sinful inclinations and are not as pure as we would like to be. You will not entirely sweep out of your heart all this rubbish, because we are still flesh and blood. This much can surely be done: outward wicked deeds can be prevented and carnal, shameful words and works avoided, although it is attained with difficulty. But it will never come to pass here that you are free from lust and evil inclination. Saint Jerome undertook to root such inclinations out of his heart by prayer, fasting, work, and torture of the body, but he found out what he accomplished. It was of no avail; the concupiscence remained. Works and words can be restrained, but lust and inclinations no one can root out of himself.

12. In short, if you desire to attain the true righteousness that avails before God, you must despair altogether of yourself and trust in God alone; you must surrender yourself entirely to Christ and accept him, so that all that he has is yours, and all that is yours, becomes his. For in this way you begin to burn with divine love and become quite another man, completely born anew, and all that is in you is converted. Then you will have as much delight in chastity as before you had pleasure in unchastity, and so forth with all lusts and inclinations.

13. This now is the first work of God, that we know ourselves, how condemned, miserable, weak, and sickly we are. It is then good and God's will, that a man desponds and despairs of himself, when he hears, This shalt thou do and that shalt thou do. For everybody must feel and experience in himself, that he does not and cannot do it. The law is neither able nor is it designed

to give you this power of obeying it; but it effects what Saint Paul says, "The law worketh wrath," in Romans 4:15, that is, nature rages against the law, and wishes the law did not exist.

14. Therefore, they who presume to satisfy the law by outward deeds, become hypocrites; but in the others it works wrath only, and causes sins to increase, as Saint Paul says in another place, "The power of sin is the law," in 1 Corinthians 15:56. For the law does not take sin away, aye, it multiplies sin, and causes me to feel my sin. So he says again to the Corinthians, "The letter killeth," in 2 Corinthians 3:6, that is, the law works death in you; in other words, it reduces you to nothing; "but the Spirit giveth life." For when he comes through the Gospel, the law is already fulfilled, as we shall hear.

15. Therefore, the world errs when it tries to make men righteous through laws; only pretenders and hypocrites result from such efforts. But reverse this and say, as Saint Paul says, The law produces sin. For the law does not help me the least, except that it teaches me to know myself; there I find nothing but sin; how then should it take sin away? We will now see how this thought is set forth in this Gospel. The text says,

> *When therefore it was evening, on that day, the first day of the week,*
> *and the doors were shut where disciples were for fear of the Jews.*

16. What do the disciples fear? They fear death; aye, they were in the very midst of death. Whence came their fear of death? From sin; for if they had not sinned, they would not have feared. Nor could death have injured them; for the sting of death, by means of which it kills, is sin, in 1 Corinthians 15:56. But they, like us all, had not yet a true knowledge of God. For if they had esteemed God as God, they would have been without fear and in security; as David says, "Whither shall I go from thy Spirit? Or whither shall I flee from thy presence? If I ascend up into heaven, thou art there: if I make my bed in Sheol, behold, thou art there. If I take the wings of the morning, and dwell in the uttermost parts of the sea; even there shall thy hand lead me, and thy right hand shall hold me," in Psalm 139:7–10. And, as he says in another place, "In peace will I both lay me down and sleep; for thou, Jehovah, alone makest me dwell in safety," in Psalm 4:8. It is easy to die, if I believe in God; for then I fear no death. But whoever does not believe in God, must fear death, and can never have a joyful and secure conscience.

17. Now God drives us to this by holding the law before us, in order that through the law we may come to a knowledge of ourselves. For where there is not this knowledge, one can never be saved. He that is well needs no physician; but if a man is sick and desires to become well, he must know that

he is weak and sick; otherwise, he cannot be helped. But if one is a fool and refuses to take the remedy that will restore him to health, he must certainly die and perish. But our papists have closed our eyes, so that we were not compelled, and not able, to know ourselves, and they failed to preach the true power of the law. For where the law is not properly preached, there can be no self-knowledge.

18. David had such knowledge, when he said, "Have mercy upon me, O God, according to thy lovingkindness; according to the multitude of thy mercies blot out my transgressions. Wash me thoroughly from mine iniquity, and cleanse me from my sin. For I know my transgressions; and my sin is ever before me. Against thee, thee only, have I sinned, and done that which is evil in thy sight, that thou mayest be justified when thou speakest, and be clear when thou judgest. Behold, I was brought forth in iniquity; and in sin did my mother conceive me," in Psalm 51:1ff. Just as if David wished to say, Behold, I am so formed of flesh and blood, which of itself is sin, that I cannot but sin. For although you restrain your hands and feet or tongue that they sin not; the inclinations and lusts always remain, because flesh and blood are present, you may go whither you please, to Rome or to Saint James.

19. If now an upright heart that comes to the point of knowing itself is met by the law, it verily will not begin and seek to help itself by works; but it confesses its sin and helplessness, its infirmity and sickness, and says, Lord God, I am a sinner, a transgressor of thy divine commandments: help thou, for I am lost. Now when a man is in such fear and cries out thus to God, God cannot refrain from helping him; as in this case, Christ was not long absent from the disciples tormented by fear; but he is soon present, comforts them, and says, "Peace be unto you!" Be of good courage; it is I; fear not. The same happens now. When we come to a knowledge of ourselves through the law and are now in deep fear, God arouses us and has the Gospel preached to us, by which he gives us a joyful and secure conscience.

20. But what is the Gospel? It is this, that God has sent his Son into the world to save sinners, in John 3:16, and to crush hell, overcome death, take away sin, and satisfy the law. But what must you do? Nothing but accept this and look up to your Redeemer and firmly believe that he has done all this for your good and freely gives you all as your own, so that in the terrors of death, sin, and hell you can confidently say and boldly depend upon it, and say, Although I do not fulfill the law, although sin is still present and I fear death and hell, nevertheless, from the Gospel I know that Christ has bestowed upon me all his works. I am sure he will not lie, his promise he will surely fulfill. And as a sign of this, I have received baptism. For he says to his apostles and

disciples, "Go ye into all the world, and preach the Gospel to the whole creation. He that believeth and is baptized shall be saved; but he that disbelieveth shall be condemned," in Mark 16:15–16. Upon this I anchor my confidence. For I know that my Lord Christ has overcome death, sin, hell, and the devil all for my good. For he was innocent, as Peter says, "Who did no sin, neither was guile found in his mouth," in 1 Peter 2:22. Therefore, sin and death were not able to slay him, hell could not hold him, and he has become their Lord, and has granted this to all who accept and believe it. All this is effected not by my works or merits; but by pure grace, goodness, and mercy.

21. Now, whoever does not appropriate this faith to himself, must perish; and whoever possesses this faith, shall be saved. For where Christ is, the Father will come and also the Holy Spirit. There will then be pure grace, no law; pure mercy, no sin; pure life, no death; pure heaven, no hell. There I will comfort myself with the works of Christ, as if I myself had done them. There I will no longer concern myself about cowls or tonsures, Saint James or Rome, rosaries or scapulars, praying or fasting, priests or monks.

22. Behold, how beautiful the confidence toward God that arises in us through Christ! You may be rich or poor, sick or well, yet you will always say, God is mine, I am willing to die; for this is acceptable to my Father, and death cannot harm me; it is swallowed up in victory, as Saint Paul says in 1 Corinthians 15:57, yet not through us, but "Thanks be to God," says he, "who giveth us the victory through our Lord Jesus Christ." Therefore, although we must die, we have no fear of death, for its power and might are broken by Christ, our Savior.

23. So then you understand that the Gospel is nothing but preaching and glad tidings, how Christ entered into the throes of death for us, took upon himself all our sins and abolished them; not that it was needful for him to do it, but it was pleasing to the Father; and that he has bestowed all this upon us, in order that we might boldly stand upon it against sin, death, Satan, and hell. Hence arises great, unspeakable joy, such as the disciples here experience. The text says, "The disciples therefore were glad, when they saw the Lord"—not a Lord, who inspired them with terror or burdened them with labor and toil, but who provided for them and watched over them like a father is the lord of his estate and cares for his own. Aye, then first they rejoiced most on his account, when he spoke to them, "Peace be unto you! It is I," and when he had showed them his hands and feet, that is, his works, all which were to be theirs.

24. In the same manner, he still comes to us through the Gospel, offers us peace, and bestows his works upon us: if we believe, we have them; if we believe not, we have them not. For the Lord's hands and feet really signify

nothing but his works, which he has done here upon earth for men. And the showing of his side is nothing but the showing of his heart, in order that we may see how kind, loving, and fatherly his mind is toward us. All this is set forth for us in the Gospel as certainly and clearly as it was revealed and shown to the disciples bodily in our text. And it is much better that it is done through the Gospel than if he now entered here by the door; for you would not know him, even if you saw him standing before you, even much less than the Jews recognized him.

25. This is the true way to become righteous, not by human commandments, but by keeping the commandments of God. Now nobody can do this except by faith in Christ alone. From this flows love that is the fulfillment of the law, as Saint Paul says in Romans 13:10. And this results not from the exercise of virtues and good works, as was taught hitherto, which produced only true martyrs of Satan and hypocrites; but faith makes righteous, holy, chaste, humble, and so forth. For as Paul says to the Romans, "The Gospel is the power of God unto salvation to every one that believeth; to the Jew first and also to the Greek. For therein is revealed a righteousness of God from faith unto faith: as is written, But the righteous shall live by faith," in Romans 1:16–17. As if Saint Paul should say, Your works will not save you but the Gospel will, if you believe; your righteousness is nothing, but Christ's righteousness avails before God; the Gospel speaks of this and no other writing does. Whoever now wishes to overcome death and blot out sins by his works, says that Christ has not died; as Saint Paul says to the Galatians, "If righteousness is through the law, then Christ died for naught," in Galatians 2:21. And they who preach otherwise are wolves and seducers.

26. This has been said of the first part of our Gospel, to show what is to be our attitude toward God, namely, we are to cling to him in faith; and it shows what true righteousness is that is availing before God and how it is attained, namely, by faith in Christ, who has redeemed us from the law, from death, sin, hell, and the devil; and who has freely given us all this in order that we may rely upon it in defiance of the law, death, sin, hell, and the devil. Now follows how we are to conduct ourselves toward our neighbor; this is also shown to us in the text, where the Lord speaks thus:

II. OF LOVE TO YOUR NEIGHBOR

"As the Father hath sent me, even so send I you."

27. Why did God the Father send Christ? For no other purpose than to do the Father's will, namely, to redeem the world. He was not sent to merit

heaven by good works or to become righteous thereby. He did many good works, aye, his whole life was nothing else than a continual doing good. But for whom did he do it? For the people who stood in need of it, as we read here and there in the evangelists; for all he did, he did for the purpose of serving us. "As the Father hath sent me," he says here, "even so send I you." My Father hath sent me to fulfill the law, take the sin of the world upon myself, slay death, and overcome hell and the devil; not for my own sake, for I am not in need of it; but all for your sakes and in your behalf, in order that I may serve you. So shall you also do.

28. By faith you will accomplish all this. It will make you righteous before God and save you, and likewise also overcome death, sin, hell, and the devil. But this faith you are to show in love, so that all your works may be directed to this end; not that you are to seek to merit anything by them; for all in heaven and earth is yours beforehand; but that you serve your neighbor thereby. For if you do not give forth such proofs of faith, it is certain that your faith is not right. Not that good works are commanded us by this Word; for where faith in the heart is right, there is no need of much commanding good works to be done; they follow of themselves. But the works of love are only an evidence of the existence of faith.

29. This also is the intent of Saint Peter, when he admonishes us in 2 Peter 1:5, to give diligence to make our faith sure and to prove it by our good works. But good works are those we do to our neighbor in serving him, and the only one thing demanded of a Christian is to love. For by faith he is already righteous and saved; as Saint Paul says in Romans 13:8, "Owe no man anything, save to love one another: for he that loveth his neighbor hath fulfilled the law." Therefore Christ says to his disciples in John 13:34–35: "A new commandment I give unto you, that ye love one another; even as I have loved you, that ye also love one another. By this shall all men know that ye are my disciples, if ye have love one to another."

30. In this way, we must give proof of ourselves before the world, that everyone may see that we keep God's commandment; and yet not that we would be saved or become righteous thereby. So then I obey the civil government for I know that Christ was obedient to the government, and yet he had no need to be; he did it only for our sakes. Therefore, I will also do it for Christ's sake and in behalf of my neighbor, and for the reason alone that I may prove my faith by my love; and so on through all commandments. In this manner, the apostles exhort us to good works in their writings; not that we become righteous and are saved by them, but only to prove our faith both to ourselves and others, and to make it sure. The Gospel continues,

"Receive ye the Holy Spirit: Whose soever sins ye forgive, they are
forgiven unto them; whose soever sins ye retain, they are retained."

31. This power is here given to all Christians, although some have appropriated it to themselves alone, like the pope, bishops, priests, and monks have done: they declare publicly and arrogantly that this power was given to them alone and not to the laity. But Christ here speaks neither of priests nor of monks, but says, "Receive ye the Holy Spirit." Whoever has the Holy Spirit, power is given to him, that is, to everyone that is a Christian. But who is a Christian? He that believes. Whoever believes has the Holy Spirit. Therefore, every Christian has the power, which the pope, bishops, priests, and monks have in this case, to forgive sins or to retain them.

32. Do I hear then, that I can institute confession, baptize, preach, and administer the Lord's Supper? No. Saint Paul says in 1 Corinthians 14:40, "Let all things be done decently and in order." If everybody wished to hear confession, baptize, and administer the Lord's Supper, what order would there be? Likewise, if everybody wished to preach, who would hear? If we all preached at the same time, what a confused babble it would be, like the noise of frogs! Therefore, the following order is to be observed: the congregation shall elect one, who is qualified, and he shall administer the Lord's Supper, preach, hear confession, and baptize. True we all have this power; but no one shall presume to exercise it publicly, except the one who has been elected by the congregation to do so. But in private, I may freely exercise it. For instance, if my neighbor comes and says, Friend, I am burdened in my conscience; speak the absolution to me; then I am free to do so, but I say it must be done privately. If I were to take my seat in the church, and another and all would hear confession, what order and harmony would there be? Take an illustration: If there are many heirs among the nobility, with the consent of all the others they elect one, who alone administers the estate in behalf of the others; for if everyone wished to rule the country and people, how would it be? Still they all alike have the power that he has who rules. So also is it with this power to forgive sins and to retain them.

33. But this word, to forgive sins or to retain sins, concerns those who confess and receive more than those who are to impart the absolution. And thereby we serve our neighbor. For in all services the greatest is to release from sin, to deliver from the devil and hell. But how is this done? Through the Gospel, when I preach it to a person and tell him to appropriate the words of Christ, and to believe firmly that Christ's righteousness is his own and his sins are Christ's. This I say, is the greatest service I can render to my neighbor.

34. Accursed be the life, where one lives only for himself and not for his neighbor; and on the contrary, blessed be the life, in which one lives not for himself but for his neighbor and serves him by teaching, by rebuke, by help, and by whatever manner and means. If my neighbor errs, I am to correct him; if he cannot immediately follow me, then I am to bear patiently with him; as Christ did with Judas, who had the purse with the money and went wrong and stole from it. Christ knew this very well; yet he had patience with him, admonished him diligently, although it did no good, until he disgraced himself.

35. So we are to give heed to do everything in behalf of our neighbor, and ever to be mindful, that Christ has done this and that for me; why should I not also for his sake freely do all for my neighbor? And see to it that all the works you do are directed not to God, but to your neighbor. Whoever is a ruler, a prince, a mayor, a judge, let him not think that he is a ruler to gain heaven thereby or to seek his own advantage; but to serve the public. And so with other works, I assume to do for the good of my neighbor. For example, if I take a wife, I make myself a captive; why do I do this? In order that I may not do harm to my neighbor's wife and daughters, and thus may bring my body into subjection; and so forth with all other works.

36. Thus then you have finely portrayed in this Gospel, as in almost all the Gospel lessons, these two thoughts, faith and love. Through faith we belong above to God, through love below to our neighbor. That we may thus lay hold of this truth, may God give us his help! Amen.

The Second Sunday After Easter

❧✦❧

Christ's Office and Kingdom: A Sermon on the Good Shepherd

I am the good shepherd: the good shepherd layeth down his life for
the sheep. He that is a hireling, and not a shepherd, whose own the
sheep are not, beholdeth the wolf coming, and leaveth the sheep, and
fleeth, and the wolf snatcheth them, and scattereth them: he fleeth
because he is a hireling, and careth not for the sheep. I am the good
shepherd; and I know mine own, and mine own know me, even as the
Father knoweth me, and I know the Father; and I lay down my life for
the sheep. And other sheep I have, which are not of this fold: them also
I must bring, and they shall hear my voice; and they shall become one
flock, one shepherd." — JOHN 10:11–16

1. This is a comforting Gospel, which so beautifully portrays the Lord
Jesus and teaches us what manner of person he is, what kind of works he
does, and how he is disposed toward men. And there is no better way to understand it than to contrast light and darkness, and day and night; that is, the
good shepherd with the wicked one, as the Lord himself does.

2. Now, you have often heard that God has given the world two different
proclamations. One is that which is declared in the Word of God when it says,
Thou shalt not kill, not commit adultery, not steal, in Exodus 20:13–15, and
when it adds the threat that all who do not keep these commandments shall
die. But this declaration will make no one godly at heart. For though it may
compel a man outwardly to appear godly before men, inwardly it leaves the
heart at enmity with the law, and wishing that there were no such law.

3. The other proclamation is that of the Gospel. It tells where one may obtain that which will meet the demands of the law. It does not drive or threaten,
but tenderly invites us. It does not say, Do this and do that, but rather, Come,
I will show you where you may find and obtain what you need to make you
godly. See, here is the Lord Jesus; he will give it to you. Therefore, the two
are as contrary to each other as taking and giving, demanding and presenting;

and this distinction must be well observed. Thus God ever has ruled and still rules the world today. To coarse and rude persons, who are not influenced by the Gospel, the law must be declared, and they must be driven until they are humbled and acknowledge their imperfections. When this has been accomplished, the Gospel is to be applied.

4. These are the two divine proclamations, which come from heaven. Besides these, there are others that are not from heaven, but are human prattle, which the pope and our bishops have invented that they might terrify our consciences. Such men are not worthy of being called shepherds or hirelings, but they are here designated by the Lord Jesus as thieves, murderers, and wolves. For if men are to be savingly governed, it must be done with the Word of God; and if it is not done by the Word of God, they are not properly governed.

I. THE NATURE OF THE OFFICE AND KINGDOM OF CHRIST EXPLAINED

5. Now, here Jesus has in mind the second proclamation. He explains it and sets himself forth as the chief shepherd, yea, as the only shepherd; for that which he does not tend is not kept. This comforting and sweet proclamation we will now consider.

6. You have heard that after his sufferings and death, Christ our Lord arose from the dead and entered upon, and was enthroned in, an immortal existence. Not that he might sit up there in heaven idly and find pleasure in himself, but that he might take charge of the kingdom of which the prophets and all the Scriptures have so fully spoken, and might rule as a king. Therefore, we should think of him as being present and reigning among us continually, and never think of him as sitting up there doing nothing, but rather that he from above fills and rules all things, as Paul says to the Ephesians, in Ephesians 4:10, and especially that he is taking care of his kingdom, which is the Christian faith, and that, therefore, his kingdom among us here on earth must prosper. This kingdom, as we have said, is so constituted that we all must daily increase and grow in holiness, and it is not governed by any other power save the oral proclamation of the Gospel.

7. This proclamation is not of men, but Christ himself sent it forth, and then put it into the hearts of the apostles and their successors so that they understood it, and into their mouths so that they spoke and declared it. This is his kingdom, and so does he rule that all of his power is comprehended in and connected with the Word of God. They who hear and believe it belong to this kingdom, and the Word then becomes so mighty that it provides all that man may need and bestows all the blessings that we may desire. For it

is the power of God, and it can and will save all who believe it, as Saint Paul declared to the Romans, in Romans 1:16. If you believe that Christ died to save you from all evil, and will hold fast to that Word, you will find it so certain and sure that no creature can overthrow it; and as no one can overthrow the Word, neither can anyone harm you who believe it. Accordingly, with the Word you will overcome sin, death, the devil, and hell, and you will find a refuge in the Word and attain that which is found where the Word is, namely, everlasting peace, joy, and life. In short, you will be participants in all the power that is in the Word. Therefore, it is a peculiar kingdom. The Word is present and is orally proclaimed to all the world, but its power is deeply hidden, so that none but they who believe realize that it is so effective and that it accomplishes such great things. It must be experienced and realized by the heart.

8. Hence all that we preachers can do is to become the mouthpieces and instruments of Christ our Lord, through whom he proclaims the Word bodily. He sends forth the Word publicly so that all may hear it, but that the heart inwardly experiences it, that is effected through faith and is wrought by Christ in secret where he perceives that it can be done according to his divine knowledge and pleasure. That is why he says, "I am the good shepherd." And what is a good shepherd? "The good shepherd," says Christ, "layeth down his life for the sheep; and I lay down my life for the sheep." In this one virtue, the Lord comprehends and exemplifies all others in the beautiful parable of the sheep. Sheep, you know, are most foolish and stupid animals. When we want to speak of anybody's stupidity we say, "He is a sheep." Nevertheless, it has this trait above all other animals, that it soon learns to heed its shepherd's voice and will follow no one but its shepherd and, though it cannot help and keep and heal itself, nor guard itself against the wolf, but is dependent upon others, yet it always knows enough to keep close to its shepherd and look to him for help.

9. Now, Christ uses this trait or nature of the animal as an illustration in explaining that he is the good shepherd. In this manner, he plainly shows what his kingdom is, and wherein it consists, and would say, My kingdom is only to rule the sheep; that is, poor, needy, wretched men, who well see and realize that there is no other help or counsel for them.

10. But that we may make it the plainer, and may understand it the better, we will cite a passage from the prophet Ezekiel, where he speaks of the wicked shepherds that are against Christ, when he says, in Ezekiel 34:2ff., "Should not the shepherds feed the sheep? Ye eat the fat, and ye clothe you with the wool, ye kill the fatlings; but ye feed not the sheep. The diseased have ye not strengthened, neither have ye healed that which was sick, neither

have ye bound up that which was broken, neither have ye brought back that which was driven away, neither have ye sought that which was lost; but with force and with rigor have ye ruled over them. And they were scattered, because there was no shepherd; and they become food to all the beasts of the field and were scattered. My sheep wandered through all the mountains, and upon every high hill: yea, my sheep were scattered upon all the face of the earth; and there was none that did search or seek after them," and so forth. Accordingly, God reproves the shepherds who do not keep the sheep. And now mark well what he has written. His earnest intent in this paragraph is that the weak, sick, broken, those who are driven away, and the lost, are to be strengthened, bound up, healed, and sought again, and that they are not to be torn to pieces and scattered. This you should have done, says he to the shepherds, but you have not done it; therefore, I will do it myself. As he says further on, in verse 16, "I will seek that which was lost, I will bring back that which was driven away, and will bind up that which was broken, and will strengthen that which was sick."

11. Here you see that Christ's kingdom is to be concerned about the weak, the sick, the broken, that he may help them. That is, indeed, a comforting declaration. The only trouble is that we do not realize our needs and infirmities. If we realized them, we would soon flee to him. But how did those shepherds act? They ruled with rigor, and applied God's law with great severity; and, moreover, they added their own commandments, as they still do, and when these were not fulfilled, they raved and condemned, so that they were driving and driving and exhorting and exacting, continually. That is no proper way to tend and keep souls, says Christ. He is no such shepherd as that; for no one is benefited, but is rather wholly undone, by such a course, as we shall presently hear. Now let us consider this citation from the prophet in its order.

12. First, he says, The sheep that are weak are to be strengthened; that is, consciences weak in faith and troubled in spirit and of tender disposition are not to be driven and told, You must do this. You must be strong. If you are weak, you are lost. That is not strengthening the weak. Saint Paul, speaking to the Romans, in Romans 14:1, says, "But him that is weak in faith receive ye, yet not for decision of scruples." And shortly afterward, in Romans 15:1, he says, "Now we that are strong ought to bear the infirmities of the weak." Accordingly, they should not be driven with rigor, but should be comforted, even though they are weak, lest they be driven to despair; and in time they will grow stronger.

13. Isaiah, the prophet, speaks of Christ likewise, in Isaiah 42:3, "A bruised reed will he not break, and a dimly burning wick will he not quench." The

bruised reeds are poor, tender consciences, which are easily distracted so that they tremble and despair of God. He does not fly at them then, and trample them under foot; that is not his way. But he deals with them gently, lest he break them to pieces. Again, the dimly burning wick, which still burns at least, though there be more smoke than fire there, he does not wholly quench, but lights, and again and again trims it. That is a great consolation, indeed, to such as experience it; and, therefore, he who does not deal gently with tender consciences is no good shepherd.

14. Secondly, the prophet says, "Neither have ye healed the sick." Who are the sick? They are those who are manifestly deficient in certain of their works. The first clause has reference to tender consciences; the second, to outward conduct. As, for instance, when one growls and sulks, and now and then lapses and, in anger and other foolish ways, oversteps the bounds; even as the apostles, at times, grievously stumbled. But even those who in their outward works before men manifest their shortcomings, so that people are offended at them and say that they are rude and peculiar, he will not cast away; for his kingdom here below is not so constituted as to embrace only the strong and the whole, as it will be in the life to come. Christ is sent here that he might receive and help just such people.

15. Therefore, even though we are weak and sick, we must not despair and say we are not in the kingdom of Christ. But the more we realize our sickness, all the more should we turn to him; for that is what he is here for, to heal and make us whole. Accordingly, if you are sick and a sinner, and realize your condition, you have all the more reason to go to him, and say, Dear Lord, I come just because I am a sinner; that thou mayest help me, and make me good. Thus necessity drives you to him; for the greater your ailment, the more imperative it is that you seek relief. And that is what he wants; therefore, he tenderly bids us to be of good cheer, and to come unto him. They who are not good shepherds, however, expect to make people good by hatefully scolding and driving them, whereas they are thereby only making matters worse. And this may be seen when we look upon present conditions, brought about by this wrong method, when everything is so piteously scattered, even as the prophet has here said.

16. Thirdly, "Neither have ye bound up that which was broken." To be broken is as though one had a bone fractured or were otherwise wounded. As when a Christian is not only weak and infirm, so that he makes a misstep at times, but when he falls into such great temptation that he breaks his leg; for instance, if he should fall and deny the Gospel, as Saint Peter did, when he denied Christ. Well, even though one should make such a misstep as to be

impeded or overthrown—even then you should not cast him away, as though he no more belonged to this kingdom. For you must not rob Christ of his characteristic, that in his kingdom abounding grace and mercy alone prevail, so that he helps those who realize their misery and wretchedness, and desire to be helped, and that his kingdom is wholly one of consolation, and that he is a comforting, friendly shepherd, who tenderly invites, and would induce, all men to come unto him.

17. Now, all this is effected through the Gospel alone, by means of which we are to strengthen all the weak and heal all the sick; for this Word will satisfy every want of those whose consciences are troubled, and will give full consolation to all, so that no one, no matter how great a sinner he has been, need despair. Hence Christ alone is the good shepherd, who heals all our infirmities and raises up again those who have fallen. He who does not do that is no shepherd.

18. Fourthly, the prophet says, "Neither have ye brought back that which was driven away." What is meant by "that which was driven away"? It is that despised soul that is fallen so low that all efforts to reclaim it seem to be in vain. Nevertheless, Christ would not have even such dealt with rigorously. He would not have his kingdom narrowed down so as to include only such as are strong and healthy and perfect. That will be the case in the future kingdom that follows this life, as has been said, Now, because he reigns, pure grace and bliss only shall prevail. Even as God promised the children of Israel, in Exodus 3:8, that the Promised Land would be a land flowing with milk and honey, likewise Saint Paul says that our uncomely parts shall have more abundant comeliness, in 1 Corinthians 12:23.

19. Fifthly, he concludes, "Neither have ye sought that which was lost." That which was lost is that which is given up as already condemned, so that there is no expectation that it ever will return; as the publicans and harlots mentioned in the Gospel, and as the dissolute and intractable in our day, were and are. And yet, even these he would not have us pass by, but would have everything possible done to reclaim them. This was done by Saint Paul, on different occasions; as, for example, when he delivered two men unto Satan, as he said to Timothy, in 1 Timothy 1:20, "Whom I delivered unto Satan that they might be taught not to blaspheme." And, again, to the Corinthians he said, in 1 Corinthians 5:5, "I have concluded to deliver such a one unto Satan for the destruction of the flesh, that the spirit may be saved in the day of the Lord Jesus." He had cast these away as condemned, and yet he goes after them again.

20. Therefore, we should so preach Christ as one who will reject nobody, however weak he may be, but will gladly receive and comfort and strengthen

everybody; that we may always picture him to ourselves as a good shepherd. Then hearts will turn to him of their own accord, and need not be forced and driven. The Gospel graciously invites and makes men willing, so that they desire to go, and do go, to him with all confidence. And it begets a love for Christ in their hearts, so that they willingly do what they should, whereas formerly they had to be driven and forced. When we are driven, we do a thing with displeasure and against our will. That is not what God desires; therefore, it is done in vain. But when I see that God deals with me graciously, he wins my heart, so that I am constrained to fly to him; consequently, my heart is filled with happiness and joy.

21. Now see what an evil it is when one person judges another. Christ's kingdom, as we have heard, is calculated to heal and sanctify only such souls as are sick and needy; therefore, all must err who look only upon those who are strong and holy. Consequently, the knowledge that rightly apprehends Christ is great and mighty. By our nature, we are knaves to the very hide, and yet we expect everyone to be pious. With open mouth, we do not want to look at anybody but strong Christians. We ignore the sick and weak, and think that if they are not strong then they are not Christians at all. And others who are not perfectly holy, we reckon among the wicked, and yet we, ourselves, are more wicked than they. That is what our evil nature does, and our blind reason, that wants to measure God's kingdom by its own imagination, and thinks that whatever does not appear pure in its eyes is not pure in the sight of God.

22. Therefore, we must get that idea out of our minds; for if we keep it before us too much, we will finally get into such a state of mind as to think, Oh, what will become of me if only they are Christians who are strong and healthy and holy? When will I ever reach that state? And thus we, ourselves, will make it impossible. Therefore, we must eventually be driven to say, Dear Lord, I realize that I am very weak, very sick, and despondent. Nevertheless, I will not allow that to confound me, but I will come to thee, that thou mayest help me; for thou art ever the good and pious shepherd, which I also confess thee to be and, therefore, will I despair of my own works.

23. Let us, therefore, ever be wise and learn to know Christ well, and to know that in his kingdom there are only weak and sickly people, and that it is nothing but a hospital, where the sick and infirm, who need care, are gathered. And yet there are so few who understand that! And this fact seems so obscured that even they who have the Gospel and the Spirit are lacking in the knowledge of it; for it is the most profound wisdom that man can attain. For even though they see that the Scriptures praise this kingdom and speak of its preciousness, yet they do not realize what the words mean, and do not

understand that they contain that true wisdom which is far above the wisdom of men. For it is not our wisdom that we deal with, and that we speak of and preach to sensible, prudent, and wise people; but it is this, that we go among fools and simpletons, and care for them, not because we find pleasure in so doing, but in order that we may help them to get rid of their sins and foolishness, and to find righteousness and true knowledge.

24. So you see that Christian wisdom does not consist in raising our eyes to that which is lofty and wise, to see ourselves reflected there, but in lowering our eyes to that which is lowly and foolish. Let him who knows this, thank God; for such knowledge will fit him to accommodate himself to, and guide him under, all circumstances in this life. Therefore, you will yet find many even among those who preach the Gospel, who have not yet attained it. They never taught us thus before, and we were accustomed to think we did not dare to come to Christ until we had first become perfectly pure. Now, you must get out of that way of thinking and come to a proper understanding of Jesus, and learn to know him as a true shepherd. But we have heard enough on this point for the present.

II. CHRIST ILLUSTRATES HIS OFFICE AND KINGDOM BY COMPARING THE GOOD SHEPHERD WITH THE HIRELING

25. Now, he contrasts the good shepherd with a wicked one, or a hireling, and says,

> *"The good shepherd layeth down his life for the sheep. He that is a hireling, and not a shepherd, whose own the sheep are not, beholdeth the wolf coming, and leaveth the sheep, and fleeth, and the wolf snatcheth them and scattereth them: he fleeth because he is a hireling, and careth not for the sheep."*

26. In the strictest sense, he alone is the shepherd; and yet, as he alone is Christ but nevertheless calls us by the same name, Christians, even so, though he alone is the shepherd, he designates all those who exercise the office of the ministry among Christians by that name also. In like manner in Matthew 23:9, he forbids us to call any man on earth father, for one is our father, even he who is in heaven, yet Paul calls himself a father of the Corinthians when he says, "I begat you through the Gospel," in 1 Corinthians 4:15. Thus God acts as though he alone would be our father, and yet he attributes the name to men also, so that they are called fathers. But they have no right to this name in themselves; only in Christ is it theirs: even as we are called Christians though we have nothing of our own, but all we have has been given to us, in him. Now, "the hireling," says he, "whose own the sheep are not, beholdeth

the wolf coming, and leaveth the sheep, and fleeth," etc. That is a hard saying, indeed, that some who truly preach and administer the Gospel and strengthen and heal the sheep, finally allow themselves to be carried away and leave the sheep when they are most in need of help. As long as no wolf is in sight, they are active and tend the sheep; but when they see the wolf breaking in, they forsake the sheep. If the sheep have been well kept, until they are strong and healthy and fat, they will then be all the more acceptable to the wolf, for whom they have been kept.

27. How does that happen? Well, says Christ, in my kingdom, whose whole object is to strengthen the weak, heal the sick, comfort the sorrowing, and so forth, the holy cross will not be wanting. For, if we preach that Christ alone must receive, strengthen, heal, and help us poor sheep, and that we cannot, by our own strength and works, help ourselves, and that, therefore, all works and whatever else the world pretends to offer in its many religious services are of no avail, the world cannot abide such preaching. Hence it is but natural that the Gospel should bring with it the holy cross, and that they who confess it before the world should risk their necks in so doing.

28. Because this is so, the good shepherds are thus distinguished from the hirelings. Whoever is a hireling will preach the Gospel only so long as they say of him that he is a learned, pious, and good man; but when he is attacked, and men begin to denounce him as a heretic and a knave, and challenge him to a dispute, he recants or runs away, and abandons the poor sheep in their distress, and things are in a worse state than they were before. For what advantage has it been to the poor sheep that they had once been well kept? Had the shepherds been faithful, they would have sacrificed their bodies and lives for the sake of the sheep, and would have given their necks to the executioner for the Gospel's sake. Accordingly, they are never true shepherds who, in preaching, have their own popularity, profit, and advantage in view. They are surely hirelings; for they seek their own advantage, even when they dispense the true doctrine and Word of God. Therefore, they continue only as long as they are honored and praised. Hence they retract and deny the Word when the wolf comes, or flee and leave the sheep in the lurch. The sheep bleat for pasture and for the shepherd to protect them from the wolves, but there is no one to succor them; thus they are deserted when they most need someone to help them.

29. Such will be the result when men once begin to lay hands on and persecute us in earnest. There will be preachers who will hold their tongues and flee, and the sheep will be pitiably scattered, the one running here and

the other there. God grant that there may be at least some who will stand firm and risk their lives to rescue the sheep. Thus Christ has here portrayed the hireling. He then proceeds,

"I am the good shepherd; and I know mine own."

30. There is a great deal contained in these words, far too much to be exhaustively treated here. He speaks here of his own peculiar calling. "I know mine own," he says, "and mine own know me." How is this to be understood? That he explains further when he says,

"Even as the Father knoweth me, and I know the Father."

III. THE SPECIAL OFFICE CHRIST ADMINISTERS EXPLAINED

31. How is he known of the Father? Not with an earthly, but with a heavenly, knowledge. Of that we have spoken more fully before, and the substance of it is this: Christ recognizes us as his sheep, and we recognize him as our shepherd. Now, we have heard what a good shepherd is, and also who the weak sheep are. He knows us to be such sheep as are weak, sick, and broken. That is, It does not make any difference in his regard for them that they are weak and sickly, and he does not despise and reject them on that account; but he pities and heals them, even though they be so diseased that the whole world concludes they are not his sheep. Such is the world's knowledge, but that is not the way that Christ distinguishes them. He does not look upon their condition, but looks to see whether they are sheep, whether they may be designated sheep. He looks at the sheep, not at the wool.

32. Now, they are good shepherds who imitate Christ and know the sheep in the same way; who look at the person, not at the faults, and know how to distinguish between the sheep and the disease.

33. Even so the Father knows me also, says Christ, but the world does not know me. When the time comes for me to die a shameful death upon the cross, all the world will say, Well, is that the Son of God? That must be a malefactor, owned, body and soul, by the devil. And thus the world will look upon and know me; but my Father will say, This is my beloved Son, my King, my Savior. For he will not look upon my sorrows, nor upon my wounds, nor upon my cross and my death, but he will see the person that I am. Therefore, though I were in the midst of hell and in the jaws of the devil, I must again come forth, for the Father will not desert me. And thus I know my sheep and am known of them. They know that I am the good shepherd and know me;

and, therefore, they come to me and abide with me, and they are not afraid because they are weak and sick, for they know that I will receive such sheep. He now concludes, and says,

> *"And other sheep I have, which are not of this fold; them also must I bring, and they shall hear my voice; and they shall become one flock, one shepherd."*

34. Some have explained this passage in such a way as to make it appear that it will be fulfilled shortly before the last day, when the Antichrist appears, and Elias and Enoch. That is not true, and it is the devil himself who is responsible for this belief of some, that the whole world will become Christian. The devil did this that the true doctrine might be so obscured so that it might not be understood. Therefore, be on your guard; for this passage was verified and fulfilled shortly after Christ ascended into heaven, and is still in process of fulfillment. When the Gospel was first proclaimed, it was preached to the Jews; that nation was the sheepfold. And now he says here, "And other sheep I have, which are not of this fold: them also must I bring." Here he declares that the Gospel is to be preached to the gentiles also, so that they also might believe in Christ, that there might be one Christian communion, composed of Jews and gentiles. This was afterward brought about through the apostles, who preached to the gentiles and converted them to the faith. Accordingly, there is now but one church or communion, one faith, one hope, one love, one baptism, etc. And this continues to be so at the present day, and will continue until the day of judgment. Hence you must not understand this to mean that the whole world, and all men, will believe in Christ; for this holy cross will always be with us. They are in the majority who persecute Christ and, therefore, the Gospel must ever be preached, that some may be won for Christ. The kingdom of Christ is in process of growing and is not something that is completed. This is, in brief, the explanation of this Gospel.

The Third Sunday After Easter

❧

A Sermon of Comfort That Christ Preached to His Disciples

A little while, and ye behold me no more; and again a little while, and ye shall see me." Some of his disciples therefore said one to another, "What is this that he saith unto us, 'A little while, and ye behold me not; and again a little while, and ye shall see me:' and, 'Because I go to the Father?'" They said therefore, "What is this that he saith, 'A little while?' We know not what he saith." Jesus perceived that they were desirous to ask him, and he said unto them, "Do ye inquire among yourselves concerning this, that I said, 'A little while, and ye shall behold me not, and again a little while, and ye shall see me?' Verily, verily, I say unto you, that ye shall weep and lament, but the world shall rejoice: ye shall be sorrowful, but your sorrow shall be turned into joy. A woman when she is in travail hath sorrow, because her hour is come: but when she is delivered of the child, she remembereth no more the anguish, for the joy that a man is born into the world. And ye therefore now have sorrow: but I will see you again, and your heart shall rejoice, and your joy no one taketh away from you. And in that day ye shall ask me no question. Verily, verily, I say unto you, If ye shall ask anything of the Father, he will give it you in my name."

— JOHN 16:16–23

I. WHAT MOVED CHRIST TO DELIVER THIS SERMON OF COMFORT

1. Here in this Gospel we see how the Lord comforts and imparts courage to his children whom he is about to leave behind him, when they would come in fear and distress on account of his death or of their backsliding. We also notice what induced the evangelist John to use so many words that he indeed repeats one expression four times, which according to our thinking he might have expressed in fewer words. There is first of all presented to us

here the nature of the true Christian in the example of the dear apostles. In the second place, how the suffering and the resurrection of Christ are to become effective in us.

2. We also see that Christ announces to his disciples, how sorrowful they should be because he would leave them, but they are still so simple-minded and ignorant, and also so sorrowful on account of his recent conversation at the Last Supper, that they did not understand at all what he said unto them; yea, the nature of that which Christ presents to them is too great and incomprehensible for them. And it was also necessary that they should first become sorrowful before they could rejoice, even as Christ himself was an example to us that without the cross we could not enter into glory. Hence he says, in Luke 24:26, to the two, with whom he journeyed to Emmaus, "Behooved it not the Christ to suffer these things and to enter into his glory?" If, therefore, the dear disciples were to have joy, they must first of all pass through great sorrow. But this joy came to them through the Lord Jesus; for it is decreed in the Gospel, that without Christ there is no joy; and on the other hand, where Christ is, there is no sorrow, as is plainly stated in the text. Hence when Christ was taken from them, they were in great sorrow.

3. And these words here in this Gospel Christ the Lord spoke unto his disciples after the Last Supper, before he was apprehended. Let us look at them:

> *"A little while and ye behold me no more, and again a little*
> *while and ye shall see me, for I go to the Father."*

II. THE SERMON OF COMFORT ITSELF

A. Contents of This Sermon

4. "A little while," he says, "and ye behold me no more," for I shall be taken prisoner and they shall deliver me to death. But it will not last long and, during this short time, ye shall be sorrowful, but only remain steadfast in me and follow me. It will soon have an end. Three days I will be in the grave; then the world will rejoice as though it had gained a victory, but ye shall be sorrowful and shall weep and lament. "And again a little while, and ye shall see me; and, Because I go to the Father." That is, on the third day I will rise again; then ye shall rejoice and your joy no man shall take from you; and this will not be a joy of only three days, like the joy of the world, but an eternal joy. Thus the evangelist John most beautifully expresses the death and resurrection of Christ in these words, when Christ says, "A little while, and ye behold me not; and again a little while, and ye shall see me; and, Because I go to the Father."

5. An example is here given us, which we should diligently lay hold of and take to heart; if it went with us as it did in the time of the apostles, that we should be in suffering, anxiety, and distress, we should also remember to be strong and to rejoice because Christ will arise again. We know that this has come to pass; but the disciples did not know how he should be raised, or what he meant by the resurrection, hence they were so sorrowful and so sad. They heard indeed that they should see him, but they did not understand what it was or how it should come to pass. Therefore, they said among themselves, "What is this that he saith to us, A little while? We know not what he saith." To such an extent had sadness and sorrow overcome them, that they quite despaired, and knew not what these words meant and how they would see him again.

6. Therefore, we must also feel within us this "a little while" as the dear disciples felt it, for this is written for our example and instruction, so that we may thereby be comforted and be made better. And we should use this as a familiar adage among ourselves; yea, we should feel and experience it, so that we might at all times say, God is at times near and at times he has vanished out of sight. At times I remember how the Word seems neither to move me nor to apply to me. It passes by; I give no heed to it. But to this "a little while" we must give heed and pay attention, so that we may remain strong and steadfast. We will experience the same as the disciples. We cannot do otherwise than is written here; even as the disciples were not able to do otherwise.

7. The first "a little while" in that he says, "A little while, and ye shall behold me no more," they could soon afterward understand, when they saw that he was taken prisoner and put to death, but the second "a little while" in that he says, "And again a little while, and ye shall see me," that they could not understand, and we also cannot understand it. Yea, and when he says, "Because I go to the Father," that they understand still less. Thus it also goes with us: although we know and hear that trials, misfortune, and sorrow endure but a little while, yet we see that it constantly appears different than we believe. Then we despair and waver, and cannot be reconciled to it. We hear and we know very well that it shall not last very long, but how that result shall be accomplished we can never understand, as the disciples here cannot understand it.

8. But since they are unable to understand it, why does Christ relate it to them or why is it written? In order that we should not despair but hold fast to the Word, assured that it is indeed thus and not otherwise, even though it seems to be different. And although we do at times depart from the Word, we should not, therefore, remain altogether away from it, but return again,

for he makes good his Word. Even though man cannot believe it, God will nevertheless help him to believe it, and this he does without man's reason or free will and without man's adding anything thereto. Yea, the evangelist tells us that the disciples could not understand the words the Lord spoke to them; how much less could they understand his works that followed afterward. So very little does the free will and understanding of man know of the things pertaining to the salvation of the soul. These temporal things the free will can perceive and know, such as the cock crowing, which he can hear and his reason can also understand it; but when it is a question of understanding the work and Word of God, then human reason must give it up; it cannot make head or tail of it, although it pretends to understand a great deal about it. The glory thereof is too bright, the longer he beholds it, the blinder he becomes.

9. This is presented very plainly to our minds in the disciples who, though they had been so long with the Lord, yet they did not understand what he said to them. Well, neither will we be able to learn nor to understand this until we experience it; as when we say, Such and such a thing happened to me; this I felt and thus it went with me, then I was in anxiety; but it did not last long. Then I was encompassed by this temptation and by that adversity, but God delivered me soon out of them, etc.

10. We should take to heart and firmly hold fast to these words and keep them in mind when in sorrow and distress, that it will not last long, then we would also have more constant joy, for as Christ and his elect had their "a little while," so you and I and everyone will have his "a little while." Pilate and Herod will not crucify you but, in the same manner as the devil used them, so he will also use your persecutors. Therefore, when your trials come, you must not immediately think how you are to be delivered out of them. God will help you in due time. Only wait. It is only for a little while; he will not delay long.

11. But you must not lay the cross and sorrow upon yourself as some have indeed done, who chose for themselves death and imprisonment, and said, Christ willingly entered into death; he willingly permitted himself to be apprehended and delivered. I will also do the same. No, you dare not do this. Your cross and suffering will not long delay coming. These good people did not understand it. The dear disciples also said in Matthew 26:35, that they would remain with Christ and die with him. Peter said in John 13:37, he would not deny Christ, or would give his life for him; but how was it in the end? Christ went into the garden, trembled and quaked, was apprehended, put to death; Peter, however, forsook him. Where was now this great confidence, this boldness and courage of Peter? He thought Christ would die with joyful courage, and he would also follow him, but alas he was badly mistaken.

12. Here you easily see that the sorrow and sufferings, in which we expected to remain permanently, were of our own choosing, but when the hour finally comes, of which you never thought before, you will hardly be able to stand, unless you become a new man. The old Adam despairs; he does not abide; he cannot abide, for it goes against his nature, against his purpose, and against his designs. Hence you must have your own time, then you must suffer a little. For Christ withdraws himself from you and permits you to remain in the power of sin, of death, and of hell. There the heart cannot accomplish very much to calm the conscience, do whatever it will, for Christ departs and dies. Then you will have the refrain, "A little while, and ye shall not behold me." Where will you go? There is no comfort. There is no help. You are in the midst of sin; in the midst of death; in the midst of hell. If Christ would not come now independent of any merit of your own, then you would be compelled to remain in this tribulation and terror eternally, for thus it would have happened also to the disciples, if Christ had not risen from the dead and become alive. It was, therefore, necessary for him again to arise from the dead.

13. Now, this everyone must experience and suffer, either now or upon his deathbed when he dies, but how much better it is to experience it now, for when at some future time we shall be cast into the fire for the sake of the Gospel and be counted as heretics, then we shall see of what profit this is; for if the heart is not strong at such a time, what shall become of us, for there our eyes shall see the torture and the terror of death. Whither shall we go? Therefore, if Christ is not present, and if he should then withdraw his hand, we are already lost; but if he is with us to help, the flesh may indeed die, but all is well with the soul, for Christ has taken it to himself. There it is safe; no one shall pluck it out of his hand, in John 10:28.

14. But this we cannot accomplish with words; an experience is here needed for that. Well it is for him who experiences this now; then surely it will not be hard for him to die. It is very perilous indeed if we must learn this upon our deathbed, namely, how to wrestle with and conquer death. Therefore, it was indeed a great favor and mercy of God, which he showed to the holy martyrs and apostles in whom he had first conquered death, then afterward they were prepared without fear to suffer everything that could be laid upon them.

B. This Sermon of Comfort Explained

15. All this is presented to us in our Gospel, but since the disciples could not understand what he meant in that he said "A little while" and he noticed that they were desirous to ask him, he continues and explains it to them in these simple words, and says,

"Verily, verily, I say unto you, ye shall weep and lament, but the world shall rejoice; ye shall be sorrowful, but your sorrow shall be turned into joy."

16. This is spoken to all Christians, for every Christian must have temptations, trials, anxieties, adversities, sorrows, come what may. Therefore, he mentions here no sorrow nor trial, he simply says they shall weep, lament, and be sorrowful, for the Christian has many persecutions. Some are suffering loss of goods; others there are whose character is suffering ignominy and scorn; some are drowned, others are burned; some are beheaded; one perishes in this manner, and another in that; it is, therefore, the lot of the Christian constantly to suffer misfortune, persecution, trials, and adversity. This is the rod or foxtail with which they are punished. They dare not look for anything better as long as they are here. This is the court color by which the Christian is recognized and, if anyone wants to be a Christian, he dare not be ashamed of his court color or livery.

17. Why does God do this and permit his own to be persecuted and hounded? In order to suppress and subdue the free will, so that it may not seek an expedient in their works, but rather become a fool in God's works and learn thereby to trust and depend upon God alone.

18. Therefore, when this now comes to pass, we shall not be able to accommodate ourselves to it, and shall not understand it, unless Christ himself awakens us and makes us cheerful, so that his resurrection becomes effective in us, and all our works fall to pieces and be as nothing. Therefore, the text here concludes powerfully, that man is absolutely nothing in his own strength. Here everything is condemned and thrust down that has been and may still be preached about good works; for this is the conclusion: where Christ is not, there is nothing. Ask Saint Peter how he was disposed when Christ was not with him. What good works did he do? He denied Christ. He renounced him with an oath. Like good works we do, when we have not Christ with us.

19. Thus all serves to the end that we should accustom ourselves to build alone upon Christ, and to depend upon no other work, upon no other creature, whether in heaven or upon earth. In this name alone are we preserved and blessed, and in none other, in Acts 4:12 and in Acts 10:43. But on this account, we must suffer much. The worst of all is, that we must not only suffer shame, persecution, and death, but that the world rejoices because of our great loss and misfortunes. This is indeed very hard and bitter. Surely it shall thus come to pass, for the world will rejoice when it goes ill with us. But this comfort we have, that their joy shall not last long, and our sorrow shall be

turned into eternal joy. Of this the Lord gives us a beautiful parable of the woman in travail, when he says,

> *"A woman when she is in travail hath sorrow, because her hour is come, but when she is delivered of the child, she remembereth no more the anguish for joy that a man is born into the world."*

C. This Sermon of Comfort Is Illustrated by a Parable

20. With this parable he also shows that our own works are nothing, for here we see that if all women came to the help of this woman in travail, they would accomplish nothing. Here free will is at its end and is unable to accomplish anything, or to give any advice. It is not in the power of the woman to be delivered of the child, but she feels that it is wholly in the hand and power of God. When he helps and works, then something is accomplished, but where he does not help, all is lost, even if the whole world were present. In this, God shows to the woman her power, her ability, and her strength. Before this, she could dance and leap; she rejoiced and was happy, but now she sees how God must do all. Hereby we perceive that God is our Father, who also must deliver us from the womb and bring us forth to life.

21. Christ says here to his disciples, So it will also go with you. The woman is here in such a state of mind that she is fearful of great danger, and yet she knows that the whole work lies in the hands of God; in him she trusts; upon him it is she depends; he also helps her and accomplishes the work, which the whole world could not do, and she thinks of nothing but the time that shall follow, when she shall again rejoice; and her heart feels and says, A dangerous hour is at hand, but afterward it will be well. Courage and the heart press through all obstacles. Thus it will also be with you, when you are in sorrow and adversity, and when you become new creatures. Only quietly wait and permit God to work. He will accomplish everything without your assistance.

22. This parable of the woman is a strong and stubborn argument against free will, that it is entirely powerless and without strength in the things pertaining to the salvation of our souls. The Gospel shows very plainly that divine strength and grace are needed. Man's free will is entirely too weak and insignificant to accomplish anything here. But we have established our own orders and regulations instead of the Gospel and through these we want to free ourselves from sin, from death, from hell, and from all misfortune, and finally be saved thereby. A great mistake.

23. Here you see in this example, that if a man is to be born the mother must become first as though she were dead; that is, she must be in a condition

as though she were already dead; she thinks it is now all over with her. Thus it shall be also with us. If we want to become godly, we must be as dead, and despair of all our works, yea, never think that we shall be able to accomplish anything. Here no monastic life, no priest craft, and no works will be able to help; but wait patiently and permit God to do with you according to his will. He shall accomplish it; permit him to work. We shall accomplish nothing ourselves, but at times we shall feel death and hell. This the ungodly shall also feel, but they do not believe that God is present in it and wants to help them. Just as the woman here accomplishes nothing; she feels only pain, distress, and misery, but she cannot help herself out of this state.

24. But when delivered of the child, she remembers no more her sorrow and pain, but is as though she had become alive again. She could not before even think that her sorrow and pain should have an end so soon. Thus it is also with us in the trials of sin, of death, and of hell; then we are as though we were dead; yea, we are in the midst of death, and Christ has forsaken us. He has gone a little while from us. Then we are in great pain and cannot help ourselves; but when Christ returns, and makes himself known to us, our hearts are full of joy, even though the whole world be to the contrary.

25. This no one can realize unless he has once been encompassed by death. He who has once been delivered from death must then rejoice; not that such a person cannot again fall and be sorrowful at times, but since this joy is at hand he worries about nothing. He also fears nothing, no matter by what dangers he may be surrounded. This joy can indeed be interrupted, for when I fall again into sin, then I fear even a driven leaf, in Leviticus 26:36. Why? Because Christ has departed a little while from me and has forsaken me; but I will not despair, for this joy will return again. I must not then continue and cling to the pope, nor endeavor to help myself by works; but I must quietly wait until Christ comes again. He remains but a little while without. When he then looks again upon the heart and appears and shines into it, the joy returns. Then shall I be able to meet every misfortune and terror.

26. All this is said and written that we may be conscious of our weakness and inability, and that as far as our works are concerned all is nothing, all is utterly lost. But this joy is almighty and eternal when we are dead; but now in this life, it is mixed. Now I fall and then I rise again, and it cannot be eternal, because flesh and blood are still with me. Therefore, Christ says to his disciples,

> *"And ye now have sorrow, but I will see you again, and your heart*
> *shall rejoice, and your joy no man taketh from you."*

27. All this David has described in a psalm in a most masterly and beauti-ful manner, when he says in Psalm 30:1–8, "I will extol thee, O Jehovah, for thou hast raised me up, and hast not made my foes to rejoice over me. O Jehovah, my God: I cried unto thee and thou hast healed me. O Jehovah, thou hast brought up my soul from Sheol, thou hast kept me alive, that I should not go down to the pit. Sing praise unto Jehovah, O ye saints of his, and give thanks to his holy memorial name for his anger is but for a moment; his favor is for a lifetime; weeping may tarry for the night, but joy cometh in the morning. As for me, I said in my prosperity, I shall never be moved. Thou, Jehovah, of thy favor hadst made my mountain to stand strong: thou didst hide thy face; I was troubled. I cried to Thee, O Jehovah; and unto Jehovah I made supplication." Where is now the man who just said, "I shall never be moved"? Well, he replies, when thou, Jehovah, of thy favor didst make my mountains to stand strong, then I spoke thus. "But when thou didst hide thy face, I was troubled," I fell. If Christ were continually with us, I really believe we would never be afraid; but since he occasionally departs from us, we must, therefore, at times be afraid.

28. In this psalm is beautifully portrayed to us how to recognize and experience a good conscience, for here David considers the whole world as a drop, and is not the least afraid of it, even though it should storm and rage against him, for he has the Lord with him. He has made his mountain to stand strong, but when he fell and the Lord hid his face from him, then he was afraid. Then were heart, courage, and mountain gone. Then was he afraid of a driven leaf, who before was not afraid of the whole world, as he also says in another psalm unto the Lord, "Yea, though I walk through the valley of the shadow of death, I will fear no evil, for thou art with me; thy rod and thy staff they comfort me," in Psalm 23:4. Likewise in Psalm 3:6, he says, "I will not be afraid of ten thousands of the people that have set themselves against me round about." Passages like these can be multiplied in the psalms, all of which show how an upright, good conscience stands, namely, when God is with it, it is courageous and brave, but when God has departed, it is fearful and terrified.

29. Here we rightly understand now what the words of Christ signify, "I go to the Father." Before this, no one understood them, not even the disciples. But this is the road, I must die, he saith, and ye must also die. Peter vowed boastfully, for according to the old Adam he wanted to die with the Lord, and we all think we want to die with Christ, as all the other disciples said that they would enter into death with Christ, in Matthew 26:35. But all this must perish in us. You must come to the moment of trial, when Christ does not stand by you and does not die with you, when you cannot help yourself, just like the

woman in travail. When this takes place, then you come to the Father. That is, you are filled with his power, and he makes a new man of you, who thereafter is not afraid, whose character is already here a heavenly character, as Saint Paul calls it, in Philippians 3:20; and this has its beginning here, by faith. Then you become courageous and brave, and can say as the prophet in the psalm, "I will not be afraid of ten thousands of people," and "Though I walk through the valley of the shadow of death, I will fear no evil." Why all this? Because you have come to the Father. Who can now overthrow God's omnipotence? No one. Aye, then no one can do anything to you or cause you any harm.

30. This no one will understand until it has come to pass. Have you been encompassed by death and been delivered from it, then you will say, I was in death, and if the Lord had not delivered me, I would have remained in death's grasp forever. The entire thirtieth Psalm refers to this, which you will do well to examine thoroughly and consider faithfully.

31. Here you have now the fruit and the example of the death and the resurrection of Christ, and how free will is nothing, and everything reason concludes regarding these things, which pertain to our salvation. May God give grace that we may lay hold of it and regulate our lives accordingly. Amen.

APPENDIX TO THE FOREGOING SERMON

Christ

> *"Verily, verily, I say unto you, that ye shall weep and lament,*
> *but the world shall rejoice," etc. –*JOHN 16:20

1. No one should lay his cross upon himself, as some foolish persons have done and are still doing. They even court the prison and death, and say, Since Christ of his own free will entered death, I will follow him in his example as he commanded us to do. There is no need whatever to do this, for your martyrdom and cross will not be wanting. Such people, however, do not understand divine things; they think they will suddenly enter death with Christ, whom they have never learned to know except in words. Thus was Peter also disposed, but he stood before Christ like a rabbit before one beating a drum. Notice, how the old Adam lacks courage when under the cross! The new man, however, can indeed persevere through grace. In suffering, pious persons have no aim of their own; but if it be God's will, they bear good fruit like the tree planted by the streams of water; and that is pleasing to God and, besides, all presumption is condemned, all show and every excuse, however good they may be. But he who battles heroically will receive for his suffering

here joy, the eternal in place of the temporal. Of this Christ says, "Your joy shall be turned into sorrow."

2. This saying of Christ is addressed to all Christians in general. For things may go well or ill, still a Christian must contend with persecution, need, distress, and opposition. Moreover, Christ does not specify here any special punishment, cross or martyrdom; hence he says simply, You will weep, lament, and be sorrowful; for Christians suffer many kinds of persecutions. Some have their property damaged, others have their name dishonored, some are drowned, others burned or beheaded. Thus Christians die, being put to death by many different hands, each with greater contempt than the other, so that misfortune, persecution, and adversity are constantly weighing upon the neck of Christians, by which they are stricken, and there is nothing more certain for them to hope for as long as they crawl here upon the earth. And this is the court dress by which Christians are identified. Now, whoever wishes to be a Christian dare not be ashamed of his colors.

3. But why has God appointed his own children to be driven here and there by persecution? On account of free will, that it may be humbled to the ground and become a perfect fool in the works of God, and learn to trust in God alone; as a result give to God good works, things, and at last give ourselves and thus rightly trust in God and cling to Christ. It may, however, well grieve one that the world rejoices over our misfortunes. It is a common thing, the jaybird can never stop jumping. But the comfort of the Christian is, that the world's joy will not last long, and that his own distress shall be changed into joy eternal. Amen.

The Fourth Sunday After Easter

❧

Of Sin, of Righteousness, and of the Cross

B ut now I go unto him that sent me; and none of you asketh me, Whither goest thou? But because I have spoken these things unto you, sorrow hath filled your heart. Nevertheless I tell you the truth: It is expedient for you that I go away; for if I go not away, the Comforter will not come unto you; but if I go, I will send him unto you. And he, when he is come, will convict the world in respect of sin, and of righteousness, and of judgment: of sin, because they believe not on me; of righteousness, because I go to the Father, and ye behold me no more; of judgment, because the prince of this world hath been judged. I have yet many things to say unto you, but ye cannot bear them now. Howbeit when he, the Spirit of truth, shall come, he shall guide you into all the truth; for he shall not speak from himself; but what things soever he shall hear, these shall he speak; and he shall declare unto you the things that are to come. He shall glorify me: for he shall take of mine, and shall declare it unto you. All things whatsoever the Father hath are mine; therefore said I, that he taketh of mine, and shall declare it unto you." — JOHN 16:5–15

I. THE HOLY SPIRIT CONVICTS THE WORLD OF SIN

1. Christ pictures to us in this Gospel what his kingdom is and what takes place in it, how it is governed, and what it accomplishes. Here you learn that there is a kingdom upon the earth and that it is invisible, and that it cleaves to and rests upon the Word of God alone. Christ does not say that he wishes his disciples to follow him up into heaven at once; but that he will send them the Holy Spirit and that he departs from them for the very purpose of sending them the Holy Spirit, in order that thereby his kingdom may be further developed. Therefore, he says, "I have yet many things to say unto you, but ye cannot bear them now." They could not understand that kingdom, how it should exist and be administered. Their reason and senses were still too

carnal; they had never seen a spiritual kingdom, nor heard of one; therefore, they continually thought of a temporal, outward kingdom. And here as in other Gospels, faith and trust in Christ are preached. We wish now to consider the leading thoughts in this Gospel and to explain them as far as God gives us his grace to do so. The Lord addresses his disciples thus:

> *"When the Comforter is come, he will convict the world in respect of sin, and of righteousness, and of judgment; of sin, because they believe not on me."*

2. Here we must let that be "sin" which is ascribed to, and included in, sin by the high Majesty of heaven. In the text, only unbelief is mentioned as sin, "because," says the Lord, "they believe not on me."

3. But what is it to believe on Christ? It is not simply to believe that he is God, or that he reigns in heaven in equal power with God the Father; many others believe that: But I believe on Christ when I believe that he is a gracious God to me and has taken my sins upon himself and reconciled me with God the Father, that my sins are his and his righteousness mine, that there is an intermingling and an exchange, that Christ is a mediator between me and the Father. For the sins of the whole world were laid upon Christ, and the righteousness of the Father, that is in Christ, will swallow up all our sins.

No sins dare and can remain upon Christ. Such faith makes me pure and acceptable to the Father. Of this faith, the pope and our highly educated leaders know nothing to speak, much less to believe. They teach that man should do many good works if he is to be acceptable to God and be free from sin, and that then God imparts to him his grace.

4. However, here the Lord speaks quite differently, and says, "The Holy Spirit will convict the world in respect of sin, because they believe not on me." Unbelief only is mentioned here as sin, and faith is praised as suppressing and extinguishing the other sins, even the sins in the saints. Faith is so strong and overpowering that no sin dare put it under any obligation. Although sins are present in pious and believing persons, they are not imputed to them, nor shall their sins condemn them. This is Paul's meaning when he says in Romans 8:1, "There is therefore now no condemnation to them that are in Christ Jesus, who walk not after the flesh, but after the Spirit." Their hearts are cleansed by faith, as Peter says in Acts 15:9. Therefore, whatever they do in this faith, in this assurance is all good, pure, and pleasing to God. On the contrary, without this faith, all their doings are sin and destruction, though their good works may shine and glitter as beautifully as they will, and even though they raise the dead. For Paul says, "Whatsoever is not of faith is sin," in Romans 14:23.

5. What will now become of all the priests, nuns, and monks who, wishing to escape sin, run into cloisters and undertake to do many good works without this faith? Unbelief is called sin, as I said, but to believe on Christ—that he takes my sins upon himself, reconciles me to the Father and at the same time makes me his heir of all that is in heaven and earth—this is good works. In John 6:28–29, the Jews asked Christ, "What must we do, that we may work the works of God?" Jesus answered, "This is the work of God, that ye believe on him whom he hath sent." Yea, and should we preach thus, who will then enter the cloisters or contribute anything for them? The purses of the monks would then surely become flat, their kitchens scanty, their cellars empty and neglected. For this reason, they will not allow faith to be preached; nay, they condemn this doctrine and banish its preachers. Indeed they have already set about it in good earnest. Christ further says,

"Of righteousness, because I go to the Father."

II. THE HOLY SPIRIT CONVICTS THE WORLD OF RIGHTEOUSNESS

6. Here all the learned come armed, yea, the whole world besides, and tell us what kind of righteousness this is. Yes, and they shall err. For the world has never known this righteousness; it does not yet know it, and it does not wish to know it. Hence the Lord says here that the Holy Spirit will convict the world of this righteousness.

7. But what are we to understand here by "the world"? We dare not understand by it the coarse, outward sins, as adultery, murder, stealing, and theft. There are instituted for such characters the wheels and gallows, with which the worldly powers, the kings, emperors, and princes, have to do. But we will interpret "the world" as the subtle and secret sins, of which the Holy Spirit convicts, which the world does not know as sin. Yea, it pronounces them divine works; it applauds them and will not permit them to be called sins. How else can unbelief and other secret sins live in the heart while the heart itself is not conscious of them and knows not that they are sins? But those who convict the world must, on that account, be reviled as heretics and be banished from the country, as we see at present. Therefore, the Holy Spirit must convict the world.

8. The rod, however, by which the world is convicted and punished, is the divine Word and the holy Gospel, proclaimed by the apostles and preachers, as God the Father says to his Son in Psalm 2:9, "Thou shalt break them with a rod of iron; thou shalt dash them in pieces like a potter's vessel." That is, you

shall humble them with the holy Gospel. But the world resents such conviction and punishment; yet it punishes severely, and even more severely than the Holy Spirit does. The Holy Spirit takes rods, but the world uses swords and fire. Isaiah also speaks in like terms of Christ our Lord in Isaiah 11:4, "He shall smite the earth with the rod of his mouth; and with the breath of his lips shall he slay the wicked."

9. What is now the righteousness the Lord means here? Some say righteousness is a virtue that gives to every person his own. Although this is a fine definition, yet it is misleading, in that we do not know how we are indebted to everyone, to God and to man. This God desires and demands of us. Therefore, his righteousness is nothing more than the faith and grace of God, by which God makes us pious and righteous. Such righteousness we must have and thus be righteous, if we are to be found righteous and unblamable before God, and not only before man. For the smallest letter or tittle of the law shall not fail, but all will be fulfilled.

10. Noah was found to be such a righteous man. It is written of him in Genesis 6:8–9, "Noah was a righteous man, and blameless in his generation; he walked with God. Therefore he found favor in the eyes of Jehovah." It is also written of Job, in Job 1:1, that he was a perfect and upright man, one that feared God and turned away from evil. But that is done only by faith, when one believes that God has strangled and swallowed up one's sins in his righteousness. For this righteousness is nothing but to believe that Christ is seated at the right hand of the Father; that he is equal with God, possessing equal power; that he has become Lord by virtue of his Passion, by which he has ascended to the Father, reconciled us with God, and is there as our Mediator. This is what the prophet means in Psalm 110:1, "Jehovah saith unto my Lord, sit thou at my right hand, until I make thine enemies thy footstool." Therefore, Saint Paul calls Christ now a Mediator, in 1 Timothy 2:5 and in Hebrews 8:6; then a throne of grace, in Romans 3:25; a propitiation, in 1 John 2:2; and other like names. God requires this honor from us, and faith demands it that we possess him as our Lord and Savior; and this glory he will not concede to anyone else, as he says through the prophet, "My glory will I not give to another," in Isaiah 42:8.

11. His way to the Father is his glory. For "to go" means to die, and to pass through death to the Father and enter upon another existence. He glories in his future course when he says, "I go unto the Father." Therefore, here righteousness is nothing more than traveling by faith the road through death unto the Father. This faith makes us righteous before God, this faith by which we believe that he delivered us from sin, death, Satan, and hell, through

his Passion, and that thereby God, the Father, is reconciled, and our sins are blotted out by his blood. This is also the reason that he mentions his going, when he says, in respect of righteousness, not that he is with the Father, but that he goes to the Father. In this going, sin is swallowed up in righteousness and Christ passes cheerfully through death, so that no one is even aware of it. Therefore, it follows,

"And ye behold me no more."

12. The nature and art of faith are here set forth: faith neither feels nor gropes, nor do the things connected with it require a science; but it bestirs itself cheerfully to believe the things it neither feels nor can measure with all its powers inwardly or outwardly. Paul says in Romans 8:24, "Who hopeth for that which he seeth?" Therefore, the Lord aptly says, "And ye behold me no more." As if he would say that this way of good works which he is traveling, will not be seen nor grasped by the senses, but it must be believed. Now follows the third and last part of our Gospel.

III. THE HOLY SPIRIT CONVICTS THE WORLD OF JUDGMENT, OR THE CROSS

"Of judgment, because the prince of this world is judged."

13. The prince of this world is Satan, and his members include all unbelieving and godless persons; all flesh with all its powers is condemned by these words; and what the world praises is condemned by God, including both the godly and the ungodly, believers and unbelievers, friends and enemies, as Saint Peter cites, in 1 Peter 4:17, when he says, "For the time is come for judgment to begin at the house of God," that is, with the elect, in whom God dwells. The righteous, while they live here, have flesh and blood, in which sin is rooted. To suppress this sin, God will lead them into great misery and anxiety, poverty, persecution, and all kinds of danger, as Paul writes to the Romans, in Romans 7:18ff. and in Romans 8:4, and to the Corinthians, until the flesh becomes completely subject to the Spirit.

14. That, however, does not take place until death, when the flesh is completely turned to ashes. We must be in all points like Christ. Since he was here despised, mocked, and tried, so that, as the prophet Isaiah says, in Isaiah 53:3, he was esteemed and held as one stricken and smitten of God, the most despised and unworthy, full of grief and sorrow, his disciples must also go through the same experiences. Everyone should carefully consider this. It is so decreed, as Christ himself before declared to his disciples, saying, "Remember

the word that I said unto you, A servant is not greater than his lord. If they persecuted me they will also persecute you," in John 15:20. Hence Paul says in very plain words in 2 Timothy 3:12, "All that would live godly in Christ Jesus shall suffer persecution."

15. Therefore, Saint Peter carefully discriminates, and says, "If judgment begin first at us, what shall be the end of them that obey not the Gospel of God? And if the righteous is scarcely saved, where shall the ungodly and sinner appear?" in 1 Peter 4:17–18. This discrimination is between the sufferings of the godly and of the wicked. Godly and believing persons know their sins; they bear all their punishment patiently, and are resigned to God's judgment without the least murmur; therefore, they are punished only bodily, and here in time, and their pain and suffering have an end. Unbelievers, however, since they are not conscious of their sins and transgressions, cannot bear God's punishment patiently, but they resent it, and wish their life and works to go unpunished, yea, uncensured. Hence their punishment and suffering are in body and soul, here in time, and last forever beyond this life. The Lord says here, "The prince of this world is already judged." As if he were to say, All that the world and humanity in the world discover, praise, and condemn, amounts to nothing; and whatever God judges, the world cannot suffer nor bear, but rejects, repudiates, and condemns.

16. Thus three thoughts have been presented to us in this Gospel: Sin, righteousness, and, finally, the cross and persecution. We shall be freed from sin through faith. If we believe that Christ made satisfaction for our sins and that his satisfaction is ours, that is then the righteousness. When we are free from sin, and are just and pious, then the world, Satan, and the flesh will arise and contend and battle against us. Then come persecution and the cross. This we wish to have set forth in brief at present from this Gospel. May God grant his grace that we learn it thus, and know how to govern ourselves by it when we need it.

The Fifth Sunday After Easter
or Prayer Sunday

A Sermon by Christ on Prayer

*A*nd in that day ye shall ask me no question. Verily, verily, I say
unto you, If ye shall ask anything of the Father, he will give it
you in my name. Hitherto have ye asked for nothing in my name: ask,
and ye shall receive, that your joy may be made full.

*These things have I spoken unto you in dark sayings: the hour cometh,
when I shall no more speak unto you in dark sayings, but shall tell you
plainly of the Father. In that day ye shall ask in my name: and I say
not unto you, that I will pray the Father for you; for the Father himself
loveth you, because ye have loved me, and have believed that I came
forth from the Father. I came out from the Father, and am come into the
world: again, I leave the world, and go unto the Father. His disciples
say, Lo, now speakest thou plainly, and speakest no dark saying. Now
know we that thou knowest all things, and needest not that any man
should ask thee; by this we believe that thou camest forth from God."*
—JOHN 16:23–30

1. We are accustomed to read today's Gospel on this Sunday because it
treats of prayer, and this week is called Rogation (Supplication) week, in which
we give ourselves to prayer and to processions with crosses. Those who first
instituted it, no doubt, meant it well, but it has proved to work harm. For, in
the processions heretofore, many unchristian things have been practiced, and
there has been no praying at all or very little; so that the processions were rightly
abolished and discontinued. Often have I admonished that we should persevere
in prayer, for there is great need of it. Since the outward prating and mutter-
ing of prayer is done away with, we no longer pray in any way. This is a good
indication that we heretofore, notwithstanding our many prayers, never prayed.

2. The Lord points out here five things necessary to constitute true prayer. The first is God's promise, which is the chief thing and is the foundation and power of all prayers. For he promises here that it shall be given us if we ask; and besides he swears: "Verily, verily, I say unto you, If ye shall ask anything of the Father, he will give it you in my name." He promises that we might be sure of being heard in prayer; yea, he censures the disciples for the reason that they are lazy and have not therefore been praying. As if he would say, God is ready to give more quickly, and to give more than you ask; yea, he offers his treasures if we only take them. It is truly a great shame and a severe chastisement for us Christians that God should still upbraid us for our slothfulness in prayer, and that we fail to let such a rich and excellent promise incite us to pray. We let this precious treasure lie there, and seek it not, nor exercise ourselves to receive the power in such a promise.

3. So God himself now founds our prayer upon his promise and thereby encourages us to pray. If it were not for this promise, who would have the courage to pray? We have hitherto resorted to many ways of preparing ourselves to pray—ways with which the books are filled; but if you wish to be well prepared, take the promise and lay hold of God with it. Then your courage and desire to pray will soon grow, which courage you will never otherwise get. For those who pray without God's promise, imagine in themselves how angry God is, whom they wish to propitiate by means of their prayers. Without faith in the promise, there is then, neither courage nor desire to pray, but mere uncertain delusion and a melancholy spirit; there is, therefore, no hearing of prayers, and both prayer and labor are lost.

4. By these words, Christ now chastises the unbelief of those who, by reason of their foolish worship, consider themselves unworthy to pray, and gauge the worthiness of their prayer according to themselves and their own ability, and not according to the promise of God. There is then, to be sure, nothing but unworthiness. However, you should, by all means, be conscious of your own unworthiness, taking confidence not from your own doings, but from the promise of God, and be so completely conscious, that if you were all alone, and no one else in the world prayed, you would nevertheless pray, because of this promise. For you can point me to no true saint who prayed, depending upon his own worthiness, and who did not rely only upon God's promises, be he Peter, Paul, Mary, Elijah, or anyone else. All of them have been unworthy. I would not give a nickel for all the prayers of a saint if he prayed because of his own worthiness.

5. The second requisite of true prayer, following that of God's promise, is faith—that we believe the promise is true, and do not doubt that God will

give what he promises. For the words of the promise require faith. But faith is a firm, undoubting confidence in God's promise that it is true; as James says, "But if any of you lacketh wisdom, let him ask of God, who giveth to all liberally and upbraideth not; and it shall be given him. But let him ask in faith, nothing doubting: for he that doubteth is like the surge of the sea driven by the wind and tossed. For let not that man think that he shall receive anything of the Lord," in James 1:5–7. Moreover, he who doubts and yet prays, tempts God; for he doubts in respect to God's will and grace. Therefore, his prayer is nothing, and he gropes after God like the blind for the wall. John also speaks of this assurance of faith in 1 John 5:14–15, "And this is the boldness which we have toward him, that, if we ask anything according to his will, he heareth: and if we know that he heareth us whatsoever we ask, we know that we have the petitions which we have asked of him." John describes with these words how a truly believing heart is disposed in prayer, namely, that it is concerned about nothing else than that its prayer be heard, knowing that it has even then obtained its petition. That is also true. Such faith and definite assurance, however, the Holy Spirit must impart; therefore, without the Holy Spirit, surely no prayer will be offered.

6. Try it, now, and pray thus. Then you will taste the sweetness of God's promise. What courage and consolation of heart it awakens to pray for all things! It matters not how great and high the petitions may be. Elijah was a man of like passions with ourselves; yet when he prayed, it did not rain for three years and six months, and when he again prayed, it rained, in 1 Kings 17:1 and in 1 Kings 18:45. Notice, here you see a single man prays and by his prayer he is lord of the clouds, of heaven and earth. So God lets us see what power and influence a true prayer has, namely, that nothing is impossible for it to do.

7. Let everyone now ask his heart how often he has prayed during his whole life. Singing psalms and saying the Lord's Prayer is not called praying. These are instituted for children and untutored people, as exercises, to make them athletes in the Scriptures. Your prayer, however, no one but yourself sees and feels in your heart, and you will truly know it when it hits the mark.

8. The third requisite of true prayer is, that one must name definitely something that he brings to God or for which he prays, as for strong faith, for love, for peace, and for the comfort of his neighbor. One must actually set forth the petitions, just as the Lord's Prayer presents seven petitions. This is what Christ means by the words, "If ye shall ask anything of the Father." "Anything," that is, whatever you are in need of. Besides, he himself interprets this "anything," and says, "That your joy may be made full." That is, pray for

all things you need, until you have acquired even all and your joy is made full; and his prayer will first be fully answered on the day of judgment.

9. The fourth element in true prayer is that we must desire, or wish, that the petition be granted, which is nothing but asking; as Christ says, "Ask." Others have called this *"Ascensum mentis in Deum,"* when the soul ascends to God and desires something from him, and sighs from its depths, saying, Oh, that I had this or that! Such sighing Saint Paul praises in Romans 8:26. It is an intercession of the Spirit that cannot be uttered. That is, the mouth wants to, but cannot speak as rapidly and strongly as the heart desires; the yearning is greater that any words and thoughts. Hence it is, also, that man himself does not feel how deep his sighing or desire is. When Zacchæus sought to see the Lord, he himself did not feel how strongly his heart wished that Christ might speak with him and come into his house. However, when his desire was fulfilled, he was very happy, for he had succeeded according to all his wishes and prayers; he had received more than he had dared to ask by word of mouth, or desire, in Luke 19:2ff. Moses, likewise, cried so that God spoke to him, "Wherefore criest thou unto me?" in Exodus 14:15, and yet his mouth kept silence; but his heart, in its extremity, sighed deeply, and that was called crying unto God. In like manner, Saint Paul writes to the Ephesians, "God is able to do exceeding abundantly above all that we ask or think," in Ephesians 3:20. Now, temptation, anxiety, and trouble induce this sighing; they teach us what true sighing is.

10. The fifth requisite of true prayer is, that we ask in the name of Christ. This is nothing more than that we come before God in the faith of Christ and comfort ourselves with the sure confidence that he is our Mediator, through whom all things are given to us, without whom we merit nothing but wrath and disgrace. As Paul says to the Romans, "Through whom also we have had our access by faith into this grace wherein we stand; and we rejoice in hope of the glory of God," in Romans 5:2. It is praying aright in Christ's name, when we thus trust in him that we will be received and heard for his sake, and not for our own sake. Those, however, who pray in their own name, who presume that God will hear or regard them, because they say so many, such long, such devout, such godly prayers, will merit and obtain nothing but wrath and disgrace; for they wish to be people whom God should regard without a mediator. To them, Christ here is of no consideration, nor is he of any service.

11. We observe that all five requisites of prayer may be complied within the heart, without any utterance of the mouth. The oral part of prayer is really not to be despised, but it is necessary to kindle and encourage prayer inwardly, in the heart. The additional conditions, however, of which I have written enough elsewhere, should and must be omitted that we specify to God the time, person,

place, and measure. We must leave all that to his own free will, and cling only to asking; we must not doubt that the prayer is heard, and that what we petitioned is already ordered—that it will be given—as certainly as if we already had it. This is pleasing to God, and he will do as he here promises, "Ask, and ye shall receive." Those, however, who set the time, place, and measure, tempt God, and believe not that they are heard or that they have obtained what they asked; therefore, they also receive nothing. The Gospel lesson continues,

"Hitherto have ye asked nothing in my name."

12. It may be that they knew as yet nothing of such prayer, and of this name; besides, they felt no need that urged them to pray in this name. They imagined that so long as Christ was with them, they needed nothing and had enough of everything. But now that he is to separate from them and leave them, trouble immediately comes, and they will have reason enough to move them to pray.

"These things have I spoken unto you in parables (dark sayings)."

13. When he says "these things," he means that which he had just before spoken: "A little while, and ye behold me not; and again a little while, and ye shall see me"; and, "Because I go to the Father"; also, the parable of the woman in travail. For these were nothing but parables, that is, dark, obscure sayings that they did not understand. John calls these dark, hidden sayings "parables," although the German language does not designate them so, but calls them enigmas or veiled sayings. We are accustomed to say of one who has uttered an enigmatical saying, "That is a covered dish or a covered meal," when the words have a meaning not on the surface. In parables, the meaning to be conveyed is expressed in a way that not everyone understands. Of this nature were all the sayings of Christ, which he spoke to his disciples on the night of his farewell and his going to the Father; they could understand nothing of them. They thought his going would not be dying and coming into another existence; they thought of it as a pleasure walk and that Christ should return in the body, as one journeys to another country and returns. Therefore, although he spoke plainly and clearly, yet going and parting were a "covered meal" to them. Hence he adds,

"The hour cometh when I shall no more speak unto you in dark sayings (parables), but shall tell you plainly of the Father."

14. That is, what I now speak to you, while in the body, and my parables ye understand not, that I will thoroughly explain to you through the Holy Spirit. I will plainly speak of my Father, that you may then understand who

the Father is and what my going to the Father means. You will clearly see how I ascend through suffering into the Father's life and into his kingdom; that I sit at his right hand and represent you and am your Mediator; that all this is done for your sake, that you may likewise come to the Father. "I shall tell you plainly of the Father" is not to be understood to mean that he will tell us much about God's divine nature, as the sophists fancy; for that is unnecessary, and the divine nature of God is incomprehensible. But Christ will tell us how he goes to the Father, how he takes upon himself the kingdom and government of the Father; as a king's son returns to his father and assumes the government of the kingdom. Christ says further,

"In that day ye shall ask in my name."

15. For then, in your many tribulations, you will have not only reason to pray, but will also know and perceive what my name is and how you should esteem me. Then will you be taught by praying itself what you now do not at all understand, and that hitherto you have never prayed. Therefore, he adds,

"And I say not unto you, that I will pray the Father for you: for
the Father himself loveth you, because ye have loved me, and
have believed that I came forth from the Father."

16. How, then? Will Christ not be our Mediator? Shall we not pray in his name? How lovingly and sweetly the Lord can speak, and woo us to himself and, through himself, to the Father! Here he himself explains how it will be when we pray in his name: "Ye," he says, "have loved me, and have believed that I came forth from the Father." That is, ye love me and know me; have me and my name, and are in me as I in you. For Christ dwells in us, not because we can think, speak, sing, or write so much about him, but because we love him and believe in him. We know that he is come from the Father and returns to the Father; that is, how he emptied himself, in his Passion, of all his divine glory and returned again to the Father in his kingdom, for our sake. This faith brings us to the Father, and thus all then is done in his name.

17. So we are sure that Christ needs not to pray for us, for he has already prayed for us. We ourselves may now approach through Christ and pray. We no longer need a Christ who prays for us. This one Christ is enough, he who has prayed for us and accomplished this work. Therefore, he says, "The Father himself loveth you." It is not your merit, but his love. He loves you, but for my sake, because you believe on me and love me; that is, he has regard for my name in you. Hence thereby have I fulfilled my office, and you are now brought, through me, to where you may yourselves, in my place, appear in

his presence and pray. It is not necessary that I still pray for you. These are marvelous words, that we, through Christ, become like Christ and are his brethren, and may glory in being children of his Father, who loves us for Christ's sake. He says, in John 1:16, "Grace for Grace," that is, God is gracious unto us, because he is gracious to Christ, who is in us and we in him.

18. And here we also see that to "believe in Christ" does not mean to believe that Christ is a person who is both God and man; that does not help anyone. But that this same person is the Christ; that is, that he went forth from the Father and came into the world, and again leaves the world and goes to the Father. The words mean no less than that this is Christ, that he became man and died for us, rose again, and ascended to heaven. Because of this office of his, he is called Jesus Christ, and to believe this concerning him, that it is true, means to be and to abide in his name. There follows further in this Gospel,

"His disciples say, Lo, now speakest thou plainly, and speakest no dark sayings."

19. Here you see that to speak "plainly" ("*frei heraus*"), or to speak in clear terms, means to speak without parables or without dark and covered words. And the good disciples think they understand very well what he tells them, that Christ comes from the Father and goes to the Father; but they do this as good, pious children of Christ. They are easily able to understand it, and in love they tell him so. In ordinary conversation, people sometimes say to one another Yes or No, or give assent, saying, It is so and, in a sense, one understands, even though he is still far from the meaning of another's words. In such case, the conversation is without hypocrisy and in true simplicity. The evangelist hereby shows what a beautiful, plain, friendly, and loving life Christ led with his disciples, since they were so very able to understand him. Then the disciples say further,

"Now know we that thou knowest all things, and
needest not that any man should ask thee."

20. That is, you anticipate and explain yourself and speak no more in parables, concerning which we must question you; for you know in advance where we are lacking in understanding. All this reverts to the fact that they wished to ask what the "little while" meant, and he noticed it and explains by saying that he must go to the Father; which they still did not understand, and yet it was clearer than his words, "A little while and ye will not see me." Now, because he saw their thoughts—that they wished to question him—they confessed that he comes from God and knows all things, so that we need not to ask him, for he himself sees very well where the trouble is.

The Day of Christ's Ascension into Heaven

Christ Upbraids and Commissions His Disciples

*A*nd afterward he was manifested unto the eleven themselves as they sat at meat; and he upbraided them with their unbelief and hardness of heart, because they believed not them that had seen him after he was risen. And he said unto them, "Go ye into all the world, and preach the Gospel to the whole creation. He that believeth and is baptized shall be saved; but he that disbelieveth shall be condemned. And these signs shall accompany them that believe; in my name shall they cast out demons; they shall speak with new tongues; they shall take up serpents, and if they drink any deadly thing, it shall in no wise hurt them; they shall lay hands on the sick, and they shall recover."

So then the Lord Jesus, after he had spoken unto them, was received up into heaven, and sat down at the right hand of God. And they went forth, and preached everywhere, the Lord working with them, and confirming the word by the signs that followed. Amen. — MARK 16:14–20

1. In today's Gospel, there is again presented to us the essence of a Christian life, namely, faith and love; just what you constantly hear in all the Gospel lessons. Since the Gospel ever holds up before you this theme, we must continually preach and discuss it; for Jesus says to his disciples, "Go ye into all the world, and preach the Gospel to the whole creation. He that believeth and is baptized shall be saved." We will consider the thoughts of this Gospel text in order.

I. CHRIST UPBRAIDS HIS DISCIPLES WITH THEIR UNBELIEF

2. First, Christ upbraids his disciples with their unbelief and hardness of heart, and reproves them for it, and shows them their faults. He does not reject them, nor deal too severely with them, but reproves them; just as we

would say to a person, Are you not ashamed that you dared to do such a thing? meaning thereby to bring him to a knowledge of himself and make him blush with shame, that he may desist from his wicked intent or deed, though we do not reject him nor turn our love from him.

3. However, it is not an insignificant matter here that the Lord rebuked the disciples; for unbelief is the greatest sin that can be named. Christ tells them the cause of their unbelief when he says that their hearts are hardened, yet he deals mildly and gently with them.

4. This is given to us all for our comfort, lest we despair when, lacking in faith, we doubt, stumble, and fall; it is to help us to rise again, to strengthen our faith and lift up our hearts to God, that we may grasp and hold fast the confidence of God, who does not deal with us severely, but can indeed bear with us and overlook much. And whoever believes him to be thus, shall find him so; if we hold him to be a merciful God, he allows himself to be found merciful, and shows himself thus to us; but a bad conscience and an unbelieving heart have no such trust in God, but flee from him, and deem him a harsh judge, which he, therefore, is found to be.

5. So should we also deal with our neighbor. If we see him fall from the faith, or err and sin, we should not strengthen him in his wickedness, nor justify his cause, but admonish him, and in meekness reprove his faults, yet neither hold enmity nor turn our love from him. Thus Saint Paul speaks to the Galatians, "Brethren, even if a man be overtaken in any trespass, ye who are spiritual, restore such a one in a spirit of gentleness," in Galatians 6:1. But our lord pope, the bishops, priests, monks, and nuns allow no one to reprove them when they do evil; they are never willing to acknowledge that any fault is theirs, but always that of their subjects, and their policy toward subjects is one of strictness and severity.

6. To sum up all, We should expose and reprove what is wrong, and exercise truth and love toward everybody; we should be plainspoken, not letting ourselves be silenced, for none of us, since we are flesh and blood, will so live as to be found without blame in all things—I in this, you in that. We all see that even the apostles were lacking in the chief things, yet they were cornerstones, the foundations and the very best part of Christendom.

7. But let no one think that the apostles were altogether unbelieving; they believed what was written in the law and the prophets, although their faith was not yet perfect. There was a faith there and yet no faith; they did not yet believe all things, although they believed that God created heaven and earth, and was the Maker of every creature. So the apostles were not altogether without faith, for they had faith in part. Faith is a thing that always grows. It

is with faith as with a man who is ill and begins to get well—is increasing in strength. Therefore, the Lord shows where they did not believe, and what they lacked; it was that they did not believe the resurrection of Christ from the dead. Although they believed the other things, they were still lacking in this. I hold that they believed that they had a gracious God. Yet this was not enough; they must believe also the resurrection of Christ. The Lord upbraided them with their unbelief, reproved them, and said that in spite of all they had seen, they were not believing; they still lacked in a certain article of faith, namely, the article on the resurrection, hence Christ's words to them at the Last Supper, "Ye believe in God, believe also in me," in John 14:1.

8. What does it mean, then, to believe the resurrection of Christ, this thing which is so important, and concerning which the disciples were called unbelieving and faithless, and without which nothing else that they believed would help them? To believe the resurrection of Christ, is nothing else than to believe that we have a mediator before God. Who is Christ, who makes us holy and acceptable to God the Father? For man's possessions, by birth and nature, are but sin and corruption, by which he brings down upon himself the wrath of God. But God is eternal righteousness and purity and, therefore, from his very nature, hates sin. Hence there is always enmity between God and the natural man, and they cannot be friends and in harmony with one another.

9. For this cause, Christ became man and took upon himself our sins and also the wrath of the Father, and drowned them both in himself, thus reconciling us to God the Father. Without this faith, we are children of wrath, able to do no good work that is pleasing to God, nor can our prayers be acceptable before him. For thus it is written in Psalm 18:41, "They cried, but there was none to save; even unto Jehovah, but he answered them not." Yea, even our noblest deeds, by which we had thought to obtain from God mercy, help, and comfort, are counted to us for sin; as the prophet says, in Psalm 109:7, "Let his prayer be turned into sin," seeing God could not be reconciled by all our strength, for there is truly no strength in us.

10. Christ, therefore, must come, that he might go before the Father's face, reconcile us to him, and obtain for us everything we lacked. Through this same Christ, we must ask of God all we need. You have heard in last Sunday's Gospel that the Lord says, "If ye shall ask anything of the Father, he will give it to you in my name." Whatever we obtain from God, we must receive through this Christ, who has gained for us a merciful Father. For Christ is our support and refuge, where we may hide ourselves, like the young chickens hide under the wings of the mother hen. Through him alone is our prayer acceptable before God, and through him is it answered, and we obtain the

favor and mercy of the Father; for Christ has made atonement for our sins, and an angry judge he has changed into a gracious and merciful God. To believe in the resurrection of Christ means, then, to believe, as I said, that Christ has taken upon his head our sins, and the sins of the whole world, also the wrath of the Father, and thus drowned them both in himself, whereby we are become reconciled with God and altogether righteous.

11. Now, observe for yourselves how few Christians there are who have this faith, by which alone man is freed from his sins and becomes entirely holy; for they believe not in the resurrection of Christ, that their sins are taken away through Christ, since they attempt to become holy through their own works. This one runs to a cloister, that one becomes a nun, one does this, another that, in order to be free from sin; and yet they always say they believe in the resurrection of Christ from the dead, notwithstanding that their works prove the contrary.

12. The apostles have insisted upon and preached this article more than any other; thus Saint Paul speaks to the Corinthians, "If Christ hath not been raised, then is our preaching vain, your faith also is vain," in 1 Corinthians 15:14. And shortly after, in verse 17, he says, "If Christ hath not been raised, your faith is vain; ye are yet in your sins." What sort of a conclusion is this? What is its logical analysis? This—If Christ be not risen from the dead, then sin and death have devoured and slain him, and we cannot get rid of our sins ourselves. Jesus Christ took them upon himself, so that he might tread under foot sin, death, and hell, and become their Master. But if he be not risen, then he has not overcome sin, but has been overcome by sin. Also, if he has been overcome by sin, then he is not risen; if he be not risen, then he has not redeemed you; then you are yet in your sins. Likewise, Paul speaks to the Romans, "If thou shalt confess with thy mouth Jesus as Lord, and shalt believe in thy heart that God raised him from the dead, thou shalt be saved," in Romans 10:9. Thereto all the Scriptures of the Old and the New Testaments agree.

13. Now, it is not enough that we believe the historic fact of the resurrection of Christ; for this all the wicked believe, yea, even the devil believes that Christ has suffered and is risen. But we must believe also the meaning—the spiritual significance of Christ's resurrection, realizing its fruit and benefits, that which we have received through it, namely, forgiveness and redemption from all sins; we must believe that Christ has suffered death, and thereby has overcome and trodden under foot sin and death, yea, everything that can harm us, and is seated at the right hand of the Father in heaven as Almighty Lord over sin and devil, death and hell, and all that harms us, and that all this took place for our good. This, the wicked do not believe.

14. You see how much depends upon this article of faith on the resurrection. We can better dispense with all the other articles than with this one. What would it avail if we believed all the other articles, as that Christ was born of the Virgin Mary, died, and was buried, if we did not believe that he arose again? It is to this subject that God has reference, in Habakkuk 1:5, when he says, "I am working a work in your days, which ye will not believe though it be told you."

15. The importance of this subject is also the reason that Paul has urged and preached it, and in all his Epistles has treated of no work or miracle of Christ so frequently as of his resurrection. He is silent concerning the many works and wonders of Christ, and preaches and teaches emphatically the benefit and the import of the resurrection of Christ—what we have received from it. No other apostle has portrayed Christ to us in the light that Paul has. Christ did not without meaning say of him to Ananias, "He is a chosen vessel unto me to bear my name before the gentiles and kings, and the children of Israel; for I will show him how many things he must suffer for my name's sake," in Acts 9:15–16.

16. Now, no good work will help those who do not have this faith in the resurrection, let them play the hypocrite as they will. To virgins, their virginity or purity is no help; nor to monks, their long prayers. Here it avails nothing to preach of works, they are not even named; but everything must be obtained of God through Christ, as you have heard. So David prayed in Psalm 84:9, "Behold, O God, our shield, and look upon the face of thine anointed." This is enough on the first part of this Gospel. Now follows in the text the words,

"Go ye into all the world, and preach the Gospel to the whole creation."

II. THE MISSIONARY COMMISSION CHRIST GIVES TO HIS DISCIPLES

A. The Contents of This Commission

17. What shall they preach? Nothing else, he says, than just that I am risen from the dead and have overcome and taken away sin and all misery. He that believes this, shall be saved; faith alone is sufficient for his salvation. Therefore, the Gospel is nothing else than preaching the resurrection of Christ, "He that believeth shall be saved; but he that disbelieveth shall be condemned." Here all works are abolished. Here you see, also, the nature and character of faith. Faith will compel no one to accept the Gospel, but leaves its acceptance free to everyone and makes it a personal matter. He that believes, believes; he that comes, comes; he that stays out, stays out.

18. Thus you see that the pope errs and does the people injustice in that he ventures to drive them to faith by force; for the Lord commanded the disciples to do nothing more than to preach the Gospel. So the disciples also did; they preached the Gospel and left its acceptance to those who would take it, and they did not say, Believe, or I will put you to death.

19. A question arises about this passage, "Go ye into all the world," as to how it is to be understood, since the apostles certainly did not visit all the world. No apostle came hither to us; and many a heathen island has since been discovered, where the Gospel has never been preached. Yet the Scriptures say, "Their sound went out into all the earth," in Romans 10:18. Answer: Their preaching went out into all the world, although it has not yet come into all the world. This going out has been begun and continues, although it is not yet completed; the Gospel, however, will be preached ever farther and wider, until the judgment day. When this preaching shall have reached all parts of the world, and shall have been everywhere heard, then will the message be complete and its mission accomplished; then will the last day also be at hand.

20. The preaching of this message may be likened to a stone thrown into the water, producing ripples which circle outward from it, the waves rolling always on and on, one driving the other, until they come to the shore. Although the center becomes quiet, the waves do not rest, but move forward. So it is with the preaching of the Word. It was begun by the apostles, and it constantly goes forward, is pushed on farther and farther by the preachers, driven hither and thither into the world, yet always is being made known to those who never heard it before, although it be arrested in the midst of its course and is condemned as heresy. As we say, when one sends a message, the message has gone forth, although it has not yet arrived at its destination, but is still on its way; or as we say, the emperor's message is sent to Nurenburg, or to the Turk [Muslim], although it has not yet arrived, so we are to understand the preaching of the apostles.

B. The Promise Attached to This Commission

21. But there arises here another question from this passage of today's Gospel, "He that believeth, shall be saved," whether faith is sufficient for salvation, and alone saves; or whether we must also do good works in order to be saved. Here our highly learned doctors have desired to control the Holy Spirit, to sharpen his tongue, and to place a little stick under his tongue, as if he could not speak plainly, and have forced and strained this passage, and so worn it out and rent it that no marrow nor vitality remains in it. They have said that good works are necessary to faith, and that faith is not sufficient for

salvation. This is not true. Faith alone, of itself, without any works, as the Word of God here clearly says, brings us salvation, and works help nothing at all toward righteousness or salvation. We must let this passage stand pure and unadulterated, and without any addition. If the Holy Spirit had so desired, he could easily have said different words thus, "He that believeth and doeth works, shall be saved." But he did not do this; therefore, we should and will leave it as it is.

22. This I say to the end, that you may fortify yourselves with such passages, holding to the true meaning of the words. Though there are many passages in Scripture teaching that faith alone saves, yet they have been so covered over and obscured, so shaken to pieces and stretched, by the sophists and scholars, that their right meaning has suffered. Saint Paul says to the Galatians, "If righteousness is through the law, then Christ died for naught," in Galatians 2:21. That is to say, If we can be saved in any other way or work out our salvation, then Christ has died in vain; for to presume to be justified by the law means to think that man can become righteous through his works.

23. Therefore, to conclude, The chief righteousness is faith; the chief wickedness is unbelief. There is also no sin so great that it is able to condemn man; unbelief alone condemns all who are condemned. And again, only faith saves everyone; for faith alone deals with God; no works can appear before him. For works have to do only with man, and man lets his works be made use of as he has made use of Christ's. They make no one holy; they are only the distinguishing marks of a man that has already become righteous through faith, which alone makes the heart pure.

24. I can easily assent to the saying, Works do not make you pious, but show that you are pious; or when I hear it said, He that believes, serves his neighbor, I admit that it is so. But that the explanation of this text should be, Faith is not sufficient for salvation, we must also do good—this is a liberty which the text can stand just as little as this church could stand that I should pull down its pillars. There follows further in the text,

"He that believeth and is baptized shall be saved."

25. God has always accompanied his Word with an outward sign to make it the more effective to us, that we might be strengthened in heart and never doubt his Word, nor waver. Thus he gave Noah the rainbow in the heavens as a sure sign that he would keep his promise and not destroy the world by another flood. The rainbow is, so to speak, a seal or sign to Noah and to us all, just as a seal upon a letter certifies the document. And just as a nobleman has his own coat of arms of a particular device or color, by which he is

known, so has God evidenced his words for us with signs, as with a seal, that we should never doubt. To Abraham, he gave the rite of circumcision, to show that Christ should come and bless the world. Thus has he done here, adding to this promise of his, "He that believeth and is baptized shall be saved," an outward sign, namely, baptism, and also the sacrament of the bread and the wine, which was especially instituted for use in times of temptation, and when death draws near, that by it we might strengthen our faith, and remind God of his promise, and hold him to it.

26. A man can believe even though he be not baptized; for baptism is nothing more than an outward sign that is to remind us of the divine promise. If we can have it, it is well; let us receive it, for no one should despise it. If, however, we cannot receive it, or it is denied us, we will not be condemned if we only believe the Gospel. For where the Gospel is, there is also baptism and all that a Christian needs. Condemnation follows no sin except the sin of unbelief. Therefore, the Lord says, "He that disbelieveth shall be condemned"; he says not, He that is not baptized. He is silent concerning baptism, for baptism is worth nothing without faith, but is like seals affixed to a letter in which nothing is written. He that has the signs that we call sacraments, and has no faith, has only seals upon a letter of blank paper.

27. Here you see also what is the office of the apostles, to which all the bishops, and those that call themselves ministers, should conform, inasmuch as they boast that they are the successors of the apostles in preaching the Gospel. For the Lord says here, "Go ye into all the world, and preach the Gospel." Therefore, we should not listen to those who do not preach the Gospel. Now our papists come along and quote the passage in Luke 10:16, "He that heareth you, heareth me." This verse has hitherto been the pope's sword, by which he has swayed the whole world, and none has rightly understood this passage, which means that teachers are to be obeyed only when they preach the Gospel. So the Lord here inspires the apostles to speak the Gospel, which is his Word. Christ alone is to be heard, and the apostles are but messengers and instruments for this Word of Christ. Therefore, here again are condemned pope, bishops, monks, and priests, and all who preach something else than the Gospel.

28. But what is meant when the Lord says, "Preach the Gospel to the whole creation"? Shall I preach also to trees and stones, mountains and waters? What would that profit? Saint Gregory preached on this text and said that "all creation" means man; that man is one with all creatures—with the angels in understanding, with the animals in sensibilities, and with the trees in growth. We must, therefore, not misuse the text nor make its meaning too literal, for so we shall misconstrue it. The meaning is that the Gospel should be publicly

and universally preached, given to all; it should hide in no corner, but be preached freely in all places, as is written in Psalm 19:3–4, "There is no speech nor language where their voice is not heard. Their line is gone out through all the earth, and their words to the end of the world." The beginning and going forth has been fulfilled by the apostles, but the work is not yet finished; the Gospel has not yet reached its limit, for I know not whether Germany has ever heard the Word of God. The pope's word we have surely heard.

29. The Lord here says to the apostles, "Go ye into all the world, and preach the Gospel to the whole creation," for the reason that this Gospel may be published to everyone, so that even trees and stones might hear if they had ears, and might bear witness that we have heard the Gospel; and that pillar there might say, I have heard the Gospel preached to you. Thus generally and publicly shall it be proclaimed, and preached in all the world, being withheld from no one, until it reaches the ends of the world, as the psalm records. So it has now come to us, who are dwelling at the end of the world, for we live close to the sea. This, Paul has in mind when he says to the Ephesians, "And he gave some to be apostles, and some prophets; and some evangelists; and some pastors and teachers; for the perfecting of the saints, unto the work of ministering, unto the building up of the body of Christ: till we all attain unto the unity of the faith, and of the knowledge of the Son of God," in Ephesians 44:11–13. Next, the text speaks of the signs that shall follow faith, and names five signs, one after the other, thus,

> "And these signs shall accompany them that believe: in my name shall they cast out demons; they shall speak with new tongues; they shall take up serpents, and if they drink any deadly thing, it shall in no wise hurt them; they shall lay hands on the sick and they shall recover."

30. How shall we proceed here that we may preserve the truth of the passage: he that believeth shall have power also, and be able to show these signs? For the Lord says all these signs shall accompany them. Now we know that the apostles did not present all the signs, for we read of no other that drank poison than John the Evangelist, and there are no other individual instances. If the passage shall stand literally, then few believers will be cleared and few saints be entitled to heaven; for these signs, one and all, have not accompanied them, though they have had power to work signs, and have exhibited some of them.

31. Some rush on here and explain these signs as spiritual, so as to preserve the honor of the saints; but it will not do to strain the words. They do not carry such meaning; therefore, they will not bear such an explanation. It puts upon the Scriptures uncertain construction for us.

32. Others, with equal heedlessness, say that though not every individual has the power and does the wonders mentioned, yet the church as a whole, the multitude of Christendom, has; one may drive out devils, another heal the sick, and so on. Therefore, they say, such signs are a manifestation of the Spirit; where the signs are, there is also the Christian Church, and so on.

33. But these words do not refer to the church as a whole, but to each person separately. The meaning is, If there is a Christian who has faith, he shall have power to do these accompanying miracles, and they shall follow him, as Christ says, in John 14:12, "Verily, verily, I say unto you, he that believeth on me, the works that I do, shall he do also; and greater works than these shall he do," for a Christian has equal power with Christ, is a congregation, and sits with him in joint tenure. The Lord has given Christians power, as is written, in Matthew 10:8, also against the unclean spirits, that they might cast them out and heal every disease. Thus it is written in Psalm 91:13, "Thou shalt tread upon the lion and the adder; the young lion and the serpent shalt thou trample under foot."

34. We read also that this has been fulfilled. There was once a patriarch in the wilderness, who, when he met a serpent, took it in both hands and tore it in two, and thought no more about it, but said: O what a fine thing it is to have a clear and guiltless conscience! So, where there is a Christian, there is still the power to work these signs if it is necessary. But no one should attempt to exercise this power if it is not necessary or if need does not compel. The apostles did not always exercise it, but only made use of it to prove the Word of God, to confirm it by the miracles, as is written here in the text, "And they went forth, and preached everywhere, the Lord working with them, and confirming the Word by the signs that followed."

35. But since the Gospel has now been spread abroad, and made known to all the world, there is no need of working miracles as in the apostles' times. If need should arise, and men were to denounce and antagonize the Gospel, then we verily should have to employ wonder-working rather than permit the Gospel to be derided and suppressed. But I hope such a course will not be necessary, and that such a contingency will never arise. For another example, That I should here speak in new languages, is not at all necessary, since you all can well hear and understand me; but if God should send me where the people could not understand me, he could easily grant me their speech or language, that I might be understood.

36. Then let no one, without pressing need, undertake to work wonders. For we read of the patriarchs' children that they once brought a large number of serpents in their cloaks, and shook them out at their parents' feet;

whereupon their parents reproved them for tempting God unnecessarily. In like manner, we read of many signs that believers have done. It happened once upon a time that one of the fathers by chance got hold of a basilisk. He looked at it, and thereupon exclaimed, O Lord, I must die, or this reptile must! for the basilisk kills by its looks. At once, it bursted and flew into pieces.

37. I know not what I shall say about those who venture to do signs where they are not necessary. For example, some drive out demons. But I know that it is a dangerous undertaking. The devil, indeed, lets himself be driven out, but he does not intend to suffer for it; he allows it only that he may strengthen the sign-worker in such error. I would not like to trust him. We have many such instances in our times. I know also of many that happened not long ago.

38. There was a sexton who wished to learn alchemy from the devil, that is, the art of separating gold from sand, and of making gold from other metals. The devil agreed to come to him at the hour of eleven, but the sexton should have on a gown and chasuble. See with what fool's work the devil goes about! As though he cared much about the chasuble. The sexton went and reversed the hourglass and noted the hour. At eleven, he put on the chasuble. The devil came and knocked. The sexton was afraid and asked who was there. The devil said that the sexton should come at once to the parson and attend the sacrament. The sexton threw off the chasuble and ran out in haste, but found no one. Then the devil the second time demanded of the sexton to come out. The third time the devil came and said that the parson was awaiting him impatiently; he should come without delay. The sexton then went out, but by this time the hour was past, and the sexton had not on the chasuble. Then the sexton saw for the first time that it was the devil, and wished to hurry back to the house and get the chasuble. The devil, however, would not allow this, but said, No, my dear fellow, the time is past. He seized the sexton, broke his neck, and threw him to the ground. Such occasions the devil seeks, and acts. So much for this Gospel.

The Sunday After Christ's Ascension

A Sermon of Comfort and of Admonition

B ut when the Comforter is come, whom I will send unto you from
the Father, even the Spirit of truth, who proceedeth from the Father, he shall bear witness of me: and ye shall bear witness, because ye
have been with me from the beginning. These things have I spoken unto
you, that ye should not be caused to stumble. They shall put you out of
the synagogues: yea, the hour cometh, that whosoever killeth you shall
think that he offereth service unto God. And these things will they do,
because they have not known the Father, nor me. But these things have
I spoken unto you, that when their hour is come, ye may remember
them, how that I told you. And these things I said not unto you from
the beginning, because I was with you." — JOHN 15:26–16:4

1. Beloved, you have heretofore heard much about faith. Today you hear
also of the witness of faith and of the cross that follows. Paul says to the Romans, "With the heart man believeth unto righteousness," in Romans 10:10.
If one be pious, he must begin in his heart and believe. That serves only unto
godliness; it is not enough for salvation. Therefore, one must also do what
the Christian life requires, and continually abide in that life. Hence Paul adds,
"If thou shalt confess with thy mouth Jesus as Lord, thou shalt be saved." It
is these two things that constitute our salvation, faith, and the confession
of faith. Faith rescues from sin, hell, Satan, death, and all misfortunes. Now,
when we have this, we have enough. We then let God live here that we may
reach a hand to our neighbor and help him. Besides, God desires to have his
name praised and his kingdom developed and extended. Therefore, we must
praise his name, confess our faith, and win others to do the same, so that
God's kingdom may be extended and his name praised.

2. Thus faith must be exercised, worked, and polished; be purified by
fire, like gold. Faith, the great gift and treasure from God, must express itself
and triumph in the certainty that it is right before God and man, and before

angels, devils, and the whole world. Just as a jewel is not to be concealed, but to be worn in sight, so also will and must faith be worn and exhibited, as it is written in 1 Peter 1:7, "That the proof of your faith, being more precious than gold that perisheth though it is proved by fire," etc.

3. Now, by confession, I must take upon myself the load of Satan, hell, death, and the whole world—kings and princes, pope and bishops, priests and monks. By faith, everything falls that reason can or ever has devised for the salvation of the soul. It must chastise the apish tricks of the whole world, and its jewel alone must be praised. The world cannot endure this, therefore it rushes in, destroys, kills, and says, "It is expedient for you that one man should die for the people, and that the whole nation perish not," as Caiaphas says in John 11:50. Thus the confession must break forth, that God alone is the Savior; and the same confession brings us into danger of losing our lives. As the Lord says later to the disciples, "They shall put you out of the synagogues."

4. One cannot paint the cross differently than it is here painted; that is its true color. But the cross of illness—to lie in bed at home ill—is nothing compared with the cross of persecution. The first is indeed suffering, but the suffering is golden when we are persecuted and put to death with ignominy; when our persecutors have the praise; when right and honor apparently are on their side, while shame, disgrace, and injustice are on our side, compared with the world that wishes them thereby to have God's honor defended, so that all the world says we are served right and that God, the Scriptures, and all the angels witness against us. There can be no right in our cause and, without trial, we must be banished and isolated in shame and disgrace. So it also was the lot of Christ—they put him to death in the most scornful and disgraceful way, and crucified him between two thieves or murderers; he was regarded as chief of sinners, and they said, with blasphemous words, Aye, he called himself God's Son; let God help him now, if he wills it differently. Since he does not, God and all the angels must be against him. So Christ says in our Gospel, "They will kill you," and not in an ordinary way, but in an infamous manner, and all the world will say that they thereby offer God a service. It is, indeed, hard to hold and confess that God is gracious to us and that we have a Savior who opposes all the world, all its glitter and shine. But let the struggle be as hard and sharp as it will, faith must express itself, even though we would like to have it otherwise.

5. Faith must expect all this, and nothing follows its confession more surely than the cross. For it is certain to come to us, either in life or at death, that all our doings will appear to be opposed to God and the Scriptures. It is better that it be learned during life, from the people, than from the devil at

death; for the people cannot force it further than into the ears, but Satan has a pointed tongue that pierces the heart and makes the heart tremble. Satan torments you until you conclude that you are lost and ruined, that heaven and earth, God and all the angels, are your enemies. This is what the prophet means, in Psalm 6:7–8, when he says, "I am weary with my groaning; every night make I my bed to swim; I water my couch with my tears. Mine eye wasteth away because of grief; it waxeth old because of all mine adversaries." It is hard to endure this. Now you see how weak you are who are permitted to bear witness of this faith. One fears his wife, another his children and riches, and a third fears himself.

6. Faith is in vain where it does not continue steadfast to the end. Christ says in Matthew 10:22 and in Matthew 24:13, "But he that endureth to the end, the same shall be saved." Hence it is better to experience persecution here than punishment at the end. If one flees persecution, there is no faith in his heart—only a dead knowledge or erroneous belief, without sap and strength, marrow and bone; but where there is a true, living faith, it presses forward through sword and fire. Let us now notice how the Lord comforts his disciples. He says,

"But when the Comforter is come."

I. CHRIST'S SERMON OF COMFORT

7. That we may, under no circumstances, despair, Christ says, I will send you a Comforter, even one who is almighty. And he calls the Holy Spirit here a Comforter; for although both my sins and the fear of death make me weak and timid, he comes and stirs up the courage in my heart, and says, Ho, cheer up! Thus he trumpets courage into us; he encourages us in a friendly and comforting manner not to despair before death, but to cheerfully go forward, even though we had ten necks for the executioner, and says, Aye, although I have sinned, yet I am rid of my sins; and if I had still more, so that they overwhelmed me, I would hope that they should do me no harm. Not that one should not feel his sins, for the flesh must experience them; but the Spirit overcomes and suppresses diffidence and timidity, and conducts us through them. He is powerful enough to do that. Therefore, Christ says further,

"Whom I will send unto you from the Father."

8. For he, the Father, is the person that takes the initiative: I am the Son; and from us the Holy Spirit proceeds. And the three persons are one, and one essence, with equal power and authority, as he better expresses it when he says,

"The Spirit of truth, who proceedeth from the Father."

9. That is as much as to say, He who will comfort you is almighty and Lord over all things. How can the creatures now harm us, if the Creator stands by us? Notice how great the comfort of the Holy Spirit is. Now let all the Turks [Muslims] attack us. As long as he is our guard and rear guard, there is no danger. John also says, in 1 John 3:19–20, "Hereby shall we know that we are of the truth, and shall assure our heart before him; because if our heart condemn us, God is greater than our heart, and knoweth all things." Likewise, in the following chapter, verse 4, he says, "Ye are of God, my little children, and have overcome them: because greater is he that is in you than he that is in the world." So the Lord now says, Him will I send unto you, so that nothing can harm you. Is not that liberal comfort? Who would not be fearless and cheerful in view of this? And Christ calls him "The Spirit of truth"; that is, where he is and comes, there is a rock foundation through and through, the real truth. Neither falsehood nor hypocrisy is there, for the Spirit is not hypocritical. But wherever he is not, there is nothing but hypocrisy and falsehood. Therefore, we fall when the test comes because the Spirit of truth is not present. Christ now further says,

"He shall bear witness of me."

10. That is, if he is in the heart, he speaks through you, and assures and confirms you in the belief that the Gospel is true. Then, as a result, the confession of the Gospel springs forth. What, then, is the Gospel? It is a witness concerning Christ, that he is God's Son, the Savior, and besides him there is none other. This is what Peter means when he says, "Ye are a royal priesthood, that we are elected thereto, that we preach and show forth the excellencies of Christ," in 1 Peter 2:9. Hence there must always be witnessing. Witnessing loads upon itself the wrath of the whole world. Then the cross follows, then rebellions rise, then the lords and princes and all who are great become angry; for the world cannot hear, nor will it tolerate, this kind of preaching. Therefore, the Gospel is hated and spoken against.

11. Reason thinks, Aye, one can, nevertheless, easily preach the Gospel in a beautifully simple and plain way, without a revolution in the world, and then it will be heartily welcomed. This is the utterance of Satan; for if I believe and say that faith in Christ alone does and accomplishes all, I overthrow the monkey play of the whole world; and that they cannot allow. Therefore, Christ's teachings and man's teachings cannot stand together; one must fall. Priests and monks, as they are at present, are dependent in name, character,

and works upon human institutions, which the Gospel thrusts to the ground. Hence they dare not accept the Gospel, and they continue as they are.

12. Thus I say that the Christian faith is founded upon Christ alone, without anything additional. The priests will not permit their affairs and institutions to fall; in consequence, seditions and rebellions follow. Therefore, there must be dissension where the Gospel and the confession of Christ are; for the Gospel opposes everything that is not of its own spirit. If the teachings of Christ and the priests were not antagonistic, they could easily stand together. They are now pitted against one another. As impossible as it is for Christ not to be Christ, so impossible is it for a monk or priest to be a Christian. Therefore, a fire must be kindled. The Lord himself, in Matthew 10:34 and in Luke 12:51, says, "I came not to send peace, but a sword." Then follows in our text,

"And ye also bear witness, because ye have been with me from the beginning."

13. Yes; then, first, when you become certain of your faith through the Holy Spirit, who is your witness, you must also bear witness of me, for to that end I chose you to be apostles. You have heard my words and teachings, and have seen my works and life and all things that you are to preach. But the Holy Spirit must first be present; otherwise, you can do nothing, for the conscience is too weak. Yes, there is no sin so small that the conscience could vanquish it, even if it were so trifling a one as laughing in church. Again, in the presence of death, the conscience is far too weak to offer resistance. Therefore, another must come and give to the timid, despairing conscience, courage to go through everything, although all sins be upon it. And it must, at the same time, be an almighty courage, like he alone can give, who ministers strength in such a way that the courage, which before a rustling leaf could cause to fear, is now not afraid of all the devils, and the conscience that before could not restrain laughing, now restrains all sins.

14. The benefit and fruit of the Holy Spirit is, that sin will be changed to the highest and best use. Thus Paul boasts to Timothy, when he was converted, that whereas he had lived such a wicked life before, he now held his sin to be so contemptible that he composed a hymn and sang about it thus, in 1 Timothy 1:12–17, "I thank him that enabled me, even Christ Jesus our Lord, for that he counted me faithful, appointing me to his service; though I was before a blasphemer, and a persecutor, and injurious: howbeit I obtained mercy, because I did it ignorantly in unbelief; and the grace of our Lord abounded exceedingly with faith and love which is in Christ Jesus. Faithful is the saying, and worthy of all acceptation, that Christ Jesus came into the world to save sinners; of whom I am chief: howbeit for this cause I obtained

mercy, that in me as chief might Jesus Christ show forth all his long-suffering, for an example of them that should thereafter believe on him unto eternal life. Now unto the King eternal, immortal, invisible, the only God, be honor and glory for ever and ever. Amen."

II. CHRIST'S SERMON OF WARNING

"These things have I spoken unto you that ye should not be caused to stumble."

15. Now that Christ had comforted and strengthened his disciples, he warns them of their future sufferings, in order that they might be able to bear them valiantly. He is an especially good friend who warns one; and the evil visitation is much easier borne when one is prepared beforehand for it. Christ says,

> *"They shall put you out of the synagogues; yea, the hour cometh that*
> *whosoever killeth you shall think that he offereth service unto God."*

16. You will certainly experience this; therefore, arm yourself and be prepared. The most of all will be that, when they have treated you in the most shameless manner, they will think they did a good work in doing so, and it will appear to them as if your God had taken stand against you, and they will sing over it a Te Deum laudamus (Lord God, we praise thee), as if they had done God's will and offered unto him a service. Hence he arms them here, that they may be of good courage when it comes to pass; and he concludes with the thought that they shall have God's favor, although at the time there shall be no signs of it; for God does stand on the side of his disciples. He adds,

"And these things will they do, because they have not known the Father, nor me."

17. Therefore, be patient, be prepared, be firm. See to it that ye, by no means, take offense at me. Remember that I told you before that they have known neither the Father nor me; and therefore they will heap upon you dishonor, shame, and persecution. You should never forget this, for it will give you great comfort and make you bold, cheerful, and undismayed. Therefore, Christ concludes the admonition by saying,

> *"But these things have I spoken unto you, that when their hour is*
> *come, ye may remember them, how that I told you. And these things I*
> *said not unto you from the beginning, because I was with you."*

18. Who, now, has been considered to be worse than he who told the pope that he knew not the Father? The pope would, of course, declare the contrary

and say, Aye, Satan has commissioned you to speak that. Now, they all say that they know the Father. The Turk [Muslim] also says that he does. In like manner, they declare they believe God and the Scriptures. But there are two kinds of knowledge. The first, for example, such knowledge as one might have of the Turk [Muslim] from his noise and reputation; the other the knowledge one would have of the Turk [Muslim] through his deeds were he to capture and occupy Rome. In this latter sense, we do not know the Turk [Muslim].

19. It is this first kind of knowledge that some people have of God. They know very well how to say of him, I believe in God the Father, and in his only begotten Son. But it is only upon the tongue, like the foam on the water; it does not enter the heart. Figuratively, a big tumor still remains there in the heart; that is, they cling somewhat to their own deeds and think they must do works in order to be saved—that Christ's person and merit are not sufficient. Thy work is nothing, thy wisdom is foolishness, thy counsel is nothing, thy truth also amounts to nothing, neither does the Mass avail anything before God. Then they reply, Aye, the devil has prompted you to speak thus. They say, Christ has truly died for us, but in a way that we, also, must accomplish something by our deeds. Notice how deeply wickedness and unbelief are rooted in the heart. The puffed-up pride of the heart is the reason why man can know neither Christ nor the Father.

20. But to know Christ in the other and true sense is to know that he died for me and transferred the load of my sin upon himself; to so know this that I realize that all my doings amount to nothing. To let go all that is mine, and value only this, that Christ is given to me as a present; his sufferings, his righ-teousness, and all his virtues are at once mine. When I become conscious of this, I must in return love him; my affections must go out to such a being. After this, I climb upon the Son higher, to the Father, and see that Christ is God, and that he placed himself in my death, in my sin, in my misery, and bestows upon me his grace. Then I know also his gracious will and the highest love of the Father, which no heart of itself can discover or experience. Thus I lay hold of God at the point where he is the tenderest, and think, Aye, that is God; that is God's will and pleasure, that Christ did this for me. And with this experience I perceive the high, inexpressible mercy and the love in him because of which he offered his beloved child for me in ignominy, shame, and death. That friendly look and lovely sight then sustain me. Thus must God become known, only in Christ. Therefore, Christ himself says to his disciples, "No one knoweth the Son, save the Father; neither doth any know the Father, save the Son, and he to whomsoever the Son willeth to reveal him," in Matthew 11:27.

21. On the other hand, those who parade their own works, do not know Christ. Neither do they know what the Father has done through Christ. Nor do they know that God is not interested in their good works, but in his Son alone. Thus they do not know the Father, neither do they know what they have received from the Father, through Christ. Therefore, they must fall and perish, and behold God in his severest aspect—as a judge. They try to silence the judgment with their good works, but they find no good work that is sufficient to do this, and then they must finally despair. When people see that they, themselves, are nothing, and establish the foundation of their hearts upon Christ, esteem him as the highest good, and know God as a Father in death and life—this is to "know God." Enough has been said on this Gospel. We will pray to God, to give us grace to know him and his Christ aright. Amen.

Pentecost

✥

Or, the Festival of the Outpouring of the Holy Spirit

Jesus answered and said unto him, "If a man love me, he will keep my Word: and my Father will love him, and we will come unto him, and make our abode with him. He that loveth me not keepeth not my words: and the word which ye hear is not mine, but the Father's who sent me.

These things have I spoken unto you, while yet abiding with you. But the Comforter, even the Holy Spirit, whom the Father will send in my name, he shall teach you all things, and bring to your remembrance all that I said unto you. Peace I leave with you: my peace I give unto you: not as the world giveth, give I unto you. Let not your heart be troubled, neither let it be fearful. Ye heard how I said to you, I go away, and I come unto you. If ye loved me, ye would have rejoiced, because I go unto the Father: for the Father is greater than I. And now I have told you before it come to pass, that, when it is come to pass, ye may believe. I will no more speak much with you, for the prince of the world cometh: and he hath nothing in me; but that the world may know that I love the Father, and as the Father gave me commandment, even so I do. Arise, let us go hence." — JOHN 14:23–31

I. THE INTRODUCTION TO THIS SERMON OF COMFORT, TREATING OF CHRIST'S LOVE

1. In today's Gospel, Christ says plainly and bluntly, "If a man love me, he will keep my Word; he that loveth me not, keepeth not my words." The text stands there clear; whoever loves God, keeps his commandments and, on the contrary, whoever does not love God, does not keep his commandments. Christ here simply casts out of his kingdom all who do not keep his commandments with pleasure and love. Let us thoroughly understand this. It is briefly pictured to us here who are and who are not Christians. No one is a Christian unless he keeps Christ's Word, as he here says. And no one can

keep it, unless he first loves God. God had tested the plan of making people godly by means of force. For, in olden times, God dealt severely with his people, so that they were forced to keep his Word, and not to blaspheme God; to observe the Sabbath and to obey all the other commandments. To this end, he threatened to afflict and punish them, severely, as is written, in Leviticus 26:14ff. Thus God from without coerced the people to be pious by means of the fear of punishment; but their hearts were not obedient. The result is the same in the present day. Therefore, to keep God's Word is a thing that can be accomplished only by divine love.

2. Accordingly, in the New Testament, God ceased to punish and only administered the Word; for the means must yet come to the point that the divine love be present. Neither the stake nor bulls nor bans help in the least. Where this love is not, all amounts to nothing, do as we will. If one were to take all the swords in the world in his hands, he would not bring a single heretic to the faith. The people may, indeed, appear to accept the Word, but in their inward hearts there is no faith. Hence God has abolished the sword in this matter, and his plan of salvation aims to possess the heart. The bishops are commanded first to take the heart captive, so that it may find love and pleasure in the Word, and the work is then accomplished. Hence he who wishes to be a true bishop, arranges all his administration to the end that he may win souls and develop a love for and a delight in God's Word, and be able to oppose the false babblers with sound teaching, and to stop their mouths, in Titus 1:11. This will never be accomplished by means of commandments, bans, and bulls.

3. Thus the true spiritual leaders fight. They strike Satan dead and rescue souls from him; for to pierce Satan to death is nothing else than to rescue from him a human being whom he has taken captive by deceitful teaching. And that is the right kind of spiritual tactics. But in case people will not outwardly obey the Word, their parents should educate their children, and the civil government its subjects, to obedience. However, by this method, none are yet brought to believe. For it is affirmed in our text, "He that loveth me not keepeth not my words." Thus you hear what a Christian life is, namely, to love God; it is not to storm about, eat flesh, destroy pictures in churches, become monks or nuns—neither a married nor a single life avails here. It means to love, and they do this who keep his Word.

4. Now, what is God's Word? It is that we love one another as Christ loved us, and that we believe on him. If one truly possesses the Word, it must break forth out of the heart from pure love. One may possess the words and commands of man, even if he does not love; he may receive the command of a superior and execute it. But the only thing that will keep God's commandments

and Word is love. Therefore, observe how foolishly our princes and bishops act, in that they coerce and constrain the people to believe by means of force.

5. How does one now acquire this love? The human heart is so false that it cannot love unless it first sees the benefit of loving. When, in the Old Testament, God struck blows among the people as if among dogs, and he dealt severely and fearfully with them, they naturally had no love for him. Then God thought, I must show my love to you and be so affectionate that you cannot help but love me. Then he took his Son and sent him into our filth, sin, and misery, pouring out his mercy so freely and fully that we had to boast of all his treasures as if they were our own. He thus became a loving Father, and he declared his mercy and caused it to go forth into all the world that whosoever believes this and lays hold of it with his heart, shall have a gracious and merciful God, who never becomes angry nor deals blows, but who, instead, is kind and affectionate. Now, where a heart believes and experiences this, and gets glimpses of so much, then it must place all its confidence and affection in God, and deal with its neighbor as God has dealt with itself. As a result, the Word of God goes forth out of the heart, and his commandments will be kept with pleasure. Thus, first, there is no other God; secondly, man calls upon the name of the Lord; and thirdly, he lets God reign—God can do as he will, and he possesses his soul in quiet and observes the Sabbath. In this way, the commandments of the first table are fulfilled. Henceforth, he is kindly and humbly disposed toward all persons, he honors his father and mother, and serves his neighbor as his highest pleasure and with all the love of his heart. His thought is ever this, I will do to my neighbor as God has done to me. Thus love alone is the fulfillment of the law, as Paul says to the Romans, in Romans 13:10.

6. Now, no man can bring this love into the heart. Therefore, God struck in among the people with the law that man might experience and feel that no human being could love the divine, righteous, just, and holy law. In view of this, he gave us his Son, thus graciously poured out his greatest treasures, and sunk and drowned all our sins and filth in the great ocean of his love, so that this great love and blessing must draw man to love, and cheerfully be ready to fulfill, the divine commandments with willing heart. In no other way can the heart love or have any love; it must be assured that it was first loved. Now, man cannot do this; therefore, Christ comes and takes the heart captive, and says, Learn to know me. Then the heart replies, Aye, who art thou? I am Christ, who placed myself in your misery to drown your sins in my righteousness. This knowledge softens your heart, so that you must turn to him. Thus love is awakened when one learns who Christ is.

7. And a Christian should glory in this knowledge, as God says in Jeremiah 9:23–24, "Thus saith Jehovah, Let not the wise man glory in his wisdom, neither let the mighty man glory in his might, let not the rich man glory in his riches; but let him that glorieth in this, that he hath understanding, and knoweth me, that I am Jehovah who exerciseth lovingkindness, justice, and righteousness, in the earth: for in these things I delight, saith Jehovah." So also Peter, in 2 Peter 3:18, says, "But grow in the knowledge of our Lord and Savior Jesus Christ." In all the prophets, and especially in the psalms, and in many places in the Bible, there is much written about this knowledge. It is this knowledge of Christ that must convert or it will never be accomplished. No one is so hardened that he will not be converted and made tender if once his heart knows Christ. And the same knowledge causes one to steadfastly live a godly life. Isaiah says, The time will come when this knowledge shall flow forth like a deluge. This came to pass in the time of the apostles. Therefore, whoever loves God will keep his commandments, and that love brings a knowledge of God. Now Christ says, further, in our Gospel,

"And my Father will love him."

8. It comes to pass in this way: I know first, that Christ has served me by his whole life, and that Christ is God; thus I see that it is God's will that Christ should give himself for me and that the Father commissioned him to that end. Thus I climb to the Father through Christ. Then my confidence in him begins to grow, so that I esteem him as a loving Father. Christ here means to say, Man must begin with my love and then he will come to the Father; Christ is a mediator. Therefore, I must first be loved—must first feel the great treasure and blessing in Christ. Hence God takes the very first step and allows his dear child to die for me, before I ask him to do so, yea, before I ever know him. Then a confidence in and love to God grow in me; this I must feel. Christ also says here, "And my Father will love him"; that is, the convert will feel that he is placed with me in the same kingdom and co-inheritance, and will, through me and with me and with my voice, say to the Father in comforting confidence, Dearly beloved Father. Then the text continues,

"And we will come unto him, and make our abode with him."

9. When I come to the point of knowing that God is my Father, then I let him rule in my heart according to his pleasure, and allow him to be all in all. Therewith, my heart becomes a quiet, humble abode of God. Thus God is a co-laborer with me and assists me, as he says in Isaiah 66:1–2 and in Acts 7:49–50, "Thus saith Jehovah, Heaven is my throne, and the earth is

my footstool: what manner of house will ye build unto me? and what place shall be my rest? For all these things hath my hand made, and so all these things came to be, saith Jehovah: but to this man will I look, even to him that is poor and of a contrite spirit, and that trembleth at my Word." The heart must come to the point where it knows God's glory, God's power, and God's wisdom, and lets God rule in everything. It knows that all is God's work; therefore, it cannot fear anything: cold, hunger, hell, death, Satan, poverty, or any like thing. Then the heart says, My God, who has made his abode in me, is greater than Satan, death, and all the powers of hell.

10. Thus there develops in man a confident defiance of everything upon earth, for he has God and all that is God's. He does all that he is now required to do, and fears not. On the contrary, where there is no love of God, that heart does not keep God's Word; and if the heart does not keep God's Word, the hand never will. There God will never enter and make his abode. There the devil dwells, until the weak and despairing soul will even fear the sound of a driven leaf, as Moses says in Leviticus 26:36. Man cannot endure the gnawing of conscience. The conscience can never know any peace when oppressed by sin, nor can it experience a joyful confidence in God; yea, it will sink lower than hell, while confidence is higher than the heavens. There is then nothing but despair and fear for that heart. All creatures are above it. Such is a picture of the kingdom of Satan. Christ continues by saying,

"And the word which ye hear is not mine, but the Father's who sent me."

11. These words Christ speaks only in order to bring us to the Father, either in a gracious or ungracious way, either with pleasure and love or with fear, for all must lean and depend upon him. Hence whoever will not understand these words scorns God. Then no teaching, no words, nor anything else will help in his case. Now Christ comes, and says,

"These things have I spoken unto you, while yet abiding with you. But the Comforter, even the Holy Spirit, whom the Father will send in my name, he shall teach you all things, and bring to your remembrance all that I said unto you."

II. THE SERMON OF COMFORT

12. Here Christ says, The Father will send you the Holy Spirit, who will bring to your remembrance what I told you, and the same Spirit will explain it to you. In other words, Your hearts are as yet rough and untutored and you cannot understand what I have spoken to you; but when the Holy Spirit comes, he will make all so plain to you that you will experience the assurance

that it is as I told you before. Thus the Holy Spirit, and he alone, has explained the Scriptures and Christ, and made them clear. This knowledge, then, is sufficient for me and enables me to fulfill God's commandments. Beyond this, however, I have no obligations. Christ comforts his disciples further, and says,

> *"Peace I leave with you; my peace I give unto you; not*
> *as the world giveth, give I unto you."*

13. As if he had said, I shall now leave you. Farewell! It was a common greeting among the Jews, in the Hebrew language, when they met or parted, to say, Peace be with you! That is as much as to say, Take good care of yourself, be of good spirits, hope you may prosper; as we in German say, God greet you (*Gott grüsze euch*) or God bless you!

14. And the Lord adds the kind of peace he wishes them to have, and says, My peace I give unto you; not as the world is in the habit of giving peace. In plain words, he distinguishes between his peace and the peace of the world. The disciples, however, did not understand it, just as they did not understand what it was to love and to keep God's commandments. Now, it is the nature of the world's peace that it consists only in outward things, in eating and drinking and dancing; its pleasure is in the flesh. Christian peace, however, is in the heart, although at the same time the heart may suffer great persecution, fear, want, and opposition. The Lord had told them of all these things in the words, "Ye shall weep and lament." The world will persecute you, will reject your teaching, will scourge, banish, and finally put you to death; but in the midst of all, ye shall have peace and rejoice. Cling only to me and my Word!

15. And his words were soon fulfilled. When they had received the Holy Spirit, Luke writes in Acts 5:41, Peter, John, and the other disciples, though scourged and forbidden to preach, departed from the presence of the council, rejoicing that they were counted worthy to suffer dishonor for the Name. But the disciples did not at this time understand, and they were troubled because of the Lord's discourse. Therefore, he gives them further comfort, and says,

> *"Let not your heart be troubled, neither let it be fearful."*

16. These are consoling words, but for the time they are not effectual. Be not afraid, he says, for you have my peace. No one will harm you; only cling to me. The words they indeed hear, as do we, but without seeing their significance. Therefore, he says in clearer language,

"Ye heard how I said to you, I go away, and I come unto you."

17. As if he said, Be not fearful because I said to you I go away from you: I will come again to you; yea, it is especially for your sake that I go away, that afterward when I return to you, you may be the happier and be of good spirits. But neither did they understand this until the Holy Spirit later interpreted it to them. Just so it is with us in the time of temptation: we do not then understand what God intends to teach us; but later, when grace and comfort return, we understand it very well. The Lord says to the disciples,

"If ye loved me, ye would have rejoiced, because I go unto the Father."

18. His words mean, The only failing you have is that you do not love me, or do not understand what it is to love. If ye loved me, ye would gladly let me go; yea, ye would laugh for joy, because I depart from you. And the more you are visited with ill fortune and adversity, the happier you should be. But human reason does not understand this. It is certainly true that the more a Christian suffers persecution from without, the happier he is in heart, and the more peace he possesses. The reason is that he loves Christ. This Saint Paul well understood from his own experience when he wrote to the Corinthians, in 2 Corinthians 4:4–10, We are pressed on every side, yet not straitened; perplexed, yet not unto despair; pursued, yet not forsaken; smitten down, yet not destroyed; always bearing about in the body the dying of Jesus, that the life also of Jesus may be manifested in our body."

And again, he says, in verses 16 to 18, "Wherefore we faint not; but though our outward man is decaying, yet our inward man is renewed day by day. For our light affliction, which is for the moment, worketh for us more and more exceedingly an eternal weight of glory; while we look not at the things which are seen, but at the things which are not seen; for the things which are seen are temporal; but the things which are not seen are eternal."

19. This is the experience of the Christian heart when the Holy Spirit has entered it. Saint Paul writes more about this later, in 2 Corinthians 6. It made an impression upon the heathen when they saw the Christians thus hastening to death; they thought the Christians were foolish and intervened to spare their lives. The gentiles did not understand what it meant; but the Christians very well knew whence it came. Therefore the Lord adds,

"For the Father is greater than I."

20. Even if I should tell you many things, ye would not understand them; they reach no farther than the ears and never enter the heart. However, when

I return to the Father, then I will take upon myself the power to send into your hearts the Holy Spirit, through whose help ye may understand all that I said to you. For the present, I am in the service of my ministry upon earth; I only speak and preach the Word as it has been commanded me by my Father. The Arians paid no attention here to the words, "I go to the Father," which means nothing more than, I go and receive the honor the Father has. It is as if the Lord had said to his disciples, I have two offices. At present, I am upon the earth, where I am performing my office of preaching, for which I was sent by the Father. When I come to the Father, I will fulfill the other office, namely, this: I will send the Holy Spirit into your hearts. The disciples could not understand this, and neither do we understand how he administers the gift. He concludes by saying,

> *"And now I have told you before it come to pass, that*
> *when it is come to pass, ye may believe."*

21. The meaning is, I know very well that you do not understand this now; but I tell you it now so that, when it comes to pass as I have told you, you may remember that I declared it to you before, and you can then say, It is true. In what follows now in this Gospel, the Lord speaks of the hour of his suffering, that it is at hand, and says,

> *"I will no more speak much with you, for the prince of the world cometh; and*
> *he hath nothing in me; but that the world may know that I love the Father, and*
> *as the Father gave me commandment, even so I do. Arise, let us go hence."*

III. THE CONCLUSION OF THIS SERMON OF CONSOLATION

22. In other words, The time of my suffering and death is at hand. The prince of this world, the devil, is present in his adherents, and will seize me. But he will accomplish nothing, for he will unjustly lay hold of me, desiring to crush me. His tactics will fail; I will triumph over him, and I will do it justly.

23. One may reply, Did not Satan conquer Christ? Did he not put him to death? Christ himself answers this, and says that he dies for the very purpose of satisfying the will of the Father. It is not due to the power of Satan that Christ dies, but to the will of the Father, who would blot out sin through the death of his only begotten Son. Hence it does not rest in the power of the world nor of Satan to put to death either Christ or any of his followers. But it does rest in the will of the Father, who reveals his power through our weakness, before all his creatures; as Saint Paul says in 1 Corinthians 15:27. In view of this, Christ here says to his disciples, I will indeed die, but I will rise again.

I die to the end, that the world may know that I love the Father, and that I do what my Father hath commanded me. I seek the Father's glory in this, who wills that I should so do. And all this for the sake of your salvation and blessedness. Therefore, be of good cheer and let not your heart be troubled; for you will have great joy because of my death and my leaving you.

Trinity Sunday

⤙❦⤚

The Doctrine of the Trinity

O the depth of the riches both of the wisdom and the knowledge of God! How unsearchable are his judgments, and his ways past tracing out! For who hath known the mind of the Lord? or who hath been his counsellor? or who hath first given to him, and it shall be recompensed unto him again? For of him and through him, and unto him, are all things. To him be the glory for ever. Amen.

— ROMANS 11:33–36

1. This festival requires us to instruct the people in the dogma of the Holy Trinity, and to strengthen both memory and faith concerning it. This is the reason why we take up the subject once more. Without proper instruction and a sound foundation in this regard, other dogmas cannot be rightly and successfully treated. The other festivals of the year present the Lord God clothed in his works and miracles. For instance, on Christmas we celebrate his incarnation; on Easter his resurrection from the dead; on Whitsunday the gift of the Holy Spirit and the establishment of the Christian Church. Thus all the other festivals present the Lord in the guise of a worker of one thing or another. But this Trinity Festival discloses him to us as he is in himself. Here we see him apart from whatever guise assumed, from whatever work done, solely in his divine essence. We must go beyond and above all reason, leaving behind the evidence of created things, and hear only God's own testimony concerning himself and his inner essence; otherwise, we shall remain unenlightened.

2. Upon this subject the foolishness of God and the wisdom of the world conflict. God's declaration that he is one God in three distinct persons, the world looks upon as wholly unreasonable and foolish; and the followers of mere reason, when they hear it, regard everyone that teaches or believes it as no more than a fool. Therefore, this article has been assailed continually, from the times of the apostles and the fathers down to the present day, as history

testifies. Especially the Gospel of Saint John has been subjected to attack, which was written for the special purpose of fortifying this dogma against the attacks of Cerinthus the heretic, who in the apostolic age already attempted to prove from Moses the existence of but one God, which he assigned as reason that our Lord Jesus cannot be true God on account of the impossibility of God and man being united in one being. Thus he gave us the prattle of his reason, which he made the sole standard for heaven to conform to.

3. O shameless reason! How can we poor, miserable mortals grasp this mystery of the Trinity? we who do not understand the operation of our own physical powers—speech, laughter, sleep, things whereof we have daily experience? Yet we would, untaught by the Word of God, guided merely by our fallible head, pronounce upon the very nature of God. Is it not supreme blindness for man, when he is unable to explain the most insignificant physical operation daily witnessed in his own body, to presume to understand something above and beyond the power of reason to comprehend, something whereof only God can speak, and to rashly affirm that Christ is not God?

4. Indeed, if reason were the standard of judgment in such matters, I also might make a successful venture; but when the conclusions of even long and mature reflections upon the subject are compared with Scripture, they will not stand. Therefore, we must repeat, even though a mere stammering should be the result, what the Scriptures say to us, namely, that Jesus Christ is true God and that the Holy Spirit is likewise true God, yet there are not three Gods, not three divine natures, as we may speak of three brothers, three angels, three suns, three windows. There is one indivisible divine essence, while we recognize a distinction as to the persons.

SCRIPTURE PROOF THAT CHRIST IS GOD

Paul, speaking of Christ in Hebrews 1:3, refers to him as the express image of God's substance. Again, in Colossians 1:15, he says of Christ, "Who is the image of the invisible God, the firstborn of all creation." We must take these words for what they say—that all creatures, even angels and men, are ranked below Christ. This classification leaves room for God only: taking away the creature, only God remains. It is one and the same thing, then, to say that Christ is the firstborn of all creatures, and that Christ is true and essential God.

5. To make the matter as clear as possible, Paul uses the expression "image of the invisible God." If Christ be the image of God, he must be a person distinct from him whose image he is, but at the same time in one divine essence with the Father. He and the Father are not one person, but two, and yet Christ could not be the express image of the Father's person, or essence, if he

were not equally divine. No creature can be an image of the divine essence, for it does not possess that essence. To repeat, Christ could not be called the express image of God if he and the Father were not distinct persons; there must be one imaged and one who is the image. Expressed more clearly and according to Scripture, one person is the Father, who in eternity begets the other; the other is the Son, begotten in eternity, yet both are equally eternal, mighty, wise, and just.

6. Though the Jews and Turks [Muslims] ridicule our doctrine, as if we taught the existence of three brothers in heaven, it does not signify. Might I also cavil were it to serve any purpose here. But they do us wrong and falsify our teaching; for we do not conceive of the Trinity as in the nature of three men or of three angels. We regard it as one divine essence, an intimacy surpassing any earthly unity. The human body and soul are not so completely one as the Triune God. Further, we claim the holy Scriptures teach that in the one divine essence, God the Father begot a Son. Before any creature was made, before the world was created, as Paul says, "before the foundation of the world," in eternity, the Father begot a Son who is equal with him and in all respects God like himself. Not otherwise could Paul call Christ the express image of the invisible God. Thus it is proved that the Father and the Son are distinct persons, and that nevertheless but one God exists, a conclusion we cannot escape unless we would contradict Paul, and would become Jews and Turks [Muslims].

PAUL AND MOSES AGREE IN TESTIMONY

7. Again, Paul makes mention of Christ in different phrase, saying, "Neither let us tempt Christ, as some of them also tempted, and were destroyed of serpents," in 1 Corinthians 10:9. Now, keeping this verse in mind, note how Paul and Moses kiss each other, how clearly the one responds to the other. For Moses says, in Numbers 14:22, "All those men...have tempted me these ten times, and have not hearkened to my voice," and, in this connection, the speaker is represented by the term "Lord," everywhere in the Bible printed by us in capitals to indicate a name belonging only to the Eternal, applicable to none but the one true God. Other terms used to designate God are sometimes applied also to men, but this word "Lord" refers only to God.

Now, Moses says, "And the Lord [Adonai, the true God] said...All these men ...have tempted me these ten times." Then comes Paul, explaining who this God is—saying they tempted "Christ." Crawl through this statement if you may; the fact remains that Paul declares it was Christ who was tempted, and Moses makes him the one eternal and true God. Moreover, Christ was not at that time born; no, nor were Mary and David. Nevertheless, the apostle plainly says, They tempted Christ, let us not also tempt him.

8. Certainly enough, then, Christ is the man to whom Moses refers as God. Thus the testimony of Moses long before is identical with that of Paul. Though employing different terms, they both confess Christ as the Son of God, born in eternity of the Father, in the same divine essence and yet distinct from him. You may call this difference what you will; we indicate it by the term "person." True, we do not make a wholly clear explanation of the mystery; we but stammer when speaking of a "Trinity." But what are we to do? we cannot better the attempt. So, then, the Father is not the Son, but the Son is born of the Father in eternity; and the Holy Spirit proceeds from God the Father and God the Son. Thus there are three persons, and yet but one God. For what Moses declares concerning God, Paul says is spoken of Christ.

9. The same argument substantially Paul employs in Acts 20:28, when, blessing the church of Miletus and exhorting the assembled ministers concerning their office, he says, "Take heed unto yourselves, and to all the flock, in which the Holy Spirit hath made you bishops, to feed the church of the Lord which he purchased with his own blood." This, too, is a significant text, proving beyond all controversy that Christ our Lord, who purchased the church with his blood, is truly God, and to him the church belongs. For the apostle plainly asserts it was God who bought the church with his blood, and that the church is his own.

Now, in view of the fact already established that the persons are distinct, and of the further statement that God has purchased the church through his own blood, we inevitably conclude that Christ our Savior is true God, born of the Father in eternity, and that he also became man and was born of the Virgin Mary in time.

10. If such blood—the material, tangible, crimson blood, shed by a real man—is truly to be called the blood of God, then he who shed it must be actually God, an eternal, almighty person in the one divine essence. In that case, we truly can say the blood flowing from the side of the crucified One and spilled upon the ground is not merely the blood of an ordinary man, but God's own. Paul does not indulge in frivolous talk. He speaks of a most momentous matter; and he is in dead earnest when he, in his exhortation, reminds us that it is an exalted office to rule the church and to feed it with the Word of God. Lest we toy in the performance of such an office, we are reminded that the flock is as dear to him as the blood of his dear Son, so precious that all creatures combined can furnish no equivalent. And if we are

indolent or unfaithful, we sin against the blood of God and become guilty of it, inasmuch as through our fault it has been shed in vain for the souls which we should oversee.

11. There are many passages of similar import, particularly in the Gospel of John. So we cannot evade the truth but must say God the Father, God the Son, and God the Holy Spirit are three individual persons, yet of one divine essence. We do not, as the Jews and Turks [Muslims] derisively allege, worship three Gods; we worship only one God, represented to us in the Scriptures as three persons.

Christ said to Philip in John 14:9, "He that hath seen me hath seen the Father." There Christ claims unity and equality with the Father in the one divine essence. So does Paul, in Colossians 1:15, where he calls Christ "the image of the invisible God," at the same time indicating two distinct persons: the Father is not the Son, and the Son is not the Father, yet they are one God. Such passages, I say, are frequent. By means of them, the sainted fathers valiantly maintained this dogma of the Trinity against the devil and the world, thus making it our heritage.

12. Now, what care we that reason should regard it as foolishness? It requires no skill to cavil over these things; I could do that as well as others. But, praise God, I have the grace to desire no controversy on this point. When I know it is the Word of God that declares the Trinity, that God has said so, I do not inquire how it can be true; I am content with the simple Word of God, let it harmonize with reason as it may. And every Christian should adopt the same course with respect to all the articles of our faith. Let there be no caviling and contention on the score of possibility; be satisfied with the inquiry, Is it the Word of God? If a thing be his Word, if he has spoken it, you may confidently rely upon it; he will not lie nor deceive you, though you may not understand the how and the when.

Since, then, this article of the Holy Trinity is certified by the Word of God, and the sainted fathers have from the inception of the church chivalrously defended and maintained the article against every sect, we are not to dispute as to how God the Father, the Son, and the Holy Spirit are one God. This is an incomprehensible mystery. It is enough that God in his Word gives such testimony of himself. Both his nature and its revelation to us are far beyond our understanding.

PHYSICAL LIFE INEXPLICABLE TO REASON

13. And why should you presume to comprehend, to exactly understand, the sublime, inconceivable divine essence when you are wholly ignorant of

your own body and life? You cannot explain the action of your laughter, nor how your eyes give you knowledge of a castle or mountain ten miles away. You cannot tell how in sleep one, dead to the external world, is yet alive. If we are unable to understand the least detail of our physical selves, anything so insignificant as the growth of a mere hair, for instance, can we, unaided by the revelation of God's Word, climb by reason—that reason so blind to things within its natural realm—into the realm of heavenly mysteries and comprehend and define God in his majesty?

If you employ reason from mere love of disputation, why not devote it to questions concerning the daily workings of your physical nature? for instance, where are the five senses during sleep? just how is the sound of your own laughter produced? We might without sin occupy ourselves with such questions. But as to the absolute truth in a matter such as this, let us abide patiently by the authority of the Word. The Word says that Christ is the express image of the invisible God, the firstborn of all creatures; in other words, he is God equally with the Father.

14. Again, John 5:23 testifies that all should honor the Son as they honor the Father. And in John 12:44, we read, "He that believeth on me, believeth not on me, but on him that sent me." Also, in John 14:1, "Believe in God, believe also in me." And again, in John 16:15, "All things whatsoever the Father hath are mine." These and similar passages are armor that cannot be pierced; for they are uttered by God, who does not lie and who alone is qualified to speak the truth concerning himself. Thus the dogma of the Trinity is thoroughly founded upon the holy Scriptures.

THE THIRD PERSON OF THE TRINITY

15. Now, having established the existence of Christ in the Trinity, we must next consider the third person, the Holy Spirit, in Scripture sometimes termed the "Spirit" of God and sometimes his "Soul." This person is not spoken of as "born"; he is not born like the Son, but proceeds from the Father and the Son. To express it differently, he is a person possessing in eternity the divine essence, which he derives from the Father and Son in unity in the same way the Son derives it from the Father alone. There are, then, three distinct persons in one divine essence, one divine Majesty. According to the Scripture explanation of the mystery, Christ the Lord is the Son of God from eternity, the express image of the Father, and equally great, mighty, wise, and just. All deity, wisdom, power, and might inherent in the Father is also in Christ and, likewise, in the Holy Spirit, who proceeds from Father and Son. Now, when you are asked to explain the Trinity, reply

that it is an incomprehensible mystery, beyond the understanding of angels and creatures, the knowledge of which is confined to the revelations of Scripture.

16. Rightly did the fathers compose the creed, or symbol, in the simple form repeated by Christian children, "I believe in God the Father Almighty, Maker of heaven and earth, and in Jesus Christ his only Son...I believe in the Holy Ghost." This confession we did not devise, nor did the fathers of former times. As the bee collects honey from many fair and gay flowers, so is this creed collected, in appropriate brevity, from the books of the beloved prophets and apostles—from the entire holy Scriptures—for children and for unlearned Christians. It is fittingly called the "Apostle's Symbol," or "Apostle's Creed." For brevity and clearness, it could not have been better arranged, and it has remained in the church from ancient time. It must either have been composed by the apostles themselves, or it was collected from their writings and sermons by their ablest disciples.

17. It begins, "I believe." In whom? "In God the Father." This is the first person in the Godhead. For the sake of clear distinction, the peculiar attribute and office in which each person manifests himself is briefly expressed. With the first, it is the work of creation. True, creation is not the work of one individual person, but of the one divine, eternal essence as such. We must say, God the Father, God the Son, and God the Holy Spirit created heaven and earth. Yet that work is more especially predicated of the person of the Father, the first person, for the reason that creation is the only work of the Father in which he has stepped forth out of concealment into observation; it is the first work wrought by the divine Majesty upon the creature. By the word "Father," he is particularly and rightly distinguished from the other persons of the Trinity. It indicates him as the first person, derived from no other, the Son and the Holy Spirit having existence from him.

18. Continuing, the creed says, I believe in another who is also God. For to believe is something we owe to no being but God alone. Who is this second person? Jesus Christ. God's only begotten Son. Christians have so confessed for more than fifteen hundred years; indeed, such has been the confession of believers from the beginning of the world. Though not employing precisely these words, yet this has been their faith and profession.

19. The first designation of God the Son makes him the only Son of God. Although angels are called sons of the Lord our God, and even Christians are termed his children, yet no one of these is said to be the "only" or "only begotten" Son. Such is the effect of Christ's birth from the Father, that he is unequaled by any creature, not excepting even the angels. For he is in truth

and by nature the Son of God the Father; that is, he is of the same divine, eternal, uncreated essence.

20. Next comes the enumeration of the acts peculiar to him: "Who was conceived by the Holy Spirit, born of the Virgin Mary, suffered under Pontius Pilate, was crucified, dead and buried. He descended into hell; on the third day he rose again from the dead; he ascended into heaven, and sits at the right hand of God the Father Almighty; from thence he shall come to judge the quick and the dead." The distinct personality of the Son is thus demonstrated by acts peculiar to himself. Not the Father and not the Holy Spirit, but the Son alone, assumed human nature of flesh and blood, like unto ours, to suffer, die, rise again, and ascend into heaven.

21. In the third place we confess, "I believe in the Holy Ghost." Here again, a distinct person is named, yet one in divine essence with the Father and the Son; for we must believe in no one but the true God, in obedience to the first commandment, "I am Jehovah thy God…Thou shalt have no other gods before me."

Thus briefly this confession comprehends the unity of the divine essence—we accept and worship only one God—and the revealed truth that in the Trinity are three distinct persons. The same distinction is indicated in holy baptism; we are baptized into the faith of one God, yet Christ commands us to baptize "into the name of the Father and of the Son and of the Holy Spirit."

22. The peculiarity of this third person is the fact that he proceeds from both the Father and the Son. He is therefore called also the Spirit of the Father and the Son; he is poured into the human heart and reveals himself in the gathering of the church of Christ in all tongues. Through the Word of the Gospel, he enlightens and kindles the hearts of men unto one faith, sanctifying, quickening, and saving them.

23. So the creed confesses three persons as comprehended in one divine essence, each one, however, retaining his distinct personality; and in order that the simple Christian may recognize that there is but one divine essence and one God, who is tri-personal, a special work, peculiar to himself, is ascribed to each person. And such acts, peculiar to each person, are mentioned for the reason that thus a confusion of persons is avoided. To the Father we ascribe the work of creation; to the Son the work of redemption; to the Holy Spirit the power to forgive sins, to gladden, to strengthen, to transport from death to life eternal.

The thought is not that the Father alone is the Creator, the Son alone Redeemer, and the Holy Spirit alone Sanctifier. The creation and preservation of the universe, atonement for sin and its forgiveness, resurrection from the dead and the gift of eternal life—all these are operations of the one divine Majesty as such. Yet the Father is especially emphasized in the work of creation, which proceeds originally from him as the first person; the Son is emphasized in the redemption he has accomplished in his own person; and the Holy Spirit in the peculiar work of sanctification, which is both his mission and revelation. Such distinction is made for the purpose of affording Christians the unqualified assurance that there is but one God and yet three persons in the one divine essence—truths the sainted fathers have faithfully gathered from the writings of Moses, the prophets, and the apostles, and which they have maintained against all heretics.

24. This faith has descended to us by inheritance and, by his power, God has maintained it in his church, against sects and adversaries, unto the present time. So we must abide by it in its simplicity and not be wise. Christians are under the necessity of believing things apparently foolish to reason. As Paul says, in 1 Corinthians 1:21, "It was God's good pleasure through the foolishness of the preaching to save them that believe." How can reason adapt itself to comprehend that three are one, and one is three; that God became man; that he who is washed with water in obedience to Christ's command, is washed with the blood of our Lord Jesus Christ and cleansed from all sins? Such articles of faith appear utterly foolish to reason. Paul aptly calls the Gospel foolish preaching wherewith God saves such as do not depend on their own wisdom but simply believe the Word. They who will follow reason in the things dealt with in these articles, and will reject the Word, shall be defeated and destroyed in their wisdom.

25. Now, we have in the holy Scriptures and in the creed sufficient information concerning the Holy Trinity, and all that is necessary for the instruction of ordinary Christians. Besides, the divinity of our Lord Jesus Christ and that of the Holy Spirit is also attested by miracles not to be lightly esteemed nor disregarded. The Lord our God brings to pass miraculous things for the Christian's sake—for the strengthening of his faith—and not merely as a rebuke to false teachers. Were he to consider the false teachers alone, he might easily defer their retribution to the future life, since he permits many other transgressors to go unpunished for ten, twenty, or thirty years. But the fact is, God openly in this life lays hold upon leaders of sects who blaspheme and slander him with their false doctrines. He inflicts upon them unusual punishments for the sake of warning others. Besides being openly convicted of blasphemy and having the condemnation of their own conscience, the misguided ones receive testimony to the fact that these false leaders are instigators of blasphemy against God's name and his Word. All men are compelled to admit God can have no pleasure in their doctrine, since he visits them with special

marks of his displeasure, destroying them with severer punishments than ordinarily befall offenders.

26. History records that John the Evangelist had as contemporary a heretic, by the name of Cerinthus, who was the first to arise in opposition to the apostolic doctrine and in blasphemy against the Lord Jesus with the claim that Jesus is not God. This blasphemy spread to such an extent that John saw himself compelled to supplement the work of the other evangelists with his Gospel, whose distinct purpose it is to defend and maintain the deity of Christ against Cerinthus and his rabble.

A feature of John's Gospel patent to all is the sublime beginning of his Gospel, which renders it distinct from the others. He does not lay stress upon the miraculous doings of Christ, but upon his preaching, wherein he reveals himself powerfully as true God, born of the Father from eternity, and his equal in power, honor, wisdom, righteousness, and every other divine work.

With respect to John and Cerinthus, it is reported that the former, having gone to a public bath with some of his disciples, became aware that Cerinthus and his rabble were there also. Without hesitation, he told his disciples to be up and away, and not to abide among blasphemers. The disciples followed his advice and departed. Immediately after their departure, the room collapsed, and Cerinthus with his followers perished, not one escaping.

27. We also read concerning the heretic Arius, the chief foe of his time toward the dogma of the deity of Christ. The injury done by this man to the cause of Christ was such as to occupy the church for four centuries after his death; and still today, his heresy has not been altogether rooted out. But the Lord took the matter in hand by the performance of a miracle which could not but be understood.

History records that Arius had ingratiated himself into the favor of Constantine, the emperor, and his counselors. With an oath, he had succeeded in impressing them with the righteousness of his doctrine, so that the emperor gave command that Alexander, bishop of Constantinople, should recognize him as a member of the Christian Church and restore him to the priestly office. When the godly bishop refused to accede to this demand, knowing full well the purpose pursued by Arius and his followers, Eusebius and the other bishops who supported Arius threatened him with the imperial edict and expressed the determination to drive him out by force and to have Arius restored by the congregation as such. However, they gave him a day to think the matter over.

28. The godly bishop was fearful. The following of Arius was large and powerful, being supported by the imperial edict and the whole court. The

bishop, therefore, resolved to seek help from God, where alone it is found in all things relating to God's honor. He fell down upon his face in the church and prayed all night long that God should preserve his name and honor by methods calculated to stem the tide of evil purpose, and to preserve Christendom against the heretics. When it was morning, and the hour had come when Alexander the bishop should either restore Arius to office or be cast out of his own, Arius convened punctually with his followers. As the procession was wending its way to the church, Arius suddenly felt ill and was compelled to seek privacy. The pompous procession halted, waiting his return, when the message came that his lungs and liver had passed from him, causing his death. The narrative comments: *Mortem dignam blasphema et foetida mente*—a death worthy such a blasphemous and turpid mind.

29. We see, then, that this dogma has been preserved by God first through the writings and the conflicts of the apostles, and then by miracles, against the devil and his blasphemers. And it shall be preserved in the future likewise, so that, without a trace of doubt, we may believe in God the Father, God the Son, God the Holy Spirit. This is the faith which we confess with our children daily. To guard against a mixing of persons or the abandonment of the tripersonality, three distinct acts are predicated. This should enable the common Christian to avoid confusing the persons, while maintaining the divine unity as to essence.

We proclaim these things on this Sunday in order to call attention to the fact that we have not come upon this doctrine in a dream, but by the grace of God through his Word and the holy apostles and fathers. God help us to be found constant and without blemish in this doctrine and faith to our end. Amen.

Index by Source

The sermons included in this volume may be found in the Sermons of Martin Luther: the Church Postils, collected in volumes 1–4 of the Complete Sermons of Martin Luther, Edited by John Nicholas Lenker. Translated by John Nicholas Lenker and others. Published by Baker Books, a division of Baker Book House Company, Grand Rapids, Michigan 49516.

Index by Key Scripture Passage

John 16:23–30   The Fifth Sunday After Easter or Prayer
                                       Sunday: A Sermon by Christ on Prayer

John 20:19–31   The Sunday After Easter: Of True Piety,
                                       the Law and Faith, and of Love to Our
                                       Neighbor

Romans 11:33–36   Trinity Sunday: The Doctrine of the Trinity

Philippians 2:5–11   Palm Sunday: Christ: An Example of
                                       Love